T0330464

Multinational Firms' Location and the New Economic Geography

NEW HORIZONS IN INTERNATIONAL BUSINESS

Series Editor: Peter J. Buckley
Centre for International Business,
University of Leeds (CIBUL), UK

The New Horizons in International Business series has established itself as the world's leading forum for the presentation of new ideas in international business research. It offers pre-eminent contributions in the areas of multinational enterprise – including foreign direct investment, business strategy and corporate alliances, global competitive strategies, and entrepreneurship. In short, this series constitutes essential reading for academics, business strategists and policy makers alike.

Titles in this series include:

China and its Regions
Economic Growth and Reform in Chinese Provinces
Edited by Mary-Françoise Renard

Emerging Issues in International Business Research
Edited by Masaaki Kotabe and Preet S. Aulakh

Network Knowledge in International Business
Edited by Sarianna M. Lundan

Business Strategy and National Culture
US and Asia Pacific Microcomputer Multinationals in Europe
Denise Tsang

Learning in the Internationalisation Process of Firms
Edited by Anders Blomstermo and D. Deo Sharma

Alliance Capitalism and Corporate Management
Entrepreneurial Cooperation in Knowledge Based Economies
Edited by John H. Dunning and Gavin Boyd

The New Economic Analysis of Multinationals
An Agenda for Management, Policy and Research
Edited by Thomas L. Brewer, Stephen Young and Stephen E. Guisinger

Transnational Corporations, Technology and Economic Development
Backward Linkages and Knowledge Transfer in South East Asia
Axèle Giroud

Alliance Capitalism for the New American Economy
Edited by Alan M. Rugman and Gavin Boyd

The Structural Foundations of International Finance
Problems of Growth and Stability
Edited by Pier Carlo Padoan, Paul A. Brenton and Gavin Boyd

The New Competition for Inward Investment
Companies, Institutions and Territorial Development
Edited by Nicholas Phelps and Philip Raines

Multinational Enterprises, Innovative Strategies and Systems of Innovation
Edited by John Cantwell and José Molero

Multinational Firms' Location and the New Economic Geography
Edited by Jean-Louis Mucchielli and Thierry Mayer

Multinational Firms' Location and the New Economic Geography

Edited by

Jean-Louis Mucchielli

Professor of Economics, University of Paris I Panthéon-Sorbonne, Professor Affiliate, ESCP-EAP and Director, TEAM Pôle Economie Mondiale, CNRS, University of Paris I, France

and

Thierry Mayer

Professor of Economics, University of Paris-Sud, Scientific Advisor, CEPII, Research Affiliate, CERAS-ENPC, France and Research Affiliate, CEPR, UK

NEW HORIZONS IN INTERNATIONAL BUSINESS

Edward Elgar

Cheltenham, UK • Northampton, MA, USA

Published by
Edward Elgar Publishing Limited
The Lypiatts
15 Lansdown Road
Cheltenham
Glos GL50 2JA
UK

Edward Elgar Publishing, Inc.
William Pratt House
9 Dewey Court
Northampton
Massachusetts 01060
USA

A catalogue record for this book
is available from the British Library

Library of Congress Cataloguing in Publication Data

Multinational firms' location and the new economic geography/edited by
Jean-Louis Mucchielli and Thierry Mayer.
p. cm. (New horizons in international business)
'This volume is the outcome of a workshop held in the University of Paris I Pantheon-Sorbonne in May 2002'—General introduction.
Includes bibliographical references and index.
1. Industrial location—Congresses. 2. Economic geography—Congresses. 3. International business enterprises—Congresses.
I. Mucchielli, Jean-Louis. II. Mayer, Thierry. III. New horizons in international business.
HD58.M76 2004
338.8'8—dc22 2003068782

ISBN 978 1 84376 654 4

Printed on FSC approved paper
Printed and bound in Great Britain by Marston Book Services Ltd, Oxfordshire

Contents

List of figures vii
List of tables viii
List of contributors xi

Introduction 1
Jean-Louis Mucchielli and Thierry Mayer

PART I AGGLOMERATION AND MULTINATIONAL FIRMS' LOCATION

1 Geographical concentration of production by leading firms in EU manufacturing 11
Leo Sleuwaegen and Reinhilde Veugelers

2 Globalization, agglomeration and FDI location: the case of French firms in Europe 35
Jean-Louis Mucchielli and Florence Puech

3 Trade, border effects and individual characteristics: a panel specification with instrumental variables estimators 59
José De Sousa and Anne-Célia Disdier

4 North–south integration and multinationals: the case of the automobile industry in Mexico 76
Sylvie Montout and Habib Zitouna

5 Trade liberalization and the internal geography of countries 91
Matthieu Crozet and Pamina Koenig-Soubeyran

PART II HOME MARKET EFFECTS, MARKET SIZE AND LOCATION STRATEGIES

6 Market size and agglomeration 113
Keith Head, Thierry Mayer and John Ries

7 The home market effect in a Ricardian model with a continuum of goods 140
Federico Trionfetti

8 Footloose capital, market access and the geography of regional state aid 156
Gianmarco I.P. Ottaviano

9 Empirical evidence on the strategic behaviour of US MNEs within the framework of dynamic differentiated networks 178
Fragkiskos Filippaios, Constantina Kottaridi, Marina Papanastassiou and Robert Pearce

10 Intellectual property rights and international location choices: theoretical modelling and simulations 205
Etienne Pfister

Index 229

Figures

1.1	Change in distribution of Relative Entropy across industries, 1987 versus 1997	25
2.1	Distribution of the French multinationals in European regions in 2000	38
2.2	The tree structure of the location set: seven countries and 47 regions (46 regions NUTS 1 + Portugal NUTS 0)	45
2.3	Average of regional PMEU (1987–94)	53
2.4	Average of regional wages per capita (1987–94)	54
4.1	Mexican production in the automobile industry by country of origin of firms	80
4.2	Destination of Mexican automobile production (shares)	82
5.1	Real wage difference for three different external transaction costs	98
5.2	Bifurcation diagram	99
5.3	Sustain point for K91 and KL96	103
5.4	Sustain point for three different external transaction costs	104
5.5	Real wage difference when the two regions have different external transaction costs	107
6.1	Shares of demand, firms and employment	120
6.2	Predicted values of the raw concentration index (G)	121
6.3	G for the Helpman-Krugman model	137
6.4	G for the Ottaviano-Tabuchi-Thisse model	138
7.1	Technology and home bias	146
7.2	Free trade equilibrium	148
7.3	Market size and specialization in free trade	149
7.4	Magnification effect in free trade	149
7.5	Magnification effect with transport costs	152
7.6	Market size and trade costs	153
8.1	EU structural funds	159
8.2	EU aid caps	160

Tables

1.1	Country share of production, 1987–97 (percentage)	18
1.2	Number of leading firms and average home production per firm, 1987–97	20
1.3a	Share of foreign firm production in total matrix production by country, 1987–97 (percentage)	21
1.3b	Concentration of foreign firm production, 1987–97 (percentage)	22
1.4	Overall geographical concentration of matrix production within the EU, 1987–97	23
1.5	Industries with highest and lowest level of geographical concentration, 1997	24
1.6	Industries with largest positive and negative change in geographical concentration, 1987–97	26
1.7	Industries with largest positive and negative change in Entropy Between, 1987–97	27
1.8	Geographical concentration by different product-type industries, 1987–97	28
1.9	Changes in transnationality of EU matrix firms, 1987–97	29
1.10	Changes in geographic concentration of production of EU matrix firms, 1987–97	29
1.11	Geographical concentration of production of EU matrix firms by country of origin (Relative Entropy), 1987–97	29
1.12	Geographical concentration of EU versus non-EU firms, 1987–97 (average values)	31
2.1	Recent studies on multinationals' location choice in manufacturing sectors based on a discrete choice model	40
2.2	The 16 industrial sectors of activity (NACE two-digit)	44
2.3	Description of independent variables at national level	48
2.4	Description of independent variables at regional level	49
2.5	Maximum likelihood estimation results of the conditional logit models	50
2.6	Maximum likelihood estimation results of the nested logit models	51
3.1	Border effects: OLS estimator	66
3.2	Border effects: random effects estimator	67

3.3 Border effects: fixed effects estimator 69
3.4 Border effects: Hausman and Taylor (1981) estimator 70
3.5 Border effects: Amemiya and MaCurdy (1986) estimator 71
3.6 Border effects: Breusch, Mizon and Schmidt (1989) estimator 72
4.1 Production shares (% of total production) of the five largest automobile constructors in Mexico 81
4.2 Variables used in regressions (sources in parentheses) 84
4.3 Regressions (OLS) 86
4.4 Regressions (Tobit) 88
6.1 Discriminating hypotheses 123
6.2 Summary statistics on *G* 124
6.3 Summary statistics on conditional logit 126
6.4 Summary statistics on home market effects 128
6.5 Results on discriminating hypotheses 129
6.6 Concentration of Japanese FDI in the USA and the EU 132
9.1 Im, Pesaran, Shin unit root test 186
9.2 Chow tests (F-statistic) for structural breaks in the sample 186
9.3 Economic results for the full sample, Europe and non-Europe OECD, with US FDI flows as dependent variable 187
9.4 Economic results for time-divided full sample, Europe and non-Europe OECD, with US FDI flows as dependent variable 189
A9.1 Variables description and descriptive statistics 192
A9.2 Fixed effects of the samples 194
A9.3 Correlation matrices for the samples 199
10.1 No strategic effect 217
10.2 Positive strategic impact of FDI in both countries 218
10.3 Negative strategic impact of FDI in both countries 221
10.4 Asymmetric strategic effect 223

Contributors

Matthieu Crozet TEAM, University of Paris I Panthéon-Sorbonne, 106–112 Bd de l'hôpital, 75647 Paris Cedex 13, France.

José De Sousa LESSOR, University of Rennes II, and ROSES, University of Paris I Panthéon-Sorbonne, 106–112 Bd de l'hôpital, 75647 Paris Cedex 13, France.

Anne-Célia Disdier TEAM, University of Paris I Panthéon-Sorbonne, 106–112 Bd de l'hôpital, 75647 Paris Cedex 13, France.

Fragkiskos Filippaios Athens University of Economics and Business, Department of International and European Economic Studies, 76 Patission St, 10434 Athens, Greece.

Keith Head Faculty of Commerce, University of British Columbia, 2053 Main Mall, Vancouver, BC, V6T 1Z2, Canada.

Pamina Koenig-Soubeyran CREST and TEAM, University of Paris I Panthéon-Sorbonne, CREST, timbre J360, 15 Bd Gabriel Péri, 92245 Malakoff Cedex, France.

Constantina Kottaridi Athens University of Economics and Business, Department of International and European Economic Studies, 76 Patission St, 10434 Athens, Greece and Scholar of the Foundation 'Propontis'.

Thierry Mayer University of Paris-Sud, CEPII, CERAS and CEPR, CEPII, 9 rue Georges Pitard, 75015 Paris, France.

Sylvie Montout TEAM, University of Paris I Panthéon-Sorbonne, 106–112 Bd de l'hôpital, 75647 Paris Cedex 13, France.

Jean-Louis Mucchielli Professor of Economics, University of Paris I Panthéon-Sorbonne, Professor Affiliate, ESCP-EAP and Director, TEAM Pôle Economie Mondiale, CNRS, University of Paris I, UFR 06, 17 rue de la Sorbonne, 75005 Paris, France.

Gianmarco I.P. Ottaviano Università Commerciale 'L. Bocconi', Milan, GIIS, Geneva, and CEPR, London, Bocconi University, Istituto de Economica Politica, Via Gobbi 5, 20136 Milan, Italy.

Marina Papanastassiou University of Reading, Department of Economics, Reading, UK, and Athens University of Economics and Business, Department of International and European Economic Studies, 76 Patission St, 10434 Athens, Greece.

Robert Pearce University of Reading, Department of Economics, PO Box 218, Whiteknights, Reading, Berks, RG6 6AA, UK.

Florence Puech TEAM, University of Paris I Panthéon-Sorbonne, 106–112 Bd de l'hôpital, 75647 Paris Cedex 13, France.

Etienne Pfister CREDES, University of Nancy, 13 Place Carnot – C.O. no. 26, 54035 Nancy Cedex, France, and TEAM-CNRS, University of Paris I Panthéon-Sorbonne.

John Ries Faculty of Commerce, University of British Columbia, 2053 Main Mall, Vancouver, BC, V6T 1Z2, Canada.

Leo Sleuwaegen Katholieke Universiteit Leuven, Department of Applied Economics, Naamsestraat 69, 3000 Leuven, Belgium, VLGMS, and Erasmus University, Rotterdam.

Federico Trionfetti GIIS, Geneva, CEPN, University of Paris XIII, and CEPII, Paris, GIIS, 11A Avenue de la Paix, 1202 Genève, Switzerland.

Reinhilde Veugelers Katholieke Universiteit Leuven, Department of Applied Economics, Naamsestraat 69, 3000 Leuven, Belgium, and CEPR, London.

Habib Zitouna TEAM, University of Paris I Panthéon-Sorbonne, 106–112 Bd de l'hôpital, 75647 Paris Cedex 13, France.

Introduction[1]

Jean-Louis Mucchielli and Thierry Mayer

The location choices of multinational firms for their production plants is an important topic, not least because this phenomenon is accompanied by so many fears in the public debate. Recent experiences prove that the most important concerns are linked to trade integration episodes. During the process of North American Free Trade Agreement (NAFTA) adoption and implementation, expectations were strong that firms would relocate to Mexico their manufacturing activity in order to serve the North American market as a whole from this new low-cost base (the 'Giant sucking sound' of Ross Perot, being only the most vivid and famous expression of those widespread fears). The 1986 enlargement of the European Union (EU) to Spain and Portugal already witnessed similar concern. The next enlargement to 10 countries – mostly Central and Eastern European countries – programmed for May 2004, reinvigorates the arguments of those claiming that 'Old Europe' countries will lose in the process the little manufacturing industry production left from previous international opening of markets. By contrast, in 2002, some multinational firms like Canon or Philips have relocated their assembly plants or their common parts production from Mexico to China or Thailand.

Will such a large-scale change in the European economic geography take place? Faced with such questions, we believe that economists should (and actually can) provide answers. Their work can use different tools, but we will focus here on two types of methodologies typically employed. A first approach starts by noting in the examples above that *location patterns are largely the result of decisions by multinational enterprises (MNEs)*. Therefore, a clear understanding of what drives the 'internal geography' of multi-plant firms (where the MNE decides to locate each of its plant) is very useful in order to apprehend global changes in international production patterns. There is now a quite large literature aimed at assessing the theoretical and empirical determinants of the international organization of production by MNEs that can be usefully mobilized. A second path of research analyses the equilibrium pattern of international production more globally as the result of a *conflict between agglomerative and dispersive market forces*. It seems clear that the two approaches should interact.

Firm-level location choice analysis suffers when abstracted from more general phenomenons like, for instance, the local equilibria on each labour market, which is clearly both influenced by location choices of MNEs in the long run and in return affects their production costs and hence their location decision. Conversely, general equilibrium models depicting international production patterns lose a lot of their convincing power if they fail to account correctly for the individual decisions by firms. This book is an attempt to promote such interactions which, while much needed, seem not to emerge so frequently and spontaneously.

The volume is hence the result of the encounter of two types of scientific literature and researchers: the analysis of foreign direct investment location choices, on the one hand, and the work studying the forces at work in the shaping of the international economic geography, on the other hand.

The work on the determinants of location choices of multinational firms has a long and productive history based mostly on industrial organization and international business theories. The empirical applications in this field increasingly benefit from an improvement of data and methods availability – particularly at the level of the firm and of its affiliates (following this trend, most chapters in this volume use firm-level data). One of the frequently mentioned limitation of this type of research is its focus on partial equilibrium, where what happens in an industry is usually disconnected from the rest of the economy.

In parallel, the last decade has witnessed very important developments in what has been named the 'New Economic Geography'. The initial impulse was mostly theoretical and used tools familiar in international trade theory to predict general equilibrium patterns of industries' agglomeration (see Fujita, Krugman and Venables, 1999, for a complete overview). The theoretical developments were very rich but, until recently, the empirical aspects of the economic geography have clearly been left aside, to the point that the leading theorists in the field are now calling for more rigorous empirical implementations and care in the data used to explain international location patterns of increasing returns industries.

While the two fields obviously have a lot in common, it has only been recently that researchers have acknowledged the similarities of their approaches and the possible complementarities. Some were obvious but oddly left uncovered until now. On the theoretical side, one of the most interesting parallels is the analysis of location choices as a trade-off between trade costs and scale economies. This trade-off is deeply rooted in traditional regional and urban economics that led to recent new economic developments (Fujita and Thisse, 2002, p. 93, even call it the 'fundamental trade-off in spatial economics'). It is also central in the modern theory of foreign direct investment: Brainard (1993), among others, explicitly formulates the choice of a firm to invest abroad as a means to reduce trade costs to consumers (proximity) that has to be balanced with the rise in average production cost caused by the split of production between smaller plants (concentration). This is the famous 'proximity–concentration model' which is opposed to the 'factor endowments' model. The complementarities also concern the empirical assessment of likely causes of the degree of spatial concentration we observe in a lot of modern industries. This volume is the outcome of the meeting of those two strands of research, materialized in the very rich two-day workshop held in Paris in May 2002, where many scholars could exchange views on the current state of the art and the direction research should take in those topics.

The book is organized in two parts each comprising five chapters. The first part deals with agglomeration behaviours of MNEs in the context of international (mostly regional) integration. Leo Sleuwaegen and Reinhilde Veugelers propose an empirical index of agglomeration in the EU using detailed plant-level production data of the industry 'leaders'. The goal is to assess the impact of the Single Market Programme (SMP) by looking at the evolution of concentration at three points in time (1987, 1993 and 1997). The key and important improvement of their approach is that they can isolate in the overall changes what part is caused by a *reorganization of production inside the firm*. The authors find an overall trend towards dispersion of production inside the EU. They are then able to show that while leading firms still have a large share of their production at home, the share of production in other member countries inside the same firm increases significantly during the period. This 'internal' aspect is therefore important in the overall trend towards dispersion, with a slight shift towards southern member states.

In the second chapter, Jean-Louis Mucchielli and Florence Puech provide further evidence on firm-level location choices determinants inside the EU. They focus on the location choices of French affiliates abroad in seven EU countries comprising of 47 EU regions. They are particularly interested in the geographical structure of those location choices, assessing the importance of national borders in the location choice. It appears that investors consider regions as closer substitutes in their decision when those regions belong to the same nation, signalling the fact that the impact of national borders persists even within the single market. They also find stronger evidence of agglomeration effects at the regional level and detect a deterrent effect of high wages at the national level (following the way others work, in Mucchielli, 1998). The influence of borders on location choices is not limited to this aspect. Indeed, it has been shown repeatedly that national borders have a surprisingly high (negative) impact on trade flows (McCallum, 1995; Head and Mayer, 2000; Anderson and van

Wincoop, 2003). For a multinational firm, this means that locating its affiliate in a particular European country does *not* guarantee an easy access to consumers in surrounding countries, even in the EU. Also important, it means that an affiliate will be relatively insulated from third countries' competition on the specific market it is located in. Consequently, the impact of borders on trade flows has to be correctly assessed, which is the goal of José De Sousa and Anne-Célia Disdier in their chapter focusing on EU trade. They improve upon the econometric methods used in the existing literature, controlling for unobservable characteristics of bilateral trade relationships between country pairs. Their central result is that the level of market fragmentation revealed by the impact of national borders was previously slightly underestimated.

As stated above, NAFTA also yielded important issues about relocation of activity from the USA to Mexico. Sylvie Montout and Habib Zitouna study in their chapter this question for a particularly important industry: the car industry, for which Mexican production experienced drastic changes over the recent period, almost entirely due to MNE decisions. This case is particularly interesting as it deals with an example of a major North–South regional integration, for which the delocation expectations are highest. The determinants of automobile production in Mexico are analysed using here again firm-level data over a long period of time where important changes in public policies took place. Apart from confirming that the distribution of car production between Mexico and the USA is influenced in the expected way by relative labour costs and demand (with labour costs seemingly dominating the location choice), NAFTA is found to exert an important positive influence on the production of cars in Mexico.

Those first four chapters mostly deal with firms choosing a *national* location site and how regional integration affects those choices. However an increasingly important question is the impact of regional integration on location patterns *inside countries*. This issue is specifically important in Europe where regional policies rank very high on the political agenda. With the coming EU enlargement, many candidate countries fear that economic activity might become more polarized creating internal tensions as well as more pressure on the European budget if current rules for regional policy European funds allocation are kept unchanged. The vast recent changes in the Mexican economic geography underlined by Hanson (1997) suggest that those phenomenon might be important empirically. The theory is still unclear on those issues and it is important to know whether the observed recent dispersion trend in Mexico is what we should *generally* expect. Matthieu Crozet and Pamina Koenig-Soubeyran provide a much needed generalization of the original model by Krugman and Livas (1996). While Krugman and Livas (1996) claimed that external trade liberalization yields less concentration inside the liberalizing country, Chapter 5 shows that this result is in fact not robust to a generalization of the model and that the conclusions are, in fact, much more subtle. When regions inside a country have a symmetric access to the rest of the world, the original conclusion is reversed, and we should expect international trade integration to foster agglomeration. The outcome when regions have different access to international markets, is that trade integration generally favours the border region, except where competition from foreign firms is too fierce.

One of the most important result underlying the New Economic Geography is the Home Market Effect (HME). In a model with increasing returns and trade costs, there is a general tendency of countries with a large share of overall demand to attract a more than proportional share of output and/or to pay higher factor incomes. This result is a key determinant of spatial concentration, and is studied in detail in the second part of the book. Keith Head, Thierry Mayer and John Ries use this characteristic to investigate if New Economic Geography is indeed the dominant explanation of the observed agglomeration of MNEs. There can be numerous alternative explanations for spatial clustering, one of the most popular being the existence of localized technology spillovers. However this technological spillovers explanation does *not* yield a Home Market Effect as opposed to the increasing returns/trade cost theories. The authors use over 1400 individual location choices by Japanese firms in both the USA and the EU to investigate which of the two explanations seems more valid. The empirical analysis provides little support for the Home Market Effect and is much more positive for the spillovers explanation.

The HME relationship has been shown to hold in a variety of (though not in all) models with imperfect competition and trade costs, and to be inconsistent with perfect competition models where trade is caused by factor endowments differences or national product differentiation. Federico Trionfetti adds to those results through a theoretical investigation of the effect of market size on specialization and production patterns in a Ricardian model of trade. He reveals quite distinctive features of this model. The size of markets matter for production even in the absence of trade costs, which is an important difference with the factor endowments model. The more than proportional reaction of the output share to the demand share can also arise for sufficiently large demand size asymmetries. In the work on HME, the emphasis has so far been entirely focused on the theoretical foundations and the empirical quantification of this phenomenon. There has been surprisingly little work on the welfare implications of the HME, despite clear normative consequences of the location patterns of firms in this type of model. Gianmarco Ottaviano proposes a normative analysis of the existence of Home Market Effects. His main results point to a tendency towards excessive agglomeration of increasing returns to scale industries in terms of welfare. This pattern is all the more pronounced when the HME is important, that is, when scale economies are strong and trade costs are low. Policy implications are therefore that regional policies tend to have a theoretical justification, but that they should take into account the structural differences across industries in their action.

Important as market size considerations may be, they are certainly not the only determinant of location choice. The last two chapters of the volume reintroduce knowledge-related determinants in the decision as to where to locate a plant. Fragkiskos Filippaios, Constantina Kottaridi, Marina Papanastassiou and Robert Pearce study the location of US foreign direct investment (FDI) flows in Organization for Economic Co-operation and Development (OECD) countries during the past two decades. They find that their so-called 'knowledge-seeking' variables (the research and development [R&D] employment variable in particular) indeed provide additional explanatory power to more traditional determinants, and in particular to market size. Looking across time, the authors show in particular that knowledge-seeking determinants appear more important in the latest years. If knowledge is so important for FDI, then multinational firms will have an incentive strategically to use those determinants. This is the issue tackled by Etienne Pfister in the final chapter of this book. This chapter deals with location choices in a context of different intellectual property rights' protection levels across countries. There are some important, and somehow initially surprising, results arising from the interaction of FDI and property rights protection. It is shown that higher levels of protection do not systematically increase the attractiveness of a country, in particular when market size is important relative to trade costs and when imitation costs are so high that the FDI strategy by the multinational firms involves deterring entry by local competitors.

NOTE

1. This volume is the outcome of a workshop held in the University of Paris I Panthéon-Sorbonne, on May 2002, while many of the authors were visiting the international trade group of research centre TEAM. The organization of this workshop has only been made possible by the help of young researchers at TEAM and, most notably, Anne-Célia Disdier and Pamina Koenig-Soubeyran, who also took a crucial role in preparing this volume.

REFERENCES

Anderson, J. and E. van Wincoop (2003), 'Gravity with gravitas: a solution to the border puzzle', *American Economic Review*, **93** (1), 170–92.

Brainard, S.L. (1993), 'A simple theory of multinational corporations and trade with a trade-off between proximity and concentration', National Bureau of Economic Research Working Paper 4269.

Fujita, M. and J.-F. Thisse (2002), *Economics of Agglomeration; Cities, Industrial Location and Regional Growth*, Cambridge: Cambridge University Press.

Fujita, M., P. Krugman and A. Venables (1999), *The Spatial Economy: Cities, Regions, and International Trade*, Cambridge: MIT Press.

Hanson, G. (1997), 'Increasing returns, trade and the regional structure of wages', *Economic Journal*, **107** (440), 113–33.

Head, K. and T. Mayer (2000), 'Non-Europe: the magnitude and causes of market fragmentation in Europe', *Weltwirschaftliches Archiv*, **136** (2), 285–314.

Krugman, P. and R. Livas (1996), 'Trade policy and third world metropolis', *Journal of Development Economics*, **49** (1), 137–50.

McCallum, J. (1995), 'National borders matter: Canada–US regional trade patterns', *American Economic Review*, **85**, 615–23.

Mucchielli, J.-L. (ed.) (1998), 'Multinational location strategy', in *Research in Global Strategic Management*, vol. 6, London: Jai Press Inc.

PART I

Agglomeration and Multinational Firms' Location

1. Geographical concentration of production by leading firms in EU manufacturing

Leo Sleuwaegen and Reinhilde Veugelers

1.1 INTRODUCTION

The process of market integration, triggered in the European Union (EU) by the Single Market Programme (SMP), systematically changes the nature of competition, and therefore the structure of firms and industries. There is a widespread recognition of the potential benefits in terms of higher efficiency and increased competition. The 'official EU' view, summarized in the Cecchini Report on the 'Costs of non-Europe', anticipated four main effects, each having implications for the structure of industries and firms:

- direct cost savings due to the elimination of non-tariff barriers, such as fewer customs delays and costs of multiple certification;
- cost savings derived from increased volumes and more efficient location of production (scale and learning economies and better exploitation of comparative advantage);
- tightening of competitive pressures, reduced prices and increased efficiency as more firms from different Member States compete directly in the bigger marketplace;
- speedier innovation from increased competitive pressures.

At the same time, policy-makers particularly in smaller regions worry about what the effects of economic integration will be on the location of production activities. A common concern among politicians of peripheral regions in the EU is that economic integration will lead to a loss of industry production and jobs in their regions. These concerns are partly supported by recent theoretical work, which suggests that economic integration may indeed lead to increased concentration of production and larger international inequalities (for example, Krugman, 1991; Krugman and Venables, 1995).

However, the theoretical literature as it stands today fails to deliver a univocal result on the effects of market integration on geographical concentration of production, identifying both centrifugal and centripetal forces. The existing empirical studies show only modest changes in geographical concentration at the aggregate level. But studies that zero in on sectoral differences find that there is nevertheless a considerable cross-industry variation, indicating that industry characteristics on demand and technology are important to instigate the centrifugal and/or centripetal forces.

This chapter contributes to the empirical literature on the geographical concentration of production in the EU. A unique dataset of leading firms in the manufacturing sector of the EU allows us to discuss the evolution of geographical concentration of production over the period 1987–97. We are able to move beyond the aggregate and sectoral level to discuss the patterns of geographical concentration also at the firm level.

Before we present our empirical findings on the trends in geographical concentration in the EU at the aggregate and industry level in section 1.4 and at the firm level in section 1.5, we review the literature on the impact of market integration on geographical concentration of production in section 1.2. Section 1.3 explains the empirical methodology we use to measure geographical concentration.

1.2 THE IMPACT OF MARKET INTEGRATION ON GEOGRAPHICAL CONCENTRATION OF PRODUCTION

Changing Geographical Concentration at the Industry Level

The impact of market integration on the geographical concentration of production attracted much attention in the literature. The implications can be sketched fairly easily from a simple neoclassical trade perspective. When, in the pre-integration period, trade is primarily inter-industry, and driven by comparative advantage, reduced impediments to trade should heighten the impact of that comparative advantage, leading to increased specialization and hence more geographical concentration of production. If, on the other hand, trade is largely intra-industry, resulting from product differentiation, it is not obvious that geographical concentration should necessarily change – one way or the other. The 'new economic geography' literature analyses the relationship between trade integration and industrial location in an intra-industry trade setting. A series of papers by Krugman (1991), Krugman and Venables (1995) and Venables (1996) study the geographical concentration of industrial production. This literature is based on the Spence-Dixit-Stiglitz framework of product differentiation, increasing returns to scale and monopolistic competition, together with trade costs. A key feature of these models is that once production has agglomerated in a region it continues to agglomerate because of self-reinforcing demand and supply linkages. Downstream firms use an aggregate of upstream varieties as intermediate inputs. In the presence of trade costs, a larger number of upstream firms in a region implies a lower price level for intermediate inputs. This is a forward link. At the same time, more downstream firms create a larger market for upstream firms. This is a backward link. Trade costs are a force that makes it less attractive to serve markets via exports. Lower trade costs would therefore be expected to lead to less concentration of production, weakening the agglomeration forces. Low trade costs, of course, also imply a weaker dispersion force. However, as long as there is a dispersion force that is independent of trade costs, agglomeration will display a U-shaped pattern with agglomeration of economic activity for intermediate trade costs and dispersion for high and low trade costs. Examples of such trade-cost-independent dispersion forces are decreasing returns in some perfectly competitive sectors (Venables, 1996), factor-based comparative advantages (Forslid and Wooton, 1999; Fujita, Krugman and Venables, 1999) and congestion (for example, Helpman, 1999).

In summary, whether market integration will lead to more geographical concentration of production will depend on whether trade is inter- or intra-industry, the level of trade costs, and the pattern of comparative advantages and industry characteristics such as scale sensitivity and scope for product differentiation.

Empirical studies have failed to find strong conclusive evidence in favour of increased geographical concentration of production. Bearing in mind the relative growth in intra-industry trade, the EU's evaluation of the Single Market Programme (SMP) (1996) concludes that the SMP has generally not 'induced more concentration of EU industry around an industrial core' (European Commission, 1996, pp. 5–6). Most of the follow-up empirical studies report different, often opposing, results depending on the level of analysis (national or regional) and the considered time period. In general the results point to a weak tendency towards less specialisation by country and less geographical concentration in manufacturing in the 1970s, and a slight reversal of this tendency since the 1980s (Amiti, 1998; WIFO, 1999).

However, empirical studies zeroing in at the sectoral level, find important differences between industries. Brülhart and Torstensson (1996) and Amiti (1999) show that especially industries characterised by strong scale economies and high to intermediate capital intensity became more geographically concentrated following European integration. A more recent study by Midelfart-Knarvik et al. (2002), using a new measure of spatial dispersion that takes into account the relative location of clusters of industries, finds that a number of industries that were initially spatially dispersed have become more concentrated. These are mainly slow-growing and unskilled labour-intensive industries. The spatial concentration is usually in peripheral low-wage countries. Among industries that were initially spatially concentrated, significant dispersion has occurred in a number of medium- and high-tech industries. Skilled and scientific labour abundance are important considerations in determining industrial location. The pull of centrality is becoming more important for industries that are intensive users of intermediate goods. These observations provide some support for the new trade and economic geography theories.

Changing Geographical Concentration at the Firm Level

Behind the effects on industry structure, are the changing strategies of individual firms. At the firm level the removal of non-tariff barriers leads to major strategic adjustments. Within the process of change, firms hitherto protected by non-tariff barriers become suddenly confronted with a new competitive environment. Although it was widely anticipated that the scale of surviving firms would increase, providing scope for cost economies, little attention was paid to what this might imply for the structure of individual firms, that is, how firms would choose to distribute that increased scale across geographic space.

Market integration makes it easier for firms to enter other EU Member State markets. This gives rise to major cross-entries of markets within the EU (frequently through mergers and acquisitions (M&A)). At the same time, improved co-ordination possibilities and the drive for a better exploitation of scale and scope economies within Europe change the configuration of activities, such that certain sub-activities tend to become more geographically concentrated in some Member States. This concentration process goes together with the development of more efficient logistics systems that is made possible by a further deregulation of the transportation and telecommunication sectors in Europe.

Vandermerwe (1993) predicts the formation of Euro-networks in view of the ongoing market integration on a European and global scale, with the structure and location of activities of firms no longer based on specific countries. As multi-country strategy structures become less efficient, transnational firms need to reorganize to a structure that allows a complex strategy. This restructuring should lead to so-called new global and regional networks, where firms concentrate on their core activities and build close relationships with suppliers and distributors. Recent economic geography models that explicitly include transnational firms show that, because of economic integration, transnational firms relocate those activities to peripheral countries which need not be close to consumers or suppliers and that are labour intensive (Gao, 1999; Raybaudi-Massilia, 2000).

In summary, while market integration provides an incentive for firms, both EU and non-EU, to enter more Member States, it likewise provides the incentives to organize production on an EU scale, which might lead production to be concentrated in fewer geographical sites.

1.3 MEASURING GEOGRAPHICAL CONCENTRATION OF PRODUCTION WITHIN THE EU USING THE MARKET SHARE MATRIX

Rather than drawing on published aggregate data, our empirical analysis enables assessment of changes in geographic concentration of production at the firm level. At the heart of the analysis is the construction of an EU 'market share matrix' (MSM hereafter). This MSM includes estimates of the turnover of a set of leading manufacturing firms, disaggregated across industries and individual Member States. In order to show how the MSM can be used to discuss the trends in geographical concentration, we first explain the underlying methodology.

The Market Share Matrix

Briefly, the basic idea of this matrix is to identify a set of 'leading firms', and disaggregate their turnover data, extracted from individual company accounts. A firm qualifies as a 'leader', if it is one of the five largest EU producers in at least one manufacturing industry. For every such firm, the matrix includes estimates of its EU turnover (sourced from within the EU) in each industry in which it operates (not only in those where it is a 'leader'), and disaggregates firm turnover according to its production centres across EU Member States. A three-dimensional matrix built on these principles can provide estimates of various structural dimensions: market concentration and geographical concentration of production of the industries, and intra-EU transnationality and diversification of the matrix firms.

The MSM has been constructed for the years 1987, 1993 and 1997. An analysis of these three years provides a rich and detailed mapping of how market concentration, geographical concentration of production, transnationality and diversification have changed over time (Veugelers et al., 2002). It is important to keep in mind that the changes over time cannot solely be attributed to the SMP, although it is a major factor of change in the considered period. In time-comparable format, the matrix covers 67 manufacturing sectors and the old EU-12 Member States as it was in 1987: Belgium/Luxembourg, the Netherlands, Germany, the UK, France, Italy, Denmark, Spain, Portugal, Greece and Ireland.

Although the MSM data clearly offer the advantage of having firm-level data, there are some disadvantages that need to be noted. First, the analysis is restricted to the level of the country as the unit of analysis in the MSM. The regional level would be a more meaningful level of analysis for geographical concentration. Second, the analysis of geographical concentration and its changes over time are very sensitive to the composition of the matrix, being restricted to leading firms only and thus favouring firms from/in large countries. As the national breakdown of the matrix firms is broadly in line with the relative sizes of the Member States, the smaller countries are likely to be underrepresented (see also Davies et al., 1996, ch. 10). Third, because all firms' turnovers are disaggregated across a common industrial classification within manufacturing, all inter-firm or inter-industry comparisons are perfectly standardized over a common 'terrain'. But this terrain is 'ring-fenced', and does not include the firms' operations outside manufacturing and outside of the EU-12.

Measuring Geographic Concentration Using the MSM

Most measures of geographical concentration take the form:

$$\mathrm{M} = \sum_{k=1}^{n} P \cdot h(P) \tag{1.1}$$

with P the share of the kth Member State in total production in sector j, $h(P_{jk})$ an assigned weight and n the number of Member States.

This study makes use of the Entropy index as a measure for geographical concentration, because of its decomposition properties.[1] The *Entropy measure* weighs each P by the logarithm of its reciprocal ($1/P$):

$$\mathrm{E} = \sum_{k=1}^{n} P \cdot \log\left(\frac{1}{P}\right) \tag{1.2}$$

If all Member States have an equal share in an industry's production, Entropy equals log n (Maximum Entropy). If production is concentrated in only one Member State, the Entropy index is at its minimum and equals zero. The geographical concentration of production is measured through the *Relative Entropy index*. The Relative Entropy index (RE) consists of the

Entropy index divided by the Maximum Entropy (log n), and is situated in the [0,1] interval.

$$RE_j = \sum_{k=1}^{n} \frac{X_{jk}}{X_j} \cdot \log \frac{X_j}{X_{jk}} / \log n \tag{1.3}$$

with X_j production in industry j
X_{jk} production in Member State k, industry j.

At the aggregate level, the Relative Entropy becomes:

$$RE = \sum_{k=1}^{n} \frac{X_k}{X} \cdot \log\left(\frac{X}{X_k}\right) / \log n \tag{1.4}$$

with X total production, X_k total production in Member State k.

To study to what extent production has shifted from northern to southern countries in the EU (the core–periphery notion), the Entropy index can be decomposed in a within-group component and a between-group component. We consider two groups of countries within the EU, Northern Europe and Southern Europe (Italy, Spain, Portugal and Greece).[2]

The '*Entropy Between*' *index* for two country groups at matrix level is:

$$E_{between} = P_1 \log\left(\frac{1}{P}\right) + P_2 \log\left(\frac{1}{P}\right) \tag{1.5}$$

with P_i = share of country group i in total production.

The '*Entropy Within*' *index* is the weighted average of the Entropy index of each group:

$$E_{within} = E_1.P_1 + E_2.P_2 \tag{1.6}$$

with P_i = share of country group i in total matrix production
E_i = Entropy index in country group i.

The higher the *Entropy Between index*, the more production is equally spread between both groups of countries. If the Entropy Between index equals 0, production is concentrated in one of the two country groups. The maximum value of the Entropy Between index is 0.3 (log 2), indicating a perfect spread of production between both clusters of countries. The Entropy Between index will be used as an inverse measure of concentration of production in northern versus southern countries.

1.4 CHANGES IN MSM GEOGRAPHICAL CONCENTRATION AT THE INDUSTRY LEVEL

The present section examines which tendencies show up in the location of total production of the leading firms in European manufacturing industries over the period 1987–97. The first part of the section provides a view on the MSM aggregate data. It shows in which Member States EU production of leading firms is located. The second part examines the changes in geographical concentration of production of leading firms by industry.

Country Shares in the MSM

The MSM data clearly show that the location of production of leading firms within the EU is very concentrated, with two-thirds of matrix production located in Germany, France and the UK (Table 1.1). The southern Member States including Portugal, Spain, Italy and Greece, comprise less than one-fifth of total matrix production. Within this group of southern countries, Italy takes up the largest part of manufacturing production with about 12 per cent of total matrix production.

Table 1.1 Country share of production, 1987–97 (percentage)

	1987	1993	1997
GER	0.35	0.39	0.35
FR	0.21	0.20	0.18
UK	0.18	0.16	0.17
NL	0.05	0.04	0.05
BEL/LUX	0.04	0.03	0.04
IRE	0.002	0.003	0.005
DEN	0.002	0.008	0.01
IT	0.12	0.12	0.13
SP	0.04	0.04	0.06
PORT	0.003	0.004	0.007
GR	0.003	0.003	0.003

The geographical structure of production within the EU does not show dramatic changes over the period of investigation. Germany, France and the UK continue to account for the majority of total matrix production. Nevertheless, closer examination of the evolution of country shares of matrix production shows a shift of matrix production to the southern EU Member States. Spain, Italy and Portugal take up an increasing part of matrix production over the period 1987–97 (20 per cent in 1997 versus 16.6

per cent in 1987). This evolution can be explained by the three following factors: an increase in the number of leading firms originating from southern Member States, a growth in firm size of incumbent, leading firms from southern member states in their home market, or an increase in 'foreign firm production', that is, production by leading firms outside their home country in Southern Europe.

Table 1.2 shows that, with the exception of Italy, there are very few leading firms originating from the southern Member States. The first factor to explain the rising share of southern countries in EU leading production, namely a rise in the number of leading firms, can only be attributed to Italy. With the exception of the Benelux countries, leading firms from all Member States, including the southern Member States, have a clear home market bias, since the majority of their production is still located in their home market. Nevertheless there is a marked decline of this home market bias over time for all firms in the matrix (see Veugelers et al., 2003, for more on this). The only exceptions are the three Spanish matrix firms that continue to concentrate all production at home. With this strong home market bias, a second possible factor to explain the rising southern share, is a growth in home market sales for the Spanish firms.

In line with the decline in home market bias, is the rise in foreign production in Member States, that is, production accounted for by foreign owned matrix firms, as Table 1.3a illustrates. This holds both for northern and southern Member States. Hence, of growing importance in the explanation of a country's share in total matrix production is the growth in foreign firm production.

The examination of the shares of southern countries in total foreign firm production (Table 1.3b) reveals a growing attractiveness of this region for foreign firm production over the period 1987–97. The attractiveness, however, holds mostly for matrix firms originating from the EU as non-EU firms locate only 17 per cent of their foreign production in Southern Europe, compared with 33 per cent for EU firms.

In summary, the share of the southern Member States in EU leading manufacturing production has increased in the period 1987–97, albeit modestly. This can be related to more Italian firms entering the league of leading firms in their industry, but a major force is the increasing attractiveness of southern Member States for FDI, mainly from other EU leading firms.

Geographical Concentration of Matrix Production across Countries

This section examines how matrix production in European manufacturing industries is geographically concentrated across Member States at the aggregate level.

Table 1.2 Number of leading firms and average home production per firm, 1987–97

	1987			1993			1997		
	Number of firms	Average size (€ mn)	Average % production in home market	Number of firms	Average size (€ mn)	Average % production in home market	Number of firms	Average size (€ mn)	Average % production in home market
GER	51	3947	88.13	49	5471	85.88	37	7922	77.41
FR	46	2899	79.08	39	4111	66.65	29	5556	61.61
UK	51	2160	77.91	43	2468	66.10	44	2542	64.67
NL	9	4143	53.27	5	6755	49.65	8	4272	43.35
BEL/LUX	4	2432	71.09	4	2217	45.68	4	2715	41.14
IRE	0	—	—	0	—	—	1	—	—
DEN	0	—	—	3	1121	84.23	5	1384	82.91
IT	26	2638	87.48	29	2741	77.32	34	2991	73.85
SP	3	1235	100.00	3	1523	100.00	3	1451	100.00
PORT	1	—	—	0	—	—	1	—	—
GR	0	—	—	0	—	—	0	—	—

Table 1.3a *Share of foreign firm production in total matrix production by country, 1987–97 (percentage)*

	1987	1993	1997
GER	22.91	25.71	31.45
FR	23.70	31.84	41.89
UK	29.36	43.52	54.19
NL	31.62	50.29	67.14
BEL/LUX	71.85	84.11	86.74
IRE	100.00	100.00	92.89
DEN	100.00	52.96	41.34
IT	25.99	34.22	39.76
SP	85.42	87.04	91.89
PORT	98.58	100.00	98.31
GR	100.00	100.00	100.00

The EU MSM project traces changes in the geographical concentration of production over the period 1987–97. Since this is a period of ongoing market integration triggered by the SMP, a time comparison provides suggestive evidence of a trend towards geographical concentration or dispersion when EU markets integrate.

Table 1.4 shows a small increase in the Relative Entropy index over the time period 1987–97, which points to an increase in geographical dispersion as de-concentration of EU matrix production. Comparing the pre- and post-1993 period, it seems, however, that the trend towards more geographical dispersion is only observed in the post-1993 period. Although the trend seems to point towards geographical dispersion, it is important to emphasize that the changes are small on average. Also, Midelfart-Knarvik et al. (2000) find a small increase in geographical dispersion of the overall manufacturing industry.

The overall trend of increased geographical dispersion is found both within northern and southern Member States. Although the Relative Entropy index increases in both groups, the increase is most notable for the southern Member States. Nevertheless, the geographical dispersion remains considerably lower in Southern Europe as compared to the countries in Northern Europe. This can be related to the lower home market bias of the smaller northern Member States, as noted above. The stronger geographical concentration within the southern Member States is explained by the persistent dominance of Italy in southern production. Spain and Portugal, however, are catching up with a substantially higher growth rate of matrix share production over the time period 1987–97, compared with Italy (8 per cent) (see Table 1.1).

Table 1.3b Concentration of foreign firm production, 1987–97 (percentage)

	1987			1993			1997		
	Share of total foreign firm production	Share of foreign firm production by EU firms	Share of foreign firm production by non-EU firms	Share of total foreign firm production	Share of foreign firm production by EU firms	Share of foreign firm production by non-EU firms	Share of total foreign firm production	Share of foreign firm production by EU firms	Share of foreign firm production by non-EU firms
GER	26.60	24.66	29.71	26.90	22.04	33.20	23.80	16.94	31.52
FR	16.50	17.05	16.43	16.80	17.92	15.45	16.40	16.43	16.32
UK	18.00	8.01	30.16	18.20	13.47	24.45	19.60	17.58	21.81
NL	4.60	5.93	3.27	5.70	5.68	5.79	6.90	5.53	8.49
BEL/LUX	8.90	11.55	6.12	7.20	10.22	3.19	6.70	10.15	2.81
IRE	0.80	1.40	0.03	0.80	1.05	0.94	1.00	1.30	0.74
DEN	0.80	1.07	0.60	1.10	1.18	0.46	0.90	1.09	0.67
IT	10.60	12.21	9.13	10.80	10.69	10.91	11.30	11.62	11.04
SP	10.90	15.41	0.00	10.40	14.79	4.60	11.30	16.26	5.71
PORT	1.20	1.89	3.27	1.30	1.77	0.70	1.40	2.15	0.55
GR	1.00	0.82	0.04	0.80	1.21	0.30	0.70	0.95	0.33
Total	100.00	100.00	100.00	100.00	100.00	100.00	100.00	100.00	100.00

Table 1.4 Overall geographical concentration of matrix production within the EU, 1987–97

	1987	1993	1997
Relative Entropy	0.72	0.71	0.76
Entropy Between	0.20	0.20	0.22
Entropy Within	0.55	0.54	0.57
Relative Entropy North	0.58	0.56	0.60
Share North	0.83	0.83	0.80
Relative Entropy South	0.30	0.31	0.34
Share South	0.17	0.17	0.20

The evolution of the Entropy Between index over the observed time period is especially interesting as it could yield evidence of a possible shift in production to the south. Table 1.4 shows slight increases of the Entropy Between index, indicating a more equal spread of matrix production between both groups and thus, a weak trend of geographical dispersion towards Southern Europe. This confirms the increasing share of the southern countries and takes into account that in 1987 the share of total production in Northern Europe was larger than that in Southern Europe.

Geographical Concentration at the Industry Level

The aggregate level hides some interesting observations related to industry specific characteristics. To uncover these industry specificities, the geographic concentration of matrix production will be discussed at the industry level. Table 1.5 lists the most and least geographically concentrated industries. The sectors with the least geographical concentration are 'Glass' and 'Dairy products'. 'Machinery', a traditional skill-based industry, is among the most concentrated industries. Note that the car-manufacturing sector holds a Relative Entropy index of 0.61, which is close to the overall average (not shown in Table 1.5).

The overall downward trend in geographical concentration at the matrix level holds generally well at the industry level. Figure 1.1 shows the distribution of the Relative Entropy across the sample of 67 industries for the years 1987 and 1997.

Whereas in 1987 only about 40 per cent of all industries had a Relative Entropy that was higher than 0.6 (eight industries even showed a Relative Entropy smaller than 0.4), in 1997 the majority of the industries (43 out of 67, that is, 65 per cent) had a Relative Entropy that was higher than 0.6. However, although the average trend is one of increased geographical

Table 1.5 Industries with highest and lowest level of geographical concentration, 1997

SPES	Industry	Relative Entropy 1997
Lowest level of geographical concentration		
7	Glass	0.83
41	Dairy products	0.82
44	Grain milling and manufacturing of starch	0.80
39	Oils and fats	0.77
72	Toys and sports goods	0.77
Highest level of geographical concentration		
63–64	Wood manufactures	0.31
38	Clocks and watches	0.37
17	Manufacture of machine tools for working metals	0.38
18	Manufacture of other machinery	0.38
33	Cycles and motor cycles	0.44

spread of manufacturing activities across all industries, large differences exist across the industries. Table 1.6 lists the industries with the largest positive and negative change in geographical concentration.

The sectors which display a decrease in RE index, that is, for which industrial production is concentrating, are sectors which were characterized by an initial low level of production concentration and are traditional industries like 'Leather' and 'Steel tubes'. In these sectors the market integration may have forced these industries to rationalize their too dispersed production activities.

Also in the evolution of the Entropy Between index, which is our measure of geographic concentration between northern and southern Member States, an important variation exists between different industries. Table 1.7 list those industries that show a strong shift of production towards Southern Europe (largest increase in Entropy Between) and those industries that have reinforced concentration of production in Northern Europe (largest decrease in Entropy Between) over the period 1987–97.

The only two industries that were concentrating most of their matrix production in Southern Europe in 1987 are 'Pasta' and 'Cycles and motorcycles' (these industries are not shown in Table 1.7). Over 1987–97 the Entropy Between index of the pasta industry has increased from 0.22 to 0.28, indicating a shift of production toward Northern Europe. For the cycles and motorcycles industry on the other hand, the Entropy Between index has decreased, pointing at a reinforcement of concentration of production in Southern Europe.

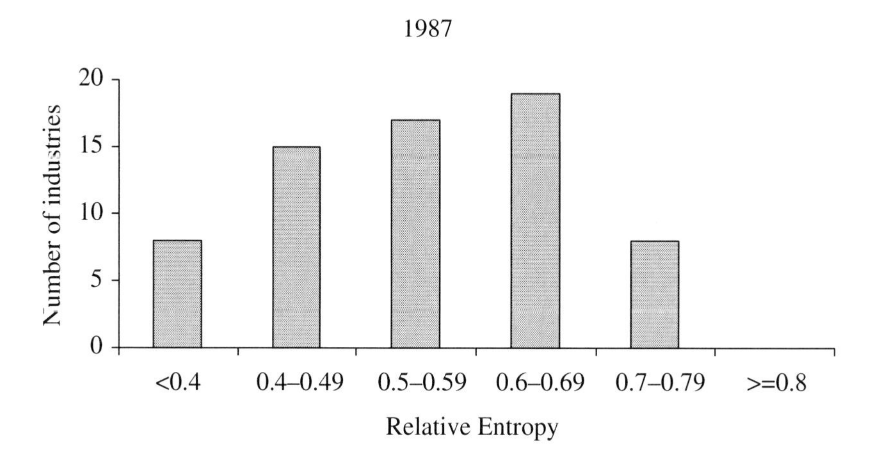

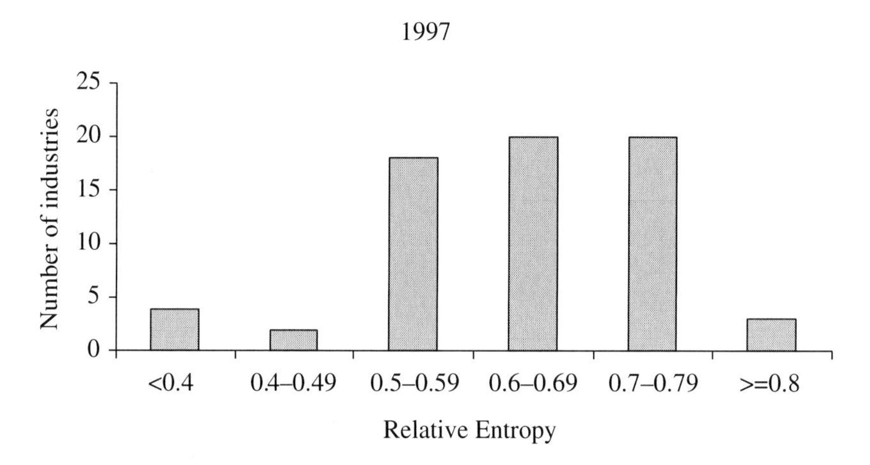

Figure 1.1 *Change in distribution of Relative Entropy across industries, 1987 versus 1997*

In search of the industry characteristics that influence the changes in geographical concentration, characteristics like scale sensitivity and scope for product differentiation affecting the intra- versus inter-industry nature of trade are likely to be important.

Following Davies et al. (1996), we will distinguish differentiated product industries from those producing homogenous goods. From a theoretical perspective, this distinction maps closely into the difference between endogenous and exogenous sunk costs in models of industry structure and

Table 1.6 Industries with largest positive and negative change in geographical concentration, 1987–97

SPES	Industry	Relative Entropy 1987	Relative Entropy 1997	Change 1987–97
Largest increase in geographical concentration				
57	Leather	0.60	0.53	−0.07
38	Clocks and watches	0.43	0.37	−0.06
33	Cycles and motorcycles	0.49	0.44	−0.05
2	Steel tubes	0.59	0.54	−0.05
Largest decrease in geographical concentration				
4	Clay products	0.34	0.73	0.39
44	Grain milling and manufacture of starch	0.50	0.80	0.30
13	Man-made fibres	0.38	0.68	0.30
45	Pasta	0.23	0.52	0.29
36	Medical instruments	0.43	0.71	0.28
43	Fish products	0.42	0.66	0.24
8	Ceramics	0.46	0.67	0.21
10	Paint and ink	0.45	0.66	0.21

vertical product differentiation (Sutton, 1991). Within the differentiated group, industries are disaggregated further according to the method of differentiation: through advertising versus R&D.[3]

Table 1.8 summarizes the time-comparable statistics for firms operating in the different industry types. Both the Relative Entropy and Entropy Between indices as measures for respectively geographical concentration of production within the EU and production shift towards Southern Europe are shown.

Table 1.8 shows that in the period 1987–97 firms active in homogenous products industries were, at the outset, more geographically concentrated than firms active in differentiated products industries. This is not surprising given the importance of fixed sunk cost and scale economies. But over time, these industries have shown the largest decrease in geographical concentration and, thus, have converged to the level of geographical concentration of the differentiated products industries in 1997.

Table 1.8 also shows that both types of industries have shifted an increasing share of production towards Southern Europe. This shift is most pronounced for homogenous products industries.

Table 1.7 *Industries with largest positive and negative change in Entropy Between, 1987–97*

SPES	Industry	Entropy Between 1987	Entropy Between 1997	Change 1987–97
Industries with largest shift of production from Northern to Southern Europe				
55	Textiles	0.06	0.29	0.24
65	Wooden furniture	0.06	0.27	0.22
58	Footwear	0.05	0.21	0.16
37	Optical instruments	0.00	0.16	0.16
67	Articles of paper	0.00	0.15	0.15
10	Paint and ink	0.05	0.19	0.14
50	Other foods	0.13	0.27	0.14
34	Aerospace	0.00	0.13	0.13
4	Clay products	0.00	0.12	0.12
28	Lighting equipment and lamps	0.05	0.16	0.11
Industries with largest increase in concentration of production in Northern Europe				
17	Manufacture of machine tools for working metals	0.25	0.22	−0.03
18	Manufacture of other machinery	0.19	0.16	−0.03
5	Cement, lime and plaster	0.26	0.21	−0.04
62	Wood boards	0.15	0.10	−0.05
19	Computer and office equipment	0.23	0.16	−0.07
32	Railway locomotives and stocks	0.23	0.16	−0.07
44	Grain milling and manufacture of starch	0.24	0.16	−0.08
42	Fruit and vegetables	0.22	0.13	−0.09
16	Manufacture of tractors and agricultural machinery	0.26	0.16	−0.10
61	Wood sawing	0.29	0.18	−0.11

1.5 GEOGRAPHICAL CONCENTRATION OF PRODUCTION AT THE FIRM LEVEL

In the previous sections we have focused on the aggregate and industry level to discuss geographical concentration. However, the aggregate geographical concentration hides the location strategies of individual firms. These location strategies of individual firms are very much influenced by the ownership dimension, as there is still a large, be it diminishing, home country bias in production, as was pointed out in section 4. Hence, when we observe in the MSM data a change in geographical concentration of

Table 1.8 Geographical concentration by different product-type industries, 1987–97

	Relative Entropy			Entropy Between		
	1987	1997	Change 1987–97	1987	1997	Change 1987–97
Type 1: Homogenous products	0.52	0.63	0.11	0.17	0.22	0.05
Type 2: Differentiated products	0.57	0.64	0.07	0.17	0.20	0.03
2A: Advertising intensive	0.61	0.68	0.07	0.16	0.19	0.03
2R: Research intensive	0.54	0.61	0.06	0.18	0.19	0.02
2AR: Adv. & res. intensive	0.59	0.65	0.06	0.18	0.22	0.04

production within an industry, this can be the result of a change in geographical concentration of production by leading firms changing their transnational production structure within the EU. But it may also simply reflect the changing geographic concentration of ownership of leading firms, which concentrate most of their production in their home country. The MSM is uniquely positioned to disentangle these effects. Table 1.2 documented that, although there is still a strong home market bias, matrix firms realize an increasingly larger share of their production outside their home market. Hence a major factor behind the increasing geographic dispersion of production activities within the EU, is the increasing transnational production of EU leading firms.

Geographical Concentration of Production by EU Leading Firms

Table 1.9 shows the increasing importance of transnational production within the EU by matrix firms based in the EU over the period 1987–1997.

As a consequence of the smaller home country bias of EU matrix firms, the geographic concentration of their production activities has decreased as the Relative Entropy index indicates both before and after 1993. In order to make an accurate comparison, the Relative Entropy index at the individual firm level is defined as Entropy divided by log n with n the fixed number of 11 Member States, as is the case at the aggregate level.[4] The reported numbers are unweighted averages of Entropy values per firm. The results are shown in Tables 1.10 and 1.11.

Table 1.11 details the differences in geographic concentration at the firm level according to the country of origin. When interpreting the empirical data, we have to re-emphasize that smaller countries are likely to be

Table 1.9 Changes in transnationality of EU matrix firms, 1987–97

	1987	1993	1997
Number of transnational EU matrix firms	117	124	138
Country entries per EU matrix firm	3.06	4.01	4.53
Average % home production	81%	76%	70%

Table 1.10 Changes in geographic concentration of production of EU matrix firms, 1987 97

	1987	1993	1997
Entropy (average values)	0.17	0.25	0.32
Relative Entropy (average values)	0.16	0.24	0.31

Table 1.11 Geographical concentration of production of EU matrix firms by country of origin (Relative Entropy), 1987–97

	Relative Entropy, 1987	Relative Entropy, 1993	Relative Entropy, 1997
GR	X	X	X
SP	0.00	0.00	0.00
IT	0.10	0.18	0.18
DEN	X	0.11	0.21
GER	0.12	0.17	0.28
UK	0.19	0.29	0.33
PORT	0.00	X	0.39
FR	0.18	0.30	0.43
BEL/LUX	0.17	0.34	0.51
NL	0.38	0.43	0.53
IRE	X	X	0.66
Average	*0.16*	*0.24*	*0.31*

underrepresented in the MSM, by using leading producers only. Therefore, any inference on the average corporate structure for those countries is distorted by a sample selection bias.

Ranking the different Member States by the level of geographic concentration of production, the large Member States are clearly situated at the upper end of the list, which appears to be due to their larger home market bias. Apart from the Spanish firms in the matrix, that are all national, the Italian, German and UK firms also have more geographically concentrated production than the EU average. Among the firms originating from the large Member States, only French firms show a high level of geographical dispersion of EU production in 1997. Over the period 1987–97 their level of geographical dispersion has increased significantly.

Geographical Concentration of Production: Comparing EU and non-EU Leading Firms

The transnational configuration of the activities of non-European firms is expected to display a somewhat different pattern to the one observed for European firms. Firms most often start their internationalization process in neighbouring or culturally related countries following a sequential process – the so-called staged model of internationalization (Johanson and Vahlne, 1977) before they move into other countries. Non-European firms can therefore be expected to be in a more advanced stage of internationalization and, as a result, will show a lower degree of geographical concentration than their European counterparts. Moreover, to compensate for the liability of foreignness (Delios and Makino, 2000), these firms should possess significant intangible assets yielding competitive advantage to sustain their leading position in Europe. As intangible assets are mostly deployed Europe-wide, most of these firms are building up transnational networks which evolve into complex organizations. At the outset such organizations display a high level of geographic dispersion. Over time, specialization within the network may lead to more geographical concentration of activities.

The empirical findings are consistent with the above arguments and show a considerable higher average number of country entries and a higher level of geographical dispersion of production for the average non-EU firm than for the average EU firm (Table 1.12). However, compared with EU firms, the level of geographic dispersion did not increase equally drastically over the period 1987–97, leaving more converging patterns of geographical concentration.

Within the group of non-EU firms, European firms based outside the EU (Austria, Finland, Norway, Sweden and Switzerland) show more geographic dispersion and have increased their geographic dispersion within the EU, as compared with non-European firms (mostly Japan and the USA). The high level of geographic dispersion displayed by non-EU, European firms is mainly explained by their small home markets, and their need to be present in the larger EU market. Non-European firms on the other hand have on average diminished their level of geographic dispersion since 1993, suggesting a rationalization and concentration of EU production by these firms.

Table 1.12 Geographical concentration of EU versus non-EU firms, 1987–97 (average values)

	Number of firms			Country entries per firm			Relative Entropy		
	1987	1993	1997	1987	1993	1997	1987	1993	1997
EU firms	191	175	166	3.06	4.01	4.53	0.16	0.24	0.31
Non-EU firms	32	43	57	4.94	5.21	5.23	0.47	0.50	0.50
Non-EU, European firms	7	9	16	6.71	5.56	6.51	0.51	0.50	0.58
Non-EU, non-European firms	25	34	41	4.20	5.12	4.73	0.45	0.50	0.47

Geographical Concentration of Production: Comparing Aggregate and Firm-Level Evidence

At the firm level a study of geographical concentration of activities analyses the location strategy of firms and changes therein. This allows checking to what extent firms have reconfigured their activities geographically. Geographical concentration at the aggregate industry level considers the concentration of production activities in an industry across Member States irrespective of the origin of the ownership of this production by firms. The MSM methodology allows for both types of analysis, and as such provides value-added to existing empirical studies, which typically focus on one dimension.

The average level of geographical concentration at the individual firm level, shown in Table 1.12 is much higher compared with the level of geographical concentration at the aggregate matrix level, shown in Table 1.4. This difference in geographical concentration at the aggregate level and individual level indicates that the location of activities by leading firms within the EU is not overlapping. The overall spread of activities within the EU is considerably higher, implying that the leading firms do not cluster production in the same countries and that the geographic distribution of ownership of leading firms is an important factor to explain aggregate geographic concentration. Leading firms still concentrate production in their home country. However, the increase in transnational production of leading firms over the investigated period is gradually reducing this home country bias.

1.6 CONCLUSION

Using a unique database on EU leading firms, we analysed the geographical concentration of production across Member States in European manufacturing industries over the time period 1987–97, along with the implementation of the European Single Market Programme. Production of leading firms is considerably concentrated in the large Member States. Tracing changes over the period 1987–97, shows a trend in the direction of more geographical dispersion of production. This trend towards geographical dispersion is found both within northern and southern Member States, and goes together with a slight shift in production toward southern Member States. A more detailed analysis at the level of the industry reveals important variation across industries.

The role of industry-specific characteristics influencing the pattern of geographical dispersion across Member States, provides some deeper insights into the geographical dispersion of industries within the EU. In homogenous products industries characterized by high fixed sunk costs and low possibilities to differentiate products, production displayed a higher level of geographic concentration. Nevertheless, also in these industries we find a trend towards more geographic dispersion, especially a shift towards the southern Member States.

Analysing geographic concentration of production activities at the firm level, the data show that, over the time period 1987–97, leading EU firms have displayed an increasing geographic dispersion of their production activities. This clearly reflects an increase in transnational activity over the considered time period. The trend towards greater cross-border production by EU firms is apparent both before and after 1993. This trend towards more transnational production appears to be broadly based across industries and countries. It indicates the strength of dispersion forces linked to lower trade and investment costs across EU Member States. For non-EU matrix firms geographical dispersion is higher than for EU matrix firms, but is not expanding at the same rate. The absence of a EU home bias effect, as well as the fact that most of these non-EU firms are in a more advanced stage of internationalization, may account for this difference.

We would like to conclude with an important caveat. By solely focusing on the production of the largest firms in Europe, our findings cannot be generalized. Further analysis should clarify to what extent our results carry over to the universe of firms in the EU.

ACKNOWLEDGEMENTS

This research was carried out as part of the project 'Determinants of Industrial Concentration, Market Integration and Efficiency in the European Union' sponsored by DGEC-FIN. The MSM data on which the analysis is based were constructed in collaboration with the University of Norwich (S. Davies), CERIS (L. Rondi) and WIFO (K. Aiginger). This chapter is based on sections 5.3, 5.4 and 5.5. of the report. The authors would like to thank Isabelle Devoldere, Joke Reynaerts and An Van Pelt for their excellent research assistence and F. Ilzkovitz and A. Dierx for their helpful comments.

NOTES

1. The Entropy measure is more sensitive than the Herfindahl index to countries with small production quantities and reduces the impact of countries with large production. The Herfindahl index which is defined as the sum of the squares of all n shares, weighs each share by itself (Jacquemin and Berry, 1979):

$$\mathrm{H} = \sum_{k=1}^{n} P \cdot P \tag{1.7}$$

2. We should note that the final choice of both groups is not crucial for the results. Including for instance Denmark, Ireland, Greece, Spain, Portugal as smaller peripheral countries versus the larger central countries Germany, France, the UK, Italy and Benelux, does not change the main results.
3. This distinction is operationalized using data on what a 'typical' industry spends on advertising and R&D: product differentiation is equated with 'high' expenditures on advertising and/or R&D. Broadly speaking, Type 2A includes industries mainly in food, drink and tobacco, Type 2R are industries in engineering, broadly defined, without significant sales to final consumers, and Type 2AR are often consumer durables (see Davies et al., 1996, pp. 26–31).
4. Normally, the number of country entries at the individual firm level differs from firm to firm, ranging between 1 and 11. However, this makes the arithmetic average of the Relative Entropy across all matrix firms not comparable with the Relative Entropy index at the matrix level. Therefore, the Relative Entropy is calculated for each firm with log n as denominator, keeping n constant ($n = 11$).

REFERENCES

Amiti, M. (1998), 'Inter-industry trade in manufactures: does country size matter?', *Journal of International Economics*, **44**, 231–55.

Amiti, M. (1999), 'Specialization patterns in Europe', *Weltwirtschaftliches Archiv*, **135** (4), 573–93.

Brülhart, M. and J. Torstensson (1996), 'Regional integration, scale economies and industry location in the European Union', CEPR Discussion Paper 1435.

Davies, S.W., B.R. Lyons, C. Matraves, L. Rondi, A. Sembenelli, J. Gual, L.

Sleuwaegen and R. Veugelers (1996), *Industrial Organisation in the European Union*, Oxford: Clarendon Press.
Delios, A. and S. Makino (2000), 'The timing of FDI: is being first always best?', AIB Conference, Phoenix, Arizona, November.
European Commission (1996), *Economic Evaluation of the Internal Market*, European Economy, Reports and Studies, 4.
Forslid, R. and I. Wooton (1999), 'Comparative advantage and the location of production', CEPR Discussion Paper 2118.
Fujita, M., P. Krugman and A. Venables (1999), *The Spatial Economy: Cities, Regions and International Trade*, Cambridge, MA: MIT Press.
Gao, T. (1999), 'Economic geography and the department of vertical multinational production', *Journal of International Economics*, **48**, 301–20.
Helpman, E. (1999), 'The structure of foreign trade', *Journal of Economic Perspectives*, **13** (2), 121–44.
Jacquemin, A. and C.H. Berry (1979), 'Entropy measure of diversification and corporate growth', *Journal of Industrial Economics*, June, 359–69.
Johanson, J. and J.E. Vahlne (1977). 'The internationalisation process of the firm – A model of knowledge development and increasing foreign market commitments', *Journal of International Business Studies*, **8**, 23–32.
Krugman, P. (1991), 'Increasing returns and economic geography', *Journal of Political Economy*, **99** (3), 483–99.
Krugman, P. and A.J. Venables (1995), 'Globalization and the inequality of nations', *Quarterly Journal of Economics*, **110**, 857–79.
Middelfart-Knarvik, K.H., H. Overman, S. Redding and T. Venables (2002), 'The location of European industry', *European Economy*, Economic Papers, 142.
Raybaudi-Massilia, M. (2000), 'Economic geography and multinational enterprise', *Review of International Economics*, **81** (1), 1–19.
Sutton, J. (1991), *Sunk Costs and Market Structure*, Cambridge, MA: MIT Press.
Vandermerwe, S. (1993), 'A framework for constructing Euro-networks', *European Management Journal*, **11** (1), 55–61.
Venables, A. (1996), 'Equilibrium locations of vertically linked industries', *International Economic Review*, **37**, 341–59.
Veugelers, R., L. Sleuwaegen, L. Rondi, S. Davies, L. Benfratello, I. Devoldere, P. Egger, M. Pfaffermayr, K. Rommens, J. Reynaerts and D. Vannoni (2002), 'Determinants of industrial concentration, market integration and efficiency in the EU', *European Economy*, forthcoming, special report no. 2, EU Publications Office.
WIFO (1999), *Specialization and (Geographic) Concentration of European Manufacturing*, Report of a Study for the Enterprise DG of the European Commission, Brussels.

2. Globalization, agglomeration and FDI location: the case of French firms in Europe

Jean-Louis Mucchielli and Florence Puech

2.1 INTRODUCTION

Even though French firms started to invest abroad only recently (French FDI flows were almost insignificant before the second half of the 1980s), nowadays France plays an important role in the world with its international investments. Despite an important decline of its FDI outflows in 2001, France became the second most important investor ($82.8 billion) behind the USA (UNCTAD, 2002). However, multinational firms' location strategies are generally developed by a concentric process illustrated by a progressive international diffusion of their activities. At the beginning of the internationalization process, plants are settled in border countries and, then, multinationals progressively invest in farther territories. But at the end of 2000, French international investments are still strongly located in the European area: more than the half of the French FDI outwards stock is located in Europe.[1]

As regards determinants of firms' internationalization, two approaches are complementary. The first is to identify the main incentives which influence the choice of producing abroad ('*why* do firms internationalize their activities?'). The second concerns firms' international location choice ('*where* do firms locate?'). With the renewal of interest of spatial economic geography, increasing numbers of articles in economic literature are devoted to multinational firms' location. An important part of these recent studies emphasizes the phenomenon of FDI agglomeration (see Ferrer, 1998, for French FDI in European regions; Ford and Strange, 1999, or Mayer and Mucchielli, 1999, concerning the location of Japanese firms in Europe). Studying multinational firms' location, some theoretical and empirical analyses suggest that firms' strategies could result from a sequential process. Several geographic scales have to be considered to evaluate firms' location determinants because multinationals seem first to choose an important geographic area in the world (like a continent), next they select a country, then a region and, finally, a specific site for their investment.

The aim of this chapter is twofold. Using a qualitative approach, we are trying to highlight the main determinants of the geographic concentration phenomenon of French firms in manufacturing sectors. Our study focuses on seven European countries: Belgium, Germany, Italy, the Netherlands, Portugal, Spain and the UK and 47 administrative European regions during the period 1987–94. Moreover, we assess if the location of French multinationals could result from a sequential process where firms at first choose a country and then a region where they are going to settle a subsidiary. The chapter is organized as follows: section 2.2 briefly underlines some stylized facts on the location of French FDI in Europe according to a perusal of our data. Section 2.3 outlines the econometric methodology (conditional logit model and nested logit model). In section 2.4 we present the database and the chosen variables. Finally, in section 2.5, we discuss the empirical results.

2.2 STYLIZED FACTS

National and Regional Geographic Concentrations of French Multinationals in Europe

A descriptive analysis based on the database *Enquête-Filiales 2000* of the French Directory of Economic and Foreign Relationships (DREE) of the French Ministry of Economics, Finance and Industry underlines that, nowadays, the main part of the French FDI (more than 38 per cent) is located in European Union countries. The analysis of the geographic distribution of French international investments highlights some strong geographic disparities at international and intra-national levels. The most attractive countries (in terms of subsidiaries located in the country) are the UK, Germany, Spain, Belgium and Italy. Those nations regroup more than 75 per cent of French FDI located in Europe. Moreover, several European regions receive a large part of French multinationals or, conversely, others are unattractive for French international investments. French FDI is located in industrialized regions or regions which include the capital of the country. For instance, considering the main host European regions in terms of the number of French FDIs, the respective shares of the Eastern region in Spain, the Lombardy in Italy or the South East in the UK are 8.1 per cent, 5.1 per cent and 3.9 per cent respectively and the ones of Madrid, Brussels and London are, respectively, equal to 7.1 per cent, 7 per cent and 6.5 per cent.[2]

Measuring the Attractiveness of European Regions

In order to more precisely describe the geographic concentration of French multinationals in European regions, a ratio denoted R for each region i is proposed. It is constructed as follows:[3]

$$R_i = \frac{\dfrac{\text{Stock of French FDI in the region } i}{\text{Stock of French FDI in Europe}}}{\dfrac{\text{GDP of the region } i}{\text{Sum of the GDP of all European regions}}} \quad (2.1)$$

This ratio can be approached as a regional attractiveness measure which takes into account the region's size. The numerator indicates the proportion of French affiliates settled in the region i and the denominator represents the share of the region i in the European gross domestic product (GDP). The benchmark is 1. Values above 1 (respectively below 1) indicate that the considered regions have a more important share (respectively a less important one) than their economic size could have been expected to. This measure enables the elimination of the regional-size effect because, all things being equal, important regions (in surface area) would tend to attract more multinationals than would smaller regions.

Using this ratio, Figure 2.1 illustrates the European regions attractiveness for the French multinational firms for the year 2000. As we mentioned, industrialized regions (as the Lombardy or the Eastern region in Spain) and regions which contain the capital have a strong attractive power. Besides, two large European areas receive an important part of French affiliates. Regions localized at the centre of the European Union constitute one of the main destinations of French FDI. This area, defined by the South of the UK, Belgium, the Netherlands and regions of West Germany, proportionally locate more French international investments than their economic size could have been predicted. The second geographic zone, comprising the northern regions of Portugal and Spain, captures a great number of French investments. Other peripheral regions are less attractive: for example, the majority of the Greek, Italian, Finnish or Swedish regions.

2.3 METHODOLOGY

We can study the French firms' location decisions by using a database which registers individually French subsidiaries in the European area.

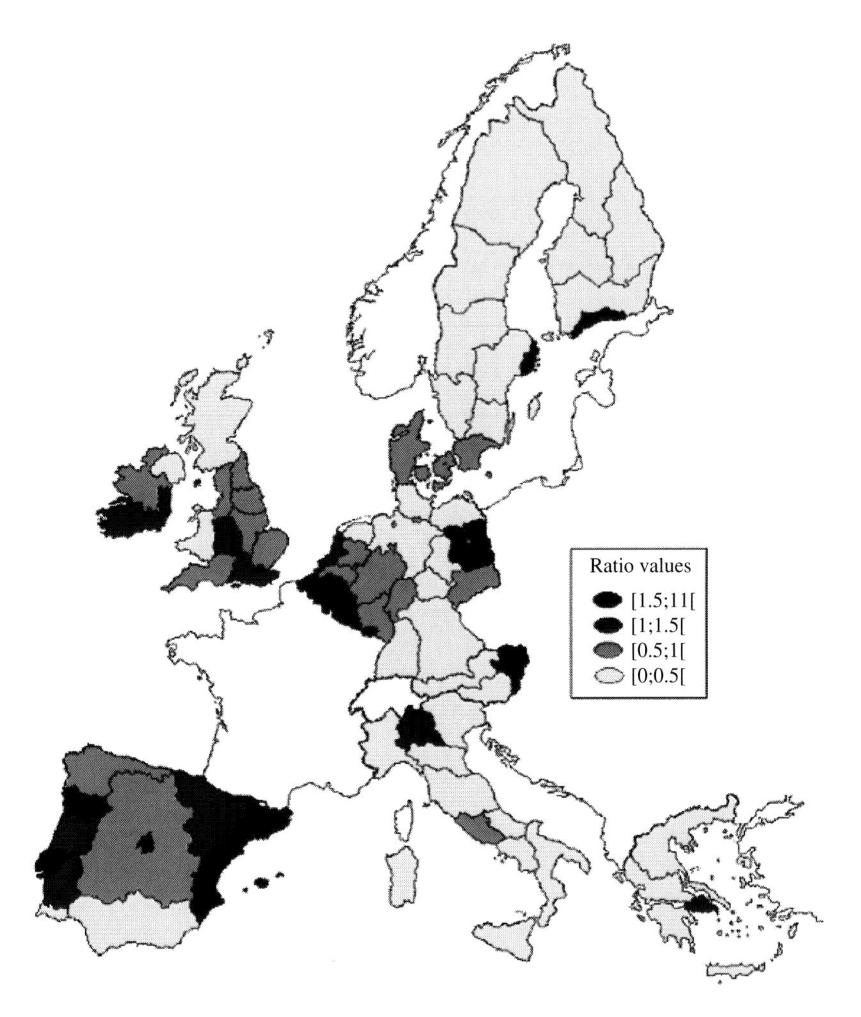

Source: Estimations calculated from the *Enquête-Filiales DREE 2000* (NUTS 1 classification).

Figure 2.1 Distribution of the French multinationals in European regions in 2000

Consequently, discrete choice models are particularly well adapted to our target. Our empirical estimations made on qualitative econometric models will enable understanding and quantification of the importance of the main determinants which influence the choice of a specific site. Also, those econometric models are able to detect whether a hierarchical geographic structure of the location choice exists.

Models *without* a Hierarchical Structure

For the first time, we are going to *separately* study determinants of French firms' location by evaluating independently the influence of location variables at national and regional levels. Table 2.1 lists some empirical studies concerning the location determinants of FDI in manufacturing sectors.

Following McFadden (1974), a lot of recent research studies firms' location determinants using a conditional logit model. The conditional logit model belongs to the discrete choice models. This model is based on the maximization of firms' profit functions: all investors will choose a particular site if and only if this specific location offers the highest profits among all possible alternatives. By assumption, we consider that when a multinational firm wants to locate a subsidiary abroad, this multinational makes a discrete choice considering all the possible alternatives (which are unranked choices).

In this theoretical framework, we consider that each firm can choose between N possible areas for its future location (the indexing is, of course, arbitrary). Profits of each firm associated with the location j can be described as $\Pi_j = V_j + \epsilon_j$ where V_j is a function of attributes of the location j and ϵ_j is an unobservable random error term. The linear expression is: $V_j = \beta X_j$ where X_j is the vector of observable characteristics of the location j and β is the vector of the parameters (which are going to be estimated). Note that each firm will choose the location j if the expected profits noted Π_j are superior to all of the expected profits of other locations: $\Pi_j = \max\{\Pi_k\}$ where $k = 1, \ldots, N$ that is to say: $P_j = P(\Pi_j > \Pi_k)$ for all k (and $k \neq j$).

In those conditions, if we assume that the random error terms are independently and identically distributed according to a Weibull distribution, McFadden (1974) proved that the probability for a firm to choose the location j is given by the conditional logit model: $P_j = \exp(\beta X_j)/\Sigma_{k=1}^{N} \exp(\beta X_k)$. Finally, coefficients which constitute the vector β are estimated by the maximum likelihood technique.

Models *with* a Hierarchical Structure

An important restriction of the conditional logit model is the hypothesis concerning random error terms: we assume that they are not correlated across alternatives. This implies a powerful property called the '*Independence of Irrelevant Alternatives*' (IIA). This well-known IIA hypothesis implies that the ratio of probabilities of any two alternatives is unaffected from the choice set. In other words, it means that adding another alternative in the sample will not change the odds ratio between two other alternatives (for more

Table 2.1 Recent studies on multinationals' location choice in manufacturing sectors based on a discrete choice model

Authors	Home country	Host country	Period	Geographic concentration	Demand	Labour costs
Chen (1996)	Foreign countries	Provinces in China grouped in three regions	1987–91	Not included	+	NS
Coughlin, Terza and Arromdee (1991)	Foreign countries	American states	1981–83	+	+	–
Crozet, Mayer and Mucchielli (2004)	Belgium, Germany, Italy, Japan, the Netherlands, Switzerland, the UK and the USA	France, 92 countries (*départments*)	1985–95	+	+	+/–
Devereux and Griffith (1998)	The USA	France, Germany, UK	1980–94	+	+	NS
Ford and Strange (1999)	Japan	7 European countries	1980–95	+	+	–
Friedman, Gerlowski and Silberman (1992)	Foreign countries	American states	1977–88	Not included	+	–
Guimarães, Figuierdo and Woodward (2000)	Foreign countries	275 Concelhos in Portugal	1985–92	+	Not included	NS
Head and Ries (1996)	Australia, Canada, Europe, Japan and the USA	54 cities in China	1984–91	+	Not included	NS
Head, Ries and Swenson (1995)	Japan	American states	1980–92	+	Not included	Not included

Head, Ries and Swenson (1999)	Japan	American states	1980–92	+	+	+/–
Jianping (1999)	China, Japan and the USA	30 Chinese provinces	1981–96	+	Not included	–
Mayer and Mucchielli (1998)	Japan	5 European countries	1984–94	+	Not included	+
Woodward (1992)	Japan	American states and counties	1980–89	+ (County)	+ (State)	NS

Notes:
NS = variable is not significant.
+ (respectively −) means that the variable has a significant positive (respectively negative) effect on firms location choice.

details, see for instance McFadden, 1974; Ben-Akiva and Lerman, 1985). As McFadden (1974) underlined, this assumption is restrictive in many applications. For example, this property is unlikely to be respected if two alternatives are close substitutes (this might be the case in our study for two regions of the same country).

A way to relax the IIA property is to use a *nested logit model.* Such an econometric model allows the statistician to partition his sample in mutually exclusive groups which seem to have similar attributes. Consequently, the nested logit model describes a location process in which individual choices can be interpreted as a multi-stage dynamic process (hierarchical decision structure). In our empirical analysis, we create a tree structure (two stages): nests are constituted by countries (first level) and each nest regroups their respective regions (bottom level). This structure seems a priori correct if we consider that two regions which belong to the same country are closer substitutes than two regions from two different countries. Therefore, we may think that a firm about to settle a subsidiary abroad hesitates at first between several potential host countries, then, after the choice of a country, the firm determines a region inside the chosen country for its subsidiary. Several articles develop this approach considering the location of firms, for instance, Hansen (1987), Guimarães, Rolfe and Woodward (1998) or Mayer and Mucchielli (1999). Also, several authors include some dummies in their model in order to absorb the correlation across choices (Bartik, 1985; Woodward, 1992; Head, Ries and Swenson, 1995; 1999).

Basically, let us denote regions $r = 1, 2, ..., R$ and countries $c = 1, 2, ..., C$. Each firm will choose the alternative which maximizes its profits: $\Pi_{cr} = V_{cr} + \epsilon_{cr}$. Here, the function of the observed characteristics V_{cr}, depends at the same time on characteristics of the nest Y_c (the country) *and* on attributes which vary across regions X_{cr}. We obtain: $V_{cr} = \beta X_{cr} + \alpha Y_c$. where β and α are vectors of parameters which are going to be estimated.

The probability for choosing a country depends at the same time on its attributes and also on characteristics of alternatives which composed the nest. We defined an expected maximum utility associated to the nest called *inclusive value* (I_c) which is equal to:

$$I_c = log\left(\sum_{i=1}^{R_c} exp(\beta X_{ic})\right) \tag{2.2}$$

Consequently, the probability P_c, to choose a country c is:

$$P_c = exp(\sigma I_c + \alpha Y_c) / \sum_{j=1}^{C} exp(\sigma I_j + \alpha Y_j)$$

The probability P_{cr} to choose a region r is: $P_{cr} = P_{r|c} \times P_c$ where (2.3)

$$P_{r|c} = exp(\beta X_{cr}) / \sum_{i=1}^{R_c} exp(\beta X_{ci}) \text{ that is to say:}$$

$$P_{cr} = (exp(\beta X_{ic}) \times exp(\sigma I_c + \alpha Y_c)) / \left(\sum_{j=1}^{C} exp(\sigma I_j + \alpha Y_j) \times exp(I_c) \right)$$

The σ coefficient of the inclusive value determines the pertinence of the tree structure. As McFadden underlined (see, for example, McFadden, 1984), $0 < \sigma < 1$ is a sufficient condition for a sequential model. On contrary, if $\sigma = 1$ or $\sigma = 0$, the model is equivalent to a conditional logit model. At last, the value $(1 - \sigma)$ gives the degree of similarity across alternatives.

2.4 LOCATION DETERMINANTS AT NATIONAL AND REGIONAL LEVELS

The Database

'*Where should we put that plant?*' This question was asked in the 1970s, by a person in charge of IBM, at the beginning of an article of a business weekly. This underlines what professionals call the intangible factors of location choice. Such factors could be enumerated as a simple list: local demand, labour cost, infrastructures, universities to a more complex one which includes economic, social, political and technique factors (Mucchielli, 1998). Those studies often denote some specificities linked to the studied multinational firm. Conversely, some annual surveys are more able to underline some generic and fundamental determinants for each multinational firm settlement.

In France, the DREE of the French Ministry of Economics, Finance and Industry annually records French multinationals or multinational firms with a French participation in the world (more than 10 per cent). In this study, we use this survey (*Enquête-Filiales DREE*), which registers all French multinationals in the world at an individual level. The *Enquête-Filiales DREE 2000* lists international French establishments created until 2001. In the sample, we only retain multinationals which belong to industrial sectors. The classification of all sectors of activity is made according to the NAF 60, which is a French nomenclature of activities. We consequently ranked those industries according to the NACE (two-digit level European nomenclature) and we only kept sectors for which we had national and regional data (see Table 2.2 for a complete list of the 16 manufacturing sectors retained in our study). Our sample is finally composed of 614 individual location choices of French multinationals settled between 1987 and 1994 in seven European countries: Belgium, Germany, Italy, the Netherlands, Portugal, Spain, the UK and in 47 regions (NUTS 1 level).[4] Figure 2.2 presents the 47 European regions.

Table 2.2 The 16 industrial sectors of activity (NACE two-digit)

22: Production and preliminary processing of metals
24: Manufacture of non-metallic mineral products
25: Chemical products
32: Mechanical engineering
33: Manufacture of office machinery and data processing machinery
34: Electrical engineering
35: Manufacture of motor vehicles and of motor vehicle parts and accessories
36: Manufacture of other means of transports
37: Instrument engineering
41 and 42: Food, drink and tobacco industry
43: Textile industry
45: Footwear and clothing industry
47: Manufacture of paper and paper products; printings and publishing
48: Processing of rubber and plastics
49: Other manufacturing industries

Variables and Expected Signs

At the national (respectively regional) level, the dependent variable is the country (respectively the region) chosen by each firm. The location decision is based on the comparison of attributes of each potential site. At both geographic scales, to understand the location patterns of new plants, we retain three main groups of explicative variables: demand, cost and agglomeration variables. We use the well-known distinction of firms' location determinants as market seeking, cost seeking and strategic seeking (the last one in order to understand the agglomeration behaviour). Those relevant attributes which may influence the location choice are discussed below.[5]

Market seeking

We do not include the GDP as a proxy of demand in the model because measuring the potential demand by the GDP has the major drawback of not taking into account the demand of the border territories. Consequently, the retained demand variables are based on a larger notion than that of the GDP and their definitions are closely related to the idea of the

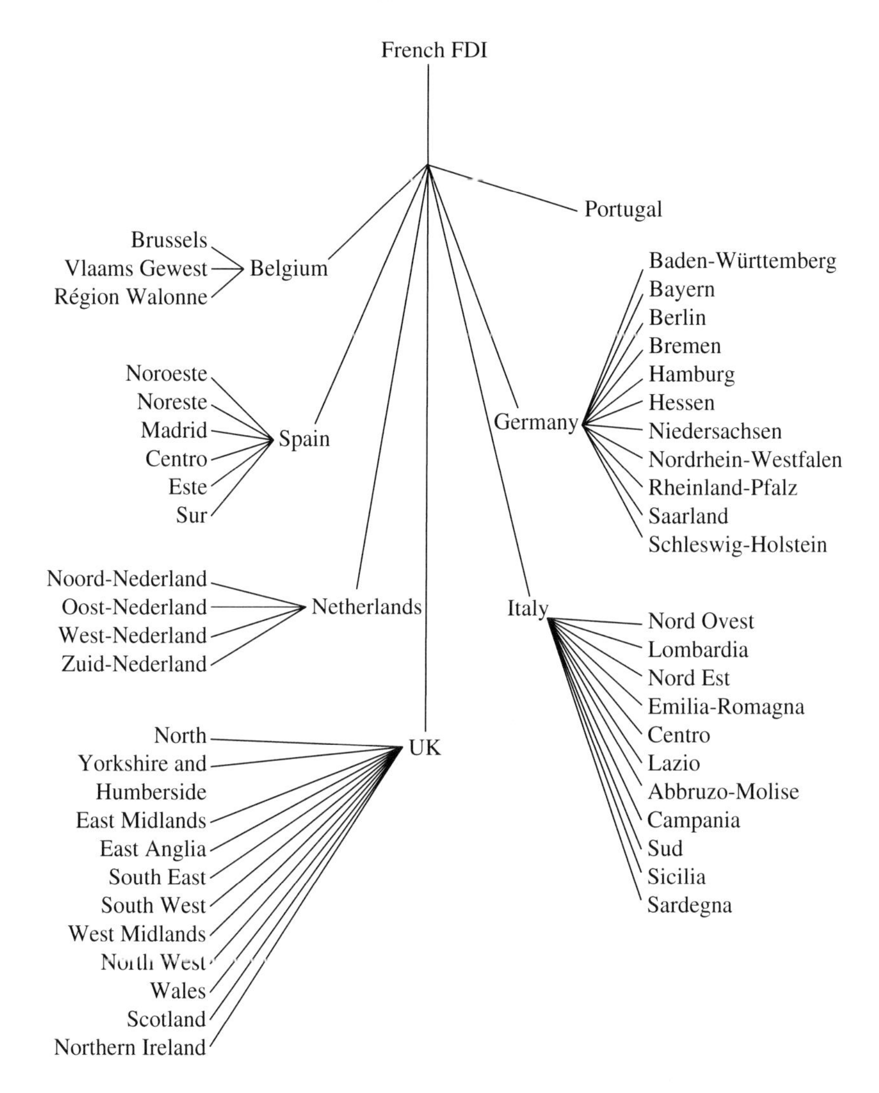

Figure 2.2 The tree structure of the location set: seven countries and 47 regions (46 regions NUTS 1 + Portugal NUTS 0)

potential market of a location site.[6] Three variables are proposed. The first, denoted $PMEU_n$, represents the sum of the GDP of the host country and of its border countries which belong to the European Union. The second variable is called $PMLARGE_n$, which is the sum of the host country GDP plus the GDP of *all* its adjacent countries (Central and Eastern European Countries – CEECs – border countries and Switzerland are included).

Finally, if we consider that the CEECs began to trade after 1991, firms may have considered the CEECs' demand only after this year. Then the variable PMLARGE91_n represents the sum of the host country GDP and of its border countries except for the CEECs adjacent countries' GDP which are only added after 1991. Analysing FDI location determinants, empirical studies generally find a positive impact of the local demand on the location choice (see Table 2.1): firms seem to have a greater incentive to settle an affiliate in areas where there is a high market potential. The expected signs of PMEU_n, PMLARGE_n and PMLARGE91_n are thus positive.

Cost seeking

The average of the annual wage cost per capita in the manufacturing sector (WAGECAP_n) is retained. A vast majority of empirical analyses find that multinationals are attracted to areas where labour costs are low (Coughlin, Terza and Arromdee, 1991; Friedman, Gerlowski and Silberman, 1992; Ford and Strange, 1999; Jianping, 1999). Consequently, the coefficient of WAGECAP_n is presumed to be negative because high wages would tend to deter and discourage French investments in the country.

Another variable included in the model is the unemployment rate labelled UNEMPLOYMENT_n (long-term unemployment rate in the country). The expected sign of this variable is unclear because firms may interpret a high unemployment rate as a result of rigidities on the labour market (negative impact), or, on the contrary, they can understand it to be a good signal of a potential availability of workers (positive impact). In the European area, empirical results of the unemployment rate on FDI are ambiguous: for instance, Ferrer (1998) found a positive significant impact whereas Mayer and Mucchielli (1998) detect a negative significant effect.

Strategic seeking

Our third group of location determinants explains the observed geographic concentration at the national level and also the agglomeration effects occurring at the regional geographic scale. Here, the strategic behaviour is analysed towards the propensity to agglomerate activities.

The idea of benefits generated by the geographic proximity of firms is not recent. As Marshall (1920) underlined, industrial concentration may provide a potential pool of skilled workers, an easier access to suppliers and a potential to benefit from knowledge spillovers. Furthermore, multinationals have imperfect information of foreign potential sites (Johanson and Wiedersheim-Paul, 1975; Hirsh, 1976). Consequently, knowing that other French or local firms are located in a particular area in the foreign market may constitute a key determinant in their location strategy. However, some theoretical debates subsist regarding the importance of forces which tend to produce an agglomeration phenomenon and those which bring a spatial dispersion of firms on a given territory (see, for instance, Krugman, 1991; Fujita, Krugman and Venables, 1999). As an example, on the one hand, the proximity to other firms could constitute a source of geographic agglomeration: for instance, after the location of one firm in a given area, all of the other firms would rather like to follow the former in order to benefit from the positive effects of intra-industry or inter-industry externalities. On the other hand, numerous firms in the same area could create some centrifugal forces: in this case, firms want to avoid their competitors generating a dispersion effect on the territory. In spite of this, empirical studies of FDI location generally support the fact that the number of local firms has a positive impact on multinationals location (Head, Ries and Swenson 1995; 1999; Head and Ries, 1996; Ford and Strange, 1999; Crozet, Mayer and Mucchielli, 2004).

The distinction between several agglomeration/dispersion forces has to be done to analyse the agglomeration patterns more precisely. First, we create a variable called INDUSTRYFDI_n, which corresponds to one plus the stock of French manufacturing FDI located in the country until the year before the settlement.[7] We expect a positive sign of INDUSTRYFDI_n because the more the cumulated count of French affiliates settled in a country, the more attractive the potential host country is. Knowing that other French multinationals had already settled in a country could be understood as a positive signal to invest in the host country. Second, we create a variable labelled SECTORFDI_n, which is the sum of French affiliates of the same sector of activity located in the country until the year before the settlement. The predicted sign of the SECTORFDI_n coefficient is unclear because it seems that there is not a general geographic concentration trend of French firms in *all* manufacturing sectors (Mucchielli and Puech, 2001). Finally, we would like to emphasize where French multinationals have a typical location behaviour or, for instance, where they only mimic the one of local firms. For this, the variable EMPLOYHOST_n represents the number of employees of the host country which belong to the same sector of the affiliate in comparison with the whole manufacturing employment in the country. We expect a positive sign associated to EMPLOYHOST_n.

We summarize sources and definitions of the national explanatory variables in Table 2.3.

The same signs for regional variables are expected as those previously described at the national level. Nevertheless, the distinction nation/region allows us to show at which geographic level determinants affect the location choice. All regional variables are described in Table 2.4.

Table 2.3 Description of independent variables at national level

Variable	Definition	Source
$PMEU_n$	Sum of the GDP of the host country (the year of the settlement) plus the GDP of its adjacent European countries	CHELEM
$PMLARGE_n$	Sum of the GDP of the host country (the year of the settlement) plus all of the GDP of its adjacent countries	CHELEM, CEPII
$PMLARGE91_n$	Sum of the GDP of the host country (the year of the settlement) plus all of the GDP of its adjacent countries; CEECs' GDP are only included after the year 1991	CHELEM, CEPII
$WAGECAP_n$	Annual average wage per capita in each sector of activity the year of the affiliate creation	STAN, OECD
$UNEMPLOYMENT_n$	Long-term unemployment rate in the country the year of the settlement	EUROSTAT
$INDUSTRYFDI_n$	One plus the stock of French affiliates in manufacturing sectors until the year before the settlement in the country	DREE 2000
$SECTORFDI_n$	One plus the stock of French affiliates which belong to the same sector until the year before the settlement in the country	DREE 2000
$EMPLOYHOST_n$	Number of employees in the country which belong to the same sector compared to the whole manufacturing industry employment in the country	STAN, OECD

2.5 RESULTS

Empirical results are depicted in Tables 2.5 and 2.6. The estimated coefficients of explanatory variables are discussed, first, considering the two geographic levels independently and, second, considering the hierarchical structure: countries/regions.

Empirical Results *without* a Sequential Structure

The econometric models 1, 2 and 3 are estimated without an eventual tree structure: investors consider separately the two geographical levels.

First, it is noteworthy that all significant variables have the expected sign.

Table 2.4 Description of independent variables at regional level

Variable	Definition	Source
$PMEU_r$	Sum of the GDP of the host region (the year of the settlement) plus the GDP of its adjacent European regions	Regio, EUROSTAT
$PMLARGE_r$	Sum of the GDP of the host region (the year of the settlement) plus all of the GDP of its adjacent regions	Regio, EUROSTAT and CHELEM
$PMLARGE91_r$	Sum of the GDP of the host region (the year of the settlement) plus all GDP of its adjacent regions; CEECs' GDP are only included after the year 1991	Regio, EUROSTAT and CHELEM
$WAGECAP_r$	Annual average wage per capita in each sector of activity the year of the affiliate creation in the region	Structure and activity of industry, EUROSTAT
$UNEMPLOYMENT_r$	Long-term unemployment rate in the region the year of the settlement	Regio, EUROSTAT
$INDUSTRYFDI_r$	One plus stock of French affiliates in manufacturing sectors until the year before the settlement in the region	DREE 2000
$SECTORFDI_r$	One plus stock of French affiliates which belong to the same sector of activity until the year before the settlement in the region	DREE 2000
$EMPLOYHOST_r$	Number of employees in the region which belong to the same sector compared to the whole manufacturing industry employment in the region	Structure and activity of industry, EUROSTAT

On the demand side, we can emphasize that the three potential market variables are not significant at a 10 per cent threshold at both geographic levels. This result is quite surprising because this leads us to think that the expected market size does not influence the location choice of French investors. Concerning the costs variable, empirical results show that labour costs have a strong repulsive impact on French multinationals: to increase the probability of locating a new subsidiary in a particular region or country it is all the more important that the local level of wages is low. Their coefficients are quite important (respectively equal to −0.60 and −0.42 at regional and national levels). This proves that firms are sensitive to the level of wages they would have to pay if they created a subsidiary in Europe: a 10 per cent increase of the wages per head in a given region will reduce its probability of attracting French FDI approximately by 6 per cent.[8] In the

Table 2.5 Maximum likelihood estimation results of the conditional logit models

	Models *without* a hierarchical structure						
	National level				Regional level		
Variables	Model 1 (a)	Model 2 (a)	Model 3 (a)	Variables	Model 1 (b)	Model 2 (b)	Model 3 (b)
PMEU_n	−0.10			PMEU_r	0.05		
	(0.12)				(0.07)		
PMLARGE_n		−0.08		PMLARGE_r		0.08	
		(0.11)				(0.07)	
PMLARGE91_n			−0.09	PMLARGE91_r			0.08
			(0.12)				(0.07)
WAGECAP_n	−0.42**	−0.44**	−0.43**	WAGECAP_r	−0.60***	−0.62***	−0.62***
	(0.20)	(0.20)	(0.20)		(0.12)	(0.13)	(0.12)
INDUSTRYFDI_n	0.47***	0.47***	0.47***	INDUSTRYFDI_r	0.57***	0.57***	0.57***
	(0.14)	(0.14)	(0.14)		(0.07)	(0.07)	(0.07)
SECTORFDI_n	0.54***	0.54***	0.54***	SECTORFDI_r	0.46***	0.46***	0.46***
	(0.11)	(0.11)	(0.11)		(0.08)	(0.08)	(0.08)
EMPLOYHOST_n	0.25***	0.25***	0.25***	EMPLOYHOST_r	0.31***	0.31***	0.31***
	(0.12)	(0.12)	(0.12)		(0.06)	(0.06)	(0.06)
UNEMPLOYMENT_n	0.09	0.09	0.09	UNEMPLOYMENT_r	−0.07	−0.06	−0.06
	(0.08)	(0.08)	(0.08)		(0.07)	(0.07)	(0.06)
Log likelihood	−1054.12	−1054.21	−1054.17	Log likelihood	−1995.21	−1994.92	−1994.91

Notes:
All variables are taken in logarithm.
Standard errors are in parentheses.
** and *** denote significance levels at 10 per cent and 5 per cent respectively.

Table 2.6 Maximum likelihood estimation results of the nested logit models

Variables	Models *with* a hierarchical structure Model 4	Model 5	Model 6
Regional level			
$PMEU_r$	0.18**		
	(0.09)		
$PMLARGE_r$		0.19**	
		(0.09)	
$PMLARGE91_r$			0.19**
			(0.09)
$WAGECAP_r$	0.44	0.46	0.46
	(0.45)	(0.45)	(0.45)
$INDUSTRYFDI_r$	0.56***	0.55***	0.55***
	(0.08)	(0.08)	(0.08)
$SECTORFDI_r$	0.35***	0.35***	0.35***
	(0.10)	(0.10)	(0.10)
$EMPLOYHOST_r$	0.29***	0.29***	0.29***
	(0.08)	(0.09)	(0.08)
$UNEMPLOYMENT_r$	−0.10	−0.08	−0.08
	(0.13)	(0.13)	(0.13)
National level			
$PMEU_n$	−0.09		
	(0.12)		
$PMLARGE_n$		−0.08	
		(0.11)	
$PMLARGE91_n$			−0.09
			(0.12)
$WAGECAP_n$	−0.96***	−0.98***	−0.97***
	(0.26)	(0.26)	(0.26)
$INDUSTRYFDI_n$	0.11	0.12	0.12
	(0.18)	(0.18)	(0.18)
$SECTORFDI_n$	0.38***	0.38***	0.38***
	(0.12)	(0.12)	(0.12)
$EMPLOYHOST_n$	0.05	0.06	0.06
	(0.13)	(0.13)	(0.13)
$UNEMPLOYMENT_n$	0.15*	0.14*	0.14*
	(0.08)	(0.08)	(0.08)
Inclusive Value	0.64***	0.63***	0.63***
	(0.20)	(0.20)	(0.20)
Log likelihood			
Regional level	−932.22	−932.77	−932.77
National level	−1048.76	−1048.80	−1048.76

Notes:
All variables are taken in logarithm.
Standard errors are in parentheses.
*, ** and *** denote significance levels at 10 per cent, 5 per cent and 1 per cent respectively.

economic literature on FDI location, some studies find a significant negative impact of labour cost variables (see Table 2.1). In particular, Mayer and Mucchielli (1999) put the stress on the wages variable which represents a key determinant at the regional level for Japanese FDI location in Europe.

Moreover, the three agglomeration variables are significant and the coefficient associated is always positive. French firms detect a positive signal from areas where some country partners (whether they belong to the same industry or not) or some local manufacturing activities are located. In other words, existing local manufacturing activity is estimated to have a positive effect on new multinationals' location. In summary, it seems that agglomeration forces tend to be stronger than dispersion forces and French FDI copy the location behaviour of local firms or of their country partners. Ferrer (1998), who studies the location of French FDI in Europe, also finds that agglomeration variables have a significant positive impact. Besides, coefficients associated with agglomeration variables INDUSTRYFDI, SECTORFDI and EMPLOYHOST are approximately equal at national and regional levels. This means that agglomeration variables have the same influence at both geographic levels. However, we could have expected that regional coefficients' values of agglomeration variables would have been stronger than national ones. Finally, we can note that regional and national unemployment rates are not significant.

Empirical Results *with* a Hierarchical Structure

Considering empirical results of nested logit models (models 4, 5 and 6), the tree structure is relevant and several variables are only significant at the national level; conversely, others are only significant at the regional level and at least one variable is pertinent at both geographical scales. It is worth noting that all significant variables have the correct expected sign.

Relevance of the tree structure

The proposed tree structure is validated (models 4, 5 and 6). Nesting regions within countries seems to be a good specification of the tree structure according to the inclusive value coefficient (all coefficients of inclusive values belong to the unit interval]0;1[) and to the coefficient significances.

As we underlined, the inclusive value coefficient is essential because it indicates the degree of choice substitutability. If the inclusive value coefficient is equal to zero or one, this implies that we can separately model both geographical levels (two conditional logit models) without the proposed hierarchical structure. However, if the coefficient of the inclusive value belongs to the unit interval]0;1[, this proves that nested regions inside countries is relevant and the value of the coefficient $(1-\sigma)$ gives the degree of similarity across alternatives. For instance, $(1-\sigma)$ close to one attests that regions which belong to the same nest are very similar; on the opposite, $(1-\sigma)$ close to zero indicates that two regions which belong to the same country are quite different. We can easily see that considering each of the three models, results rather support the second assumption (coefficient of the inclusive value is equal to 0.63 or 0.64). In summary, in our econometric models, the significance of the inclusive value coefficient demonstrates that independently modelling the location choice of French multinational firms in countries and regions constitutes an inappropriate approach and the correct econometric method is the nested logit model.

Demand and cost variables

Demand, wages and unemployment variables have an impact on the location choice decisions, but their significant influence occurs at different geographic scales.

The demand variable is only significant at the regional level. This underlines that investors consider the regional potential market in their strategies and a higher regional market size will increase the probability of choosing a particular region. If we analyse the regional potential market per country more precisely, we can show that there are some important differences between regions which belong to the same country. Figure 2.3 depicts the average regional potential market for the period 1987–94 per country and standard deviations associated (in Figure 2.3, PMEU is chosen as a proxy

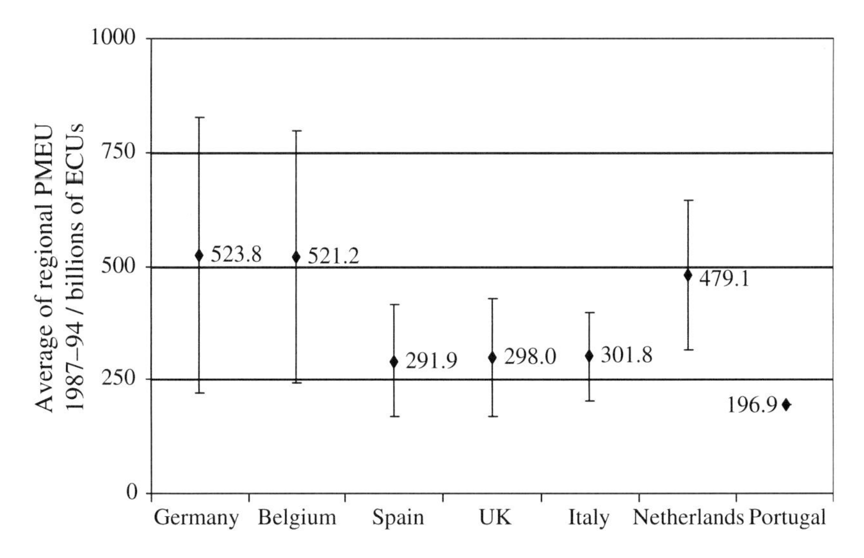

Figure 2.3 Average of regional PMEU (1987–94)

of the potential market). The variability of regional PMEU inside the same country is more important than that between countries. Estimations of nested models confirm this result: the demand variable has a significant influence on French multinationals' location strategies at the regional level. Note that differences between regions of the same country increase if PMLARGE_n or PMLARGE91_n are retained. This conclusion seems to be important because one can think that multinationals choose a country and not a region for its market size.

Conversely, analysing the regional annual value of wages per capita per country over the same period (Figure 2.4), we can point out that the mean of the annual regional wages per capita is quite different from one country to another and associated standard deviations are small. Consequently, wages per capita is likely to be a national determinant of location choice if we use a nested approach. As we find in models 4, 5 and 6, the wages variable is only significant at national geographic scale. Besides the level of this labour cost constitutes a key determinant in FDI location strategies: coefficients associated with national wages are the most important in the three nested models (coefficients vary from −0.96 to −0.98). To a certain extent, this result may revive the debate on the labour costs in Europe and the potential attractiveness of countries.

Nevertheless, we have to make additional comments. First, Figure 2.4 points out that Belgium and the UK have approximately the same average regional level of wages per capita in industrial sectors in this period,

Figure 2.4 Average of regional wages per capita (1987–94)

whereas some notable regional differences exist in Italy for this variable. Second, in our econometric model, we use two different sources of wages per capita for the two geographic scales so the national average level of wages per capita is not exactly the same as the average of regional wages per head.

Agglomeration variables
The nested results of French firms' location decisions point out some important agglomeration effects occurring at the same time at national and regional levels. Nevertheless, only one agglomeration variable is significant at the national level (SectorFDI_n), whereas all of the three variables are significant at the regional level (SectorFDI_r, IndustryFDI_r and EmployHost_r). According to a well-specified econometric model, empirical results show that agglomeration effects take place at short distances (for instance, spatial externalities generated by the geographic proximity such as externalities of technology knowledge occur in a close environment). Moreover, regional results demonstrate the simultaneous existence of intra-industry geographic concentration (from their own country partners or from local competitors) and inter-industry concentration (French firms are attracted to regions where there are other French firms). As a result, French firms are attracted to industrial areas.

2.6 CONCLUSION

Thanks to a qualitative approach, we prove in this chapter that studying location and agglomeration determinants of French firms at regional and national scales is relevant because the influence of those factors differs according to the considered geographic level. Moreover, the multi-stage process is validated. Consequently, we modelled the location patterns of the French FDI with a nested structure in order to analyse the location determinants in European countries and European regions. Econometric results indicate that several variables influence French firms' location strategies but their influence occurs generally at a single geographic scale (national *or* regional level). As a result, this study shows that policies on the location choice have to take into account the agglomeration effects which seem to be forceful at both geographic levels even though cost differences and the importance of the potential market also have a non-negligible effect, respectively, at national and regional levels.

ACKNOWLEDGEMENTS

We are grateful to the *Direction des Relations Economiques Extérieures* (DREE) of the French Ministry of Economics, Finance and Industry, which enabled us to work on the database *Enquête-Filiales DREE 2000*. We also want to thank Eric Marcon for remarks, Françoise Louët for sound advice and Thierry Mayer for providing some regional data.

NOTES

1. Source: Banque de France, 2002.
2. Estimations calculated from the *Enquête-Filiales DREE 2000* NUTS 1 level.
3. The stock of French FDI means the cumulated count of French FDI.
4. Note that at the NUTS 1 geographical level, Portugal is at the same time a country and a region.
5. Location determinants are denoted with *n* at national level and *r* at the regional one.
6. See on this literature Harris (1954), Friedman, Gerlowski and Silberman (1992) and Head, Ries and Swenson (1999) for instance.
7. It was necessary to add one to the stock of French FDI because for some sectors the first French investment was made during the period 1987–94. Consequently, we use the technique proposed by Head, Ries and Swenson (1995) to avoid any problem by taking the logarithm form.
8. All explicative variables are taken in logarithm. Thus, coefficients can be roughly interpreted as elasticities as the percentage change in new French FDI in the location *j* given 1 per cent change in the considered explicative variable:

$$\frac{\partial \ln P_j}{\partial \ln x_j} = \beta(1 - P_j) \tag{2.4}$$

   Coefficients have to be multiplied by 0.86 at the national level and by 0.98 at the regional one.

REFERENCES

Banque de France (2002), *La balance des paiements et la position extérieure de la France 2001*, Annual Report.

Bartik, T.J. (1985), 'Business location decisions in the United States: estimates of the effects of unionization, taxes, and other characteristics of states', *Journal of Business and Economic Statistics*, **3** (1), 14–22.

Ben-Akiva, M. and S.R. Lerman (1985), *Discrete Choice Analysis: Theory and Application to Travel Demand*, Cambridge: MIT Press.

Chen, C.-H. (1996), 'Regional determinants of foreign direct investment in Mainland China', *Journal of Economic Studies*, **23** (2), 18–30.

Coughlin, C.C., J.V. Terza and V. Arromdee (1991), 'State characteristics and the location of foreign direct investment within the United States', *Review of Economics and Statistics*, **73** (4), 675–83.

Crozet, M., T. Mayer and J.-L. Mucchielli (2004), 'How do firms agglomerate? A study of FDI in France', *Regional Science and Urban Economics*, **34** (1), 27–54.

Devereux, M.P. and R. Griffith (1998), 'Taxes and the location of production: evidence from panel of US multinationals', *Journal of Public Economics*, **68** (3), 335–67.
Ferrer, C. (1998), 'Patterns and determinants of location decisions by French multinationals in European countries', in J.-L. Mucchielli (ed.), *Multinational Location Strategy, Research in Global Strategic Management*, Greenwich, CT: JAI Press, pp. 117–38.
Ford, S. and R. Strange (1999), 'Where do Japanese manufacturing firms invest within Europe and why?', *Transnational Corporations*, **8** (1), 117–40.
Friedman, J., D.A. Gerlowski and J. Silberman (1992), 'What attracts foreign multinational corporations? Evidence from branch plant location in the United States', *Journal of Regional Science*, **32** (4), 403–18.
Fujita, M., P. Krugman and A. Venables (1999), *The Spatial Economy*, London: MIT Press.
Guimarães, P., O. Figuieredo and D.P. Woodward (2000), 'Agglomeration and the location of foreign direct investment in Portugal', *Journal of Urban Economics*, **47** (1), 115–35.
Guimarães, P., R.J. Rolfe and D.P. Woodward (1998), 'Regional incentives and industrial location in Puerto Rico', *International Regional Science Review*, **21** (2), 119–38.
Hansen, R.E. (1987), 'Industrial location choice in Sao Paulo, Brazil: a nested logit model', *Regional Science and Urban Economics*, **17** (1), 89–108.
Harris, C. (1954), 'The market as a factor in the localization of industry in the United States', *Annals of the Association of American Geographers*, **64**, 315–48.
Head, K. and J. Ries (1996), 'Inter-city competition for foreign investment: static and dynamic effects of China's incentive areas', *Journal of Urban Economics*, **40** (1), 38–60.
Head, K., J. Ries and D. Swenson (1995), 'Agglomeration benefits and location choice: evidence from Japanese manufacturing investments in the United States', *Journal of International Economics*, **38** (3–4), 223–47.
Head, K., J. Ries and D. Swenson (1999), 'Attracting foreign manufacturing: investment promotion and agglomeration', *Regional Science and Urban Economics*, **29** (2),197–218.
Hirsch, S. (1976), 'An international trade and investment theory of the firm', *Oxford Economic Papers*, **28** (2), 258–70.
Jianping, D. (1999), 'Agglomeration effects in manufacturing location, are there any country's preferences?', *Economia Internazionale*, **52** (1), 59–78.
Johanson, J. and F. Widersheim-Paul (1975), 'The internationalization of the firm – four Swedish cases', *Journal of Management Studies*, **12** (3), 305–22.
Krugman, P. (1991), *Geography and Trade*, London: MIT Press.
Marshall, A. (1920), *Principles of Economics*, London: Macmillan.
Mayer, T. and J.-L. Mucchielli (1998), 'Strategic location behaviour: the case of Japanese investments in Europe', in J.-L. Mucchielli, P.J. Buckley and V.V. Cordell (eds), *Globalization and Regionalization: Strategies, Policies and Economic Environments*, New York: Haworth Press.
Mayer, T. and J.-L. Mucchielli (1999), 'La Localisation à l'Etranger des Entreprises Multinationales: Une Approche d'Economie Géographique Hiéarchisée Appliquée aux Entreprises Japonaises en Europe', *Economie et Statistiques*, **326–7**, 159–76.
McFadden, D. (1974), 'Conditional logit analysis of qualitative choice behavior', in

P. Zarembka (eds), *Frontiers in Econometrics*, New York: Academic Press, pp. 105–42.
McFadden, D. (1984), 'Econometric analysis of qualitative response models', in Z. Griliches and M.D. Intriligator (eds), *Handbook of Econometrics*, vol. 2, Amsterdam: North Holland.
Mucchielli, J.-L. (1998), *Multinationales et mondialisation*, Paris: Seuil.
Mucchielli, J.-L. and F. Puech (2001) 'Location of multinational firms and agglomeration effect: an assessment of the Ellison and Glaeser index on French firms in Europe', Université Paris 1 Panthéon-Sorbonne TEAM – CNRS, mimeo.
UNCTAD (2002), *World Investment Report: Transnational Corporations and Export Competitiveness*, New York and Geneva: United Nations Publications.
Woodward, D.P. (1992), 'Location determinants of Japanese manufacturing start-ups in the United States', *Southern Economic Journal*, **58** (3), 690–708.

3. Trade, border effects and individual characteristics: a panel specification with instrumental variables estimators

José De Sousa and Anne-Célia Disdier

3.1 INTRODUCTION

Although trade flows are growing and tariff and non-tariff barriers are decreasing worldwide, borders still influence the pattern of commercial transactions. This fact is highlighted by the border effects methodology which offers an evaluation of the borders' impact on trade (McCallum, 1995; Helliwell, 1996; Wei, 1996; Wolf, 1997; Head and Mayer, 2000).[1] Size for size and distance for distance, the trade within a given geographical unity (area, country, and so on) appears higher than that observed with a given external partner. Measures of border effects are generally carried out with ordinary least squares (OLS) regressions. These estimations are sometimes conducted using the Heckman's correction in order to take into account null flows (Head and Mayer, 2000; 2002).

The objective of this chapter is to wonder about the relevance of such an econometric approach and test the robustness of the results obtained from the OLS estimates. In fact, cross-section estimations tend to ignore the unobservable characteristics[2] of bilateral trade relations, such as historical, cultural and linguistic links or the presence of minorities. The existence of a potential correlation between these unobservable characteristics and a subset of the explanatory variables runs the risk of obtaining biased estimates. The traditional method to eliminate this correlation consists in using the *within* estimator. In transforming the data into deviations from individual means, the within estimator provides unbiased and consistent estimates. However, all time-invariant variables are eliminated by the data transformation. In the setting of our study this elimination represents a serious problem as our interest is in particular attached to the coefficients on the time-invariant variables (for example, distance, 'home'). To overcome this problem several authors propose different instrumental variables estimators for panel data regressions

(Hausman and Taylor, 1981; Amemiya and MaCurdy, 1986; Breusch, Mizon and Schmidt, 1989). Using these methods this chapter offers a proper specification of trade flows and border effects measure.

Our empirical application relates to the bilateral trade flows between the nine first EU member countries. The study covers the period 1978–95 and is carried out in a sectoral way. Fixed effects capture the unobservable characteristics of each bilateral trade relation for a given sector. Also fixed time effects account for the business cycle and changes in openness across all countries (Egger and Pfaffermayr, 2003).

The remainder of the chapter is organised as follows: in section 3.2, we set out the empirical model and the data; in section 3.3, we expose the econometric method of panel data; and then the results are presented in section 3.4. Finally, we conclude in section 3.5.

3.2 EMPIRICAL MODEL AND DATA

The Gravity Equation of Trade

We adopt the gravity equation of trade which has been used extensively in the literature on border effects (McCallum, 1995; Helliwell, 1996; 1997; 1998; Wei, 1996; Wolf, 1997; Nitsch, 2000; among others). In its basic form the gravity equation relates the volume of trade between two countries to their economic size and to transaction costs. Following McCallum (1995) we have:

$$\ln(M_{ijt}) = \alpha + \gamma home + \beta_1 ln(Y_{it}) + \beta_2 ln(Y_{jt}) + \beta_3 ln(D_{ij}) + \epsilon_{ijt}, \qquad (3.1)$$

where M_{ijt} is the value of goods imported by country i from country j at time t, Y_{it} (respectively Y_{jt}) is the income of the importer (respectively of the exporter) and D_{ij} the distance between country i and j used as proxy for transaction costs.

Gross domestic product (GDP) or gross national product (GNP) is generally a proxy for the economic size. Instead of using these measures, we refer to a production measure. For the importing country we retain the apparent consumption, by subtracting its exports from its production and by adding its imports. The variable *home* is a dummy variable equal to one for intra-national trade and zero for international trade.

This basic specification is commonly augmented by various variables that are supposed to affect bilateral trade. In line with previous studies we add a measure of the exchange rate evolution and a language dummy. Our final specification is given by:

$$\ln(M_{ijt}) = \alpha + \gamma home + \beta_1 ln(Y_{it}) + \beta_2 ln(Y_{jt}) + \beta_3 ln(D_{ij}) + \beta_4 exchr_{ijt} + \beta_5 lang_{ij} + \epsilon_{ijt}, \tag{3.2}$$

where:
$exchr_{ijt}$ is the evolution of the bilateral exchange rate,
$lang_{ij} = 1$ if countries i and j share a language and 0 otherwise.

Data

Our empirical application relates to the bilateral trade flows between the nine first EU member countries (Belgium, Denmark, France, Germany, Ireland, Italy, Luxembourg, Netherlands and the UK). Data for Belgium and Luxembourg are aggregated. The study covers the period 1978–95 and is carried out in a sectoral way.

Keith Head and Thierry Mayer provide us with their data. See Head and Mayer (2000) and (2002) for a full description of the database construction. Production data come from the VISA database (Eurostat) and cover 120 NACE three-digit manufacturing industries. Trade data are taken from the COMEXT database (Eurostat) and cover 113 NACE three-digit industries for the sub-period 1978–87 and 120 NACE three-digit industries for the sub-period 1988–95. The intra-national trade of a country is calculated referring to the Wei's (1996) method. Internal and external distances are drawn up as the weighted sum of bilateral distances between the regions of the countries. Intra-regional distances are determined with the disk methodology. To capture the exchange rate influence on trade flows we introduce a variable 'exchange rate evolution' in the estimation. As defined in Head and Mayer (2002) this variable is the number of units of the importer currency for one unit of the exporter currency. Therefore a negative effect is expected.

3.3 ECONOMETRIC METHODS OF PANEL DATA

Specification Problems Resulting from Unobservable Characteristics

Compared to time-series or cross-section analyses, panel data allow us to control for unobservable characteristics which may be correlated with certain explanatory variables. Not controlling for such unobservable characteristics runs the risk of obtaining biased results. In the setting of our study this aspect is especially important. Actually, bilateral trade can be influenced by specific characteristics. For instance, the impact of historical, cultural and linguistic links on trade flows between Ireland and the UK is difficult to observe and quantify. Panel data regressions allow correcting for such effects. Consider, then, a reformulation of equation 3.2:

$$M_{nt} = \phi X_{nt} + \psi Z_n + \mu_n + v_t + \eta_{nt}, \quad (3.3)$$

where $t = 1, ..., T$ is the time index and $n = 1, ..., N$ the index identifying each couple of countries for a given sector; for instance trade between France and Italy for the sector 221 is an 'individual' n.[3] M_{nt} are import flows of 'individual' n at time t. v_t represent the fixed time effects which are obtained by the inclusion of $T - 1$ dummy variables. One of the time effects must indeed be dropped to avoid perfect collinearity. ϕ and ψ are conformably dimensioned parameter vectors associated with X_{nt} and Z_n, which are defined as follows:

X_{nt}: Time varying characteristics at time t like Y_{it}, Y_{jt} and $exchr_{ijt}$; X_{nt} is a $1 \times K$ vector of time varying variables;
Z_n: Time-invariant characteristics like *home*, D_{ij} and $lang_{ij}$; Z_n is a $1 \times G$ vector of static variables.

The unobserved individual effects μ_n are i.i.d. $N(0, \sigma_\mu^2)$ and may be correlated with parts of X and Z. The errors η_{nt} are i.i.d. $N(0, \sigma_\eta^2)$ and are assumed uncorrelated with X_{nt} and Z_n.

Ordinary Least Squares and Random Effects Estimator

Ordinary least squares estimation leads to biased results owed to the presence of correlation between certain explanatory variables and unobservable characteristics. Actually cross-section studies tend to ignore this kind of correlation by assuming that μ_n are identical for every individual. Breusch and Pagan (1980) devise a Lagrange Multiplier test for the random effects model. The Breusch and Pagan test enables us to examine the presence of individual heterogeneity in a panel. Under the null hypothesis ($\sigma_\mu^2 = 0$) the chi-squared statistic informs us on the relevance of a panel estimation. It is worth noting that our panel is unbalanced. Actually the number of periods T during which the bilateral trade is observed is not identical for each 'individual' n. As a result the Breusch and Pagan test is modified in order to take into account unbalanced data (Baltagi and Li, 1990).

Random Effects Estimator and Within Estimator

When the result of the Breusch and Pagan test rejects the null hypothesis in favour of the random effect, the OLS regression model is inappropriate.

However, in the presence of correlation of μ_n, with X_{nt} and Z_n, random effects estimator yields biased and inconsistent estimates of the parameters $(\phi, \psi, \sigma_\eta^2, \sigma_\mu^2)$. The traditional method to eliminate this correlation consists in using the *within* estimator (also known as *fixed effects* estimator). This method amounts to transforming the data into deviations from individual means. Thus the within estimator provides unbiased and consistent estimates even if μ_n are correlated with a subset of explanatory variables.

The within estimator which is consistent serves as a benchmark for the Hausman (1978) test. The specification test devised by Hausman is a test of the equality of the coefficients estimated by the within and random effects estimators. If the coefficients differ significantly, either the model is misspecified or the assumption of no-correlation between μ_n and X_{nt} and Z_n is incorrect. Under the assumption of correct specification the Hausman test examines the appropriateness of the within estimator.

Unfortunately the within estimator suffers from two important defects: (1) all time-invariant variables are eliminated by the data transformation; (2) the within estimator ignores variation across individuals in the sample. In the setting of our study the first problem is the more serious as primary interest is attached to the coefficients on time-invariant variables (ψ).

Instrumental Variables Estimators

One option to solve the foregoing problems is to use instrumental variables estimators. Traditionally this method consists in substituting correlated explanatory variables with appropriate instruments uncorrelated with unobservable characteristics (μ_n). The main drawback is the difficulty in finding instruments not taken into account by the original specification and uncorrelated with μ_n. An alternative solution consists in assuming that certain variables among X and Z are uncorrelated with μ_n (Hausman and Taylor, 1981). These variables serve as instruments for the correlated explanatory variables. The main advantage of this technique is to take explanatory variables included in the model as instruments. This instrumental-variable estimation technique can be divided into three steps. The first one corresponds to the identification of variables X and Z uncorrelated with the unobservable characteristics. In consequence we partition matrices X and Z:

$$X = (X_1, X_2) \quad \text{and} \quad Z = (Z_1, Z_2), \tag{3.4}$$

where X_1 has k_1 columns and X_2 has k_2 columns, with $k_1 + k_2 = K$, while Z_1 has g_1 columns and Z_2 has g_2 columns, with $g_1 + g_2 = G$. The variables indexed 1 are uncorrelated with μ_n (X_1 and Z_1) but the variables indexed 2 are correlated with μ_n (X_2 and Z_2).

The second step consists in transforming variables of the model. Transformed variables are used as instruments. Hausman and Taylor (1981) – hereafter HT – assume that deviations from individual means (noted Q) of varying variables provide unbiased instruments for coefficients ϕ. Besides, if the number k_1, of variables X_1, is equal to or higher than g_2, the number of variables Z_2, then the individual means (noted P) of X_1 (PX_1) are valid instruments for Z_2.[4] The HT estimator is then more efficient than the within estimator. Consequently the instrument set proposed by HT is $A_{HT} = [QX_1, QX_2, PX_1, Z_1]$. The order condition is satisfied if $k_1 \geq g_2$.

More recently improvements have been suggested in providing additional instruments. In HT's approach time varying explanatory variables uncorrelated with μ_n are used as two instruments (QX_1 and PX_1), while Amemiya and MaCurdy (1986) – hereafter AM – use such variables as $T+1$ instruments (QX_1 and also separately for each of time periods $t-X_1^*$). Consequently the instrument set proposed by AM is $A_{AM}=[QX_1, QX_2, X_1^*, Z_1]$, where X_1^* is defined as a $NT \times TK$ matrix. Each column of X_1^* contains values of X_{it} for one t only.

$$X_1^* = \begin{pmatrix} X_{11} & X_{12} & \dots & X_{1T} \\ \dots & \dots & \dots & \dots \\ X_{N1} & X_{N2} & \dots & X_{NT} \end{pmatrix} \otimes e_T, \tag{3.5}$$

where e_T is the unitary row vector of T dimension.

The order condition is satisfied if $Tk_1 \geq g_2$. The consistency of the AM estimator relies on the assumption of no-correlation between the means of X_1 variables and the unobservable characteristics for all the time periods $t=1, \dots, T$. This is a stronger exogeneity assumption than HT hypothesis of absence of correlation for all the period. However it is hard to imagine cases in which the HT assumption would hold but the AM's would not (Amemiya and MaCurdy, 1986).

Breusch, Mizon and Schmidt (1989) – hereafter BMS – demonstrate that the AM instrument set $A_{AM}=[QX_1, QX_2, X_1^*, Z_1]$ is equivalent to $A_{AM}=[QX_1, QX_2, PX_1, (QX_1)^*, Z_1]$, where $(QX_1)^*$ is defined in the same way as X_1^*, that is each column of $(QX_1)^*$ contains the deviations from means of X_{it} for one t only. They suggest that a potentially more efficient estimator can be obtained by using time invariant explanatory variables correlated with μ_n. Therefore the instrument set proposed by BMS is $A_{BMS} = [QX_1, QX_2, PX_1, (QX_1)^*, (QX_2)^*, Z_1]$ extending the AM treatment of the X_1 variables to the X_2 variables, that is $(QX_2)^*$ is defined as $(QX_1)^*$. The order condition is satisfied if $Tk_1 + (T-1)k_2 \geq g_2$.

If the instrumental variables estimators resulting from these procedures are unbiased, they are not efficient. Actually, they ignore the autocorrelation structure of the error terms related to the presence of unobservable characteristics (μ_n) (Guillotin and Sevestre, 1994, p. 123).

Thus the third step consists in improving the efficiency of these estimators. Following HT, Guillotin and Sevestre (1994) suggest to apply the instrumental variable method to the transformed model:

$$M_{nt} + (\theta_n - 1)M_{n.} = \phi(X_{nt} + (\theta_n - 1)X_{n.}) + \psi\theta_n Z_n + \theta_n\mu_n + (\eta_{nt} + (\theta_n - 1)\eta_n), \tag{3.6}$$

where:

$$\theta_n = \left(\frac{\sigma_\eta^2}{\sigma_\eta^2 + T_n\sigma_\mu^2}\right)^{1/2}. \tag{3.7}$$

Unlike Hausman and Taylor (1981, p. 1381), theta correction is here applied to an unbalanced panel. Nevertheless it remains an additional difficulty, since it is necessary to replace the variances σ_μ^2 and σ_η^2 with unbiased estimates. Obtaining these estimates from within and between regressions is more difficult than in the setting of a balanced panel because of a heteroscedasticity problem. An additional correction must be applied to achieve efficient and unbiased estimates (Guillotin and Sevestre, 1994, pp. 125–7).

3.4 RESULTS

Table 3.1 summarizes the results of border effects estimations using the OLS estimator. As did Head and Mayer (2000), we divide the sample into six sub-periods. The heteroscedasticity is corrected with the White's (1980) method. The overall fit of the estimation is globally in line with the existing comparable papers studying border effects.[5] Except for the exchange rate evolution variable,[6] the different estimated coefficients have for all sub-periods the expected signs and magnitudes and are significant at the 1 per cent level. We note a decrease of the border effect over time. Distance has a negative effect on bilateral trade and this effect is relatively strong: an increase of 1 per cent of the distance generates a decrease of the bilateral trade of about 1 per cent. Trade flows are positively influenced by the sharing of a language.

We now estimate border effects using the random effects estimates (Table 3.2). As previously mentioned fixed bilateral effects for each sector are introduced. Except again for the exchange rate evolution variable, all the estimated coefficients are significant and are very close to the ones obtained with the OLS estimator. However, the Breusch and Pagan (1980)

Table 3.1 Border effects: OLS estimator

	Dep. variable: ln of bilateral imports					
Period	[78–80]	[81–83]	[84–86]	[87–89]	[90–92]	[93–95]
Home	2.124[a]	2.026[a]	1.844[a]	1.766[a]	1.673[a]	1.745[a]
	(0.043)	(0.043)	(0.041)	(0.038)	(0.041)	(0.043)
Ln (Y_{it})	0.519[a]	0.540[a]	0.550[a]	0.585[a]	0.614[a]	0.602[a]
	(0.012)	(0.011)	(0.010)	(0.009)	(0.010)	(0.011)
Ln (Y_{jt})	0.734[a]	0.657[a]	0.671[a]	0.637[a]	0.634[a]	0.639[a]
	(0.012)	(0.011)	(0.010)	(0.010)	(0.011)	(0.011)
Ln ($Dist_{ij}$)	−1.015[a]	−0.952[a]	−1.009[a]	−1.007[a]	−1.016[a]	−0.915[a]
	(0.033)	(0.034)	(0.032)	(0.029)	(0.030)	(0.031)
Exch. Rate $Evo._{ijt}$	−1.752[a]	0.245	1.722[a]	0.846[c]	1.929[a]	0.152
	(0.357)	(0.285)	(0.290)	(0.444)	(0.450)	(0.227)
Common $Language_{ij}$	1.006[a]	0.989[a]	0.894[a]	0.878[a]	0.850[a]	0.912[a]
	(0.046)	(0.044)	(0.042)	(0.040)	(0.042)	(0.044)
Fixed time effects	2.99[c]	1.88	1.46	0.06	0.57	0.48
	F(2,10330)	F(2,9902)	F(2,10480)	F(2,11036)	F(2,10459)	F(2,10494)
N	10339	9911	10489	11045	10468	10503
R^2	0.679	0.683	0.690	0.696	0.699	0.683

Note: Standard errors in parentheses with [a] and [c] respectively denoting significance at the 1 per cent and 10 per cent levels.

Table 3.2 Border effects: random effects estimator

	Dep. variable: ln of bilateral imports					
Period	[78–80]	[81–83]	[84–86]	[87–89]	[90–92]	[93–95]
Home	2.095[a]	2.028[a]	1.808[a]	1.760[a]	1.663[a]	1.756[a]
	(0.120)	(0.123)	(0.111)	(0.104)	(0.108)	(0.112)
Ln (Y_{it})	0.526[a]	0.468[a]	0.534[a]	0.519[a]	0.603[a]	0.549[a]
	(0.016)	(0.015)	(0.014)	(0.014)	(0.015)	(0.015)
Ln (Y_{jt})	0.658[a]	0.620[a]	0.615[a]	0.626[a]	0.593[a]	0.632[a]
	(0.017)	(0.016)	(0.015)	(0.015)	(0.015)	(0.016)
Ln ($Dist_{ij}$)	−1.023[a]	−0.953[a]	−1.013[a]	−0.979[a]	−1.020[a]	−0.906[a]
	(0.057)	(0.059)	(0.053)	(0.050)	(0.052)	(0.053)
Exch. Rate $Evo._{ijt}$	−0.867[a]	0.464[a]	−0.014	−0.203[b]	0.242[b]	0.048
	(0.120)	(0.095)	(0.071)	(0.097)	(0.122)	(0.098)
Common $Language_{ij}$	0.982[a]	0.950[a]	0.887[a]	0.897[a]	0.829[a]	0.904[a]
	(0.113)	(0.114)	(0.104)	(0.097)	(0.102)	(0.105)
Breusch Pagan	8218.01[a]	8035.44[a]	8434.45[a]	9202.34[a]	9040.24[a]	8889.39[a]
Lagrangian mult. test	Chi2(1)	Chi2(1)	Chi2(1)	Chi2(1)	Chi2(1)	Chi2(1)
Fixed time effects	36.32[a]	39.24[a]	77.11[a]	13.28[a]	32.71[a]	20.43[a]
	Chi2(2)	Chi2(2)	Chi2(2)	Chi2(2)	Chi2(2)	Chi2(2)
N	10339	9911	10489	11045	10468	10503
R^2	0.677	0.681	0.688	0.695	0.699	0.682

Note: Standard errors in parentheses with [a] and [b] respectively denoting significance at the 1 per cent and 10 per cent levels.

Lagrangian Multiplier test of the difference between the OLS and random effects estimates allows us to reject the OLS regression for each sub-period. The statistic is distributed as χ^2_1 and ranged from 8035.44 to 9202.34 according to sub-periods. But a problem remains: in the random effects regression independent variables are assumed uncorrelated with the unobservable characteristics. When this assumption is rejected, the coefficients are biased and inconsistent.

To test the presence of such correlation we proceed to a within regression and to a Hausman test (Table 3.3). The transformation of the data into deviations from individual means provides, even in the presence of a correlation, unbiased and consistent coefficients. Nevertheless following this transformation all time-invariant variables (home, distance and common language) are eliminated. The comparison between Table 3.2 and Table 3.3 shows several differences concerning the estimated coefficients of time-varying explanatory variables; this suggests the effective existence of a correlation. The Hausman test of the difference between random effects and within estimates confirms this result: the null hypothesis of no correlation is rejected for the six sub-periods. The statistic is distributed a χ^2_1 under Ho and yields between 94.89 and 192.22 according to sub-periods.

In order to obtain coefficients for the time-invariant variables, estimations using HT, AM and BMS estimators are run. The results are presented in Tables 3.4, 3.5 and 3.6. As previously underlined, explanatory variables could be classified into two different groups: The time-varying explanatory variables (variables X) and the time-invariant explanatory variables (variables Z); besides each group includes variables that are correlated and uncorrelated with the unobservable characteristics.

The significant differences for estimated coefficients on Y_{it} and Y_{jt} obtained with the random effects and within regressions suggest a potential endogeneity for these variables.[7] With this hypothesis we let: $X_1 = (exchr_{ijt})$, $X_2 = (Y_{it}, Y_{jt})$, Z_1 $(home, D_{ij}, lang_{ij})$ and $Z_2 = (\emptyset)$. The order condition for identification is satisfied for each estimation.

Several conclusions could be deduced from the results. First, note that the HT estimates are close to the within estimates. This suggests the legitimacy of the chosen instruments. This fact is confirmed by the Hausman test of the difference between the within and HT estimates. The test statistic is ranging from 0.18 (sub-period: 87–89) to 2.62 (sub-period: 78–80) and is distributed as χ^2_1. The AM and BMS estimates are very close to the HT estimates. The Hausman test comparing AM to HT suggests that the additional instruments introduced by AM cannot be rejected for any time periods. This conclusion as shown by the Hausman test of the difference between BMS and AM estimates is also valid for the additional exogeneity

Table 3.3 *Border effects: fixed effects estimator*

	Dep. variable: ln of bilateral imports					
Period	[78–80]	[81–83]	[84–86]	[87–89]	[90–92]	[93–95]
Home	—	—	—	—	—	—
Ln (Y_{it})	0.519[a]	0.286[a]	0.452[a]	0.319[a]	0.505[a]	0.368[a]
	(0.033)	(0.026)	(0.028)	(0.027)	(0.034)	(0.031)
Ln (Y_{jt})	0.206[a]	0.337[a]	0.312[a]	0.331[a]	0.314[a]	0.319[a]
	(0.040)	(0.034)	(0.035)	(0.042)	(0.041)	(0.055)
Ln ($Dist_{ij}$)	—	—	—	—	—	—
Exch. Rate Evo.$_{ijt}$	−0.678[a]	0.532[a]	0.042	−0.181[c]	0.230[c]	0.052
	(0.123)	(0.096)	(0.074)	(0.098)	(0.123)	(0.102)
Common Language$_{ij}$	—	—	—	—	—	—
Hausman test	163.25[a]	192.22[a]	123.74[a]	155.15[a]	118.11[a]	94.89[a]
	Chi2(5)	Chi2(5)	Chi2(5)	Chi2(5)	Chi2(5)	Chi2(5)
Fixed bilateral effects	54.34[a]	55.65[a]	71.37[a]	56.33[a]	67.50[a]	50.47[a]
	F(3726,6607)	F(3467,6438)	F(3813,6670)	F(3772,7267)	F(3537,6925)	F(3521,6976)
Fixed time effects	64.59[a]	60.57[a]	73.73[a]	59.28[a]	23.59[a]	40.31[a]
	F(2,6607)	F(2,6438)	F(2,6670)	F(2,7267)	F(2,6925)	F(2,6976)
N	10339	9911	10489	11045	10468	10503
R^2	0.201	0.105	0.124	0.151	0.061	0.089

Note: Standard errors in parentheses with [a] and [c] respectively denoting significance at the 1 per cent and 10 per cent levels.

Table 3.4 Border effects: Hausman and Taylor (1981) estimator

	Dep. variable: ln of bilateral imports					
Period	[78–80]	[81–83]	[84–86]	[87–89]	[90–92]	[93–95]
Home	2.233[a]	2.292[a]	2.053[a]	2.078[a]	1.962[a]	2.077[a]
	(0.129)	(0.132)	(0.133)	(0.123)	(0.127)	(0.147)
Ln (Y_{it})	0.517[a]	0.285[a]	0.461[a]	0.315[a]	0.509[a]	0.367[a]
	(0.041)	(0.062)	(0.042)	(0.034)	(0.038)	(0.046)
Ln (Y_{jt})	0.228[a]	0.334[a]	0.301[a]	0.336[a]	0.309[a]	0.319[a]
	(0.040)	(0.041)	(0.038)	(0.048)	(0.052)	(0.063)
Ln ($Dist_{ij}$)	−0.931[a]	−0.853[a]	−0.809[a]	−0.958[a]	−0.917[a]	0.939[a]
	(0.071)	(0.072)	(0.055)	(0.076)	(0.089)	(0.097)
Exch. Rate $Evo._{ijt}$	−0.670[a]	0.532[a]	0.060	−0.178[c]	0.234[b]	0.050
	(0.110)	(0.089)	(0.073)	(0.100)	(0.104)	(0.097)
Common $Language_{ij}$	0.938[a]	0.863[a]	0.924[a]	0.695[a]	0.721[a]	0.628[a]
	(0.111)	(0.113)	(0.110)	(0.108)	(0.112)	(0.126)
Hausman test	2.62	0.74	0.70	0.18	0.55	0.54
	Chi2(1)	Chi2(1)	Chi2(1)	Chi2(1)	Chi2(1)	Chi2(1)
Fixed time effects	66.06[a]	54.25[a]	60.50[a]	45.67[a]	25.48[a]	34.04[a]
	F(2,10330)	F(2,9902)	F(2,10480)	F(2,11036)	F(2,10459)	F(2,10494)
N	10339	9911	10489	11045	10468	10503
R^2	0.242	0.178	0.189	0.208	0.148	0.161

Note: Standard errors in parentheses with [a], [b] and [c] respectively denoting significance at the 1 per cent, 5 per cent and 10 per cent levels.

Table 3.5 Border effects: Amemiya and MaCurdy (1986) estimator

	Dep. variable: ln of bilateral imports					
Period	[78–80]	[81–83]	[84–86]	[87–89]	[90–92]	[93–95]
Home	2.232^{a}	2.293^{a}	2.053^{a}	2.074^{a}	1.963^{a}	2.070^{a}
	(0.129)	(0.132)	(0.133)	(0.123)	(0.127)	(0.147)
Ln (Y_{it})	0.514^{a}	0.290^{a}	0.461^{a}	0.314^{a}	0.515^{a}	0.358^{a}
	(0.040)	(0.063)	(0.042)	(0.034)	(0.038)	(0.045)
Ln (Y_{jt})	0.232^{a}	0.327^{a}	0.301^{a}	0.342^{a}	0.301^{a}	0.338^{a}
	(0.039)	(0.041)	(0.037)	(0.047)	(0.052)	(0.062)
Ln ($Dist_{ij}$)	-0.931^{a}	-0.853^{a}	-0.809^{a}	-0.960^{a}	-0.916^{a}	-0.943^{a}
	(0.071)	(0.072)	(0.055)	(0.076)	(0.089)	(0.097)
Exch. Rate $Evo._{ijt}$	-0.674^{a}	0.536^{a}	0.060	-0.181^{c}	0.236^{b}	0.047
	(0.111)	(0.090)	(0.073)	(0.101)	(0.104)	(0.097)
Common $Language_{ij}$	0.938^{a}	0.863^{a}	0.924^{a}	0.695^{a}	0.721^{a}	0.629^{a}
	(0.111)	(0.113)	(0.110)	(0.108)	(0.112)	(0.126)
Hausman test	0.01	1.23	0.01	3.38	0.45	0.01
	Chi2(3)	Chi2(3)	Chi2(3)	Chi2(3)	Chi2(3)	Chi2(3)
Fixed time effects	66.03^{a}	54.40^{a}	60.43^{a}	44.97^{a}	25.47^{a}	33.71^{a}
	F(2,10330)	F(2,9902)	F(2,10480)	F(2,11036)	F(2,10459)	F(2,10494)
N	10339	9911	10489	11045	10468	10503
R^2	0.242	0.178	0.189	0.208	0.148	0.161

Note: Standard errors in parentheses with [a], [b] and [c] respectively denoting significance at the 1 per cent, 5 per cent and 10 per cent levels.

Table 3.6 Border effects: Breusch, Mizon and Schmidt (1989) estimator

	Dep. variable: ln of bilateral imports					
Period	[78–80]	[81–83]	[84–86]	[87–89]	[90–92]	[93–95]
Home	2.237[a]	2.293[a]	2.058[a]	2.064[a]	1.960[a]	2.060[a]
	(0.129)	(0.132)	(0.133)	(0.122)	(0.127)	(0.146)
Ln (Y_{it})	0.511[a]	0.290[a]	0.456[a]	0.316[a]	0.514[a]	0.369[a]
	(0.041)	(0.064)	(0.043)	(0.034)	(0.038)	(0.043)
Ln (Y_{jt})	0.228[a]	0.327[a]	0.299[a]	0.352[a]	0.306[a]	0.340[a]
	(0.039)	(0.041)	(0.037)	(0.046)	(0.051)	(0.062)
Ln ($Dist_{ij}$)	−0.927[a]	−0.853[a]	−0.804[a]	−0.966[a]	−0.918[a]	−0.946[a]
	(0.071)	(0.073)	(0.055)	(0.077)	(0.089)	(0.097)
Exch. Rate $Evo._{ijt}$	−0.674[a]	0.536[a]	0.059	−0.184[c]	0.235[b]	0.048
	(0.111)	(0.089)	(0.073)	(0.101)	(0.104)	(0.097)
Common $Language_{ij}$	0.940[a]	0.863[a]	0.925[a]	0.696[a]	0.721[a]	0.633[a]
	(0.110)	(0.113)	(0.110)	(0.109)	(0.112)	(0.126)
Hausman test	2.56	0.00	0.06	0.07	2.51	0.88
	Chi2(7)	Chi2(7)	Chi2(7)	Chi2(7)	Chi2(7)	Chi2(7)
Fixed time effects	67.11[a]	53.25[a]	60.83[a]	45.15[a]	25.42[a]	32.91[a]
	F(2,10330)	F(2,9902)	F(2,10480)	F(2,11036)	F(2,10459)	F(2,10494)
N	10339	9911	10489	11045	10468	10503
R^2	0.242	0.178	0.189	0.209	0.149	0.163

Note: Standard errors in parentheses with [a], [b] and [c] respectively denoting significance at the 1 per cent, 5 per cent and 10 per cent levels.

restriction added by BMS. The statistic of the Hausman test distributed as χ_7^2 under the null hypothesis of no correlation is never significant.

Following the elimination of the correlation the coefficients in HT, AM and BMS estimations are unbiased. Given that these coefficients are very similar, we discuss the results all together. Observe that the border effects are now slightly higher than in OLS and random effects estimates. Coefficients on Y_{it} and above all on Y_{jt} differ significantly from the theoretical unitary income elasticities. This result can be interpreted in two ways. On the one hand, one part of the production consists of non-tradable goods (see Anderson, 1979). On the other hand, before the correction of the correlation, both variables captured a part of the unobservable characteristics. After correction this effect is removed. In other words the fixed effects allow us to capture these unobservable characteristics in a more precise way. Finally, the proper estimation of both coefficients impacts on the magnitudes of the coefficients on distance and common language which are reduced.

3.5 CONCLUSION

This chapter offers an estimation of border effects using different econometric specifications. Our sample consists of sectoral bilateral trade flows between the nine first EU member countries. Our results indicate the existence of a correlation between certain explanatory variables and the individual characteristics of trade relations. So OLS and random effects yield biased and inconsistent estimates. If the within regression provides unbiased and consistent estimates, all time-invariant explanatory variables are eliminated by the transformation of data into deviations from individual means. To overcome this problem we apply efficient instrumental variables estimators for panel data regression models proposed by Hausman and Taylor (1981), Amemiya and MaCurdy (1986) and Breusch, Mizon and Schmidt (1989). An important benefit of these methods consists in using instruments variables derived from the structural equation. It allows controlling efficiently for the individual characteristics as well. These approaches therefore offer a better estimation of the empirical model. In particular, border effects are better specified and appear slightly higher. Also, the magnitudes of the coefficient on distance and on common language are reduced.

ACKNOWLEDGEMENTS

We wish to thank Keith Head and Thierry Mayer for providing us with their dataset. We are grateful to Cem Ertur, Keith Head, Miren Lafourcade, Thierry Mayer, Reinhilde Veugelers and participants at the 2002 French Economic Association Conference (AFSE 2002), Paris, 19–20 September 2002, at the Workshop 'Economic Geography and Multinational's Location', University of Paris 1, 22–23 May 2002, and at the 2nd Spring School in Economic Geography, Pau, 2–4 May 2002 for helpful comments and suggestions. We also thank Céline Carrère, Matthieu Crozet, Mathilde Maurel, Ariane Tichit and participants at the 'Ateliers de la MSE', Session on Economic Geography, University of Paris 1, 21 March 2002, and at the VIIth Spring Meeting of Young Economists (SMYE 2002), 18–20 April 2002 for their valuable comments on an earlier draft of the chapter.

NOTES

1. See Helliwell (1998) and Head and Mayer (2002) for a literature review of border effects.
2. The alternative expressions individual effects, individual heterogeneity and specific effects are often used instead.
3. Our sample consists of sectoral bilateral trade flows between the nine first EU member countries. Distinct fixed effects are introduced for each direction of trade: Trade between France (importer) and Italy (exporter) for the sector 221 and the one between France (exporter) and Italy (importer) for the sector 221 represent two different 'individuals'.
4. If Z_2 is empty, the gain obtained adding individual means of X_1 as instruments is marginal (Martinez-Espineira, 2002).
5. However, as our empirical model differs from the one used by Head and Mayer (2000), note that our results are not identical to the ones obtained by them.
6. For a detailed analysis of the exchange rate volatility impact on border effects, see Taglioni (2002).
7. Carrère (2002) who analyses the impact of preferential trade agreements on African trade using the Hausman and Taylor (1981) estimator also finds a correlation between income variables and unobservable characteristics.

REFERENCES

Amemiya, T. and T. MaCurdy (1986), 'Instrumental-variable estimation of an error-components model', *Econometrica*, **54** (4), 869–80.

Anderson, J.E. (1979), 'A theoretical foundation for the gravity equation', *American Economic Review*, **69** (1), 106–16.

Baltagi, B. and Q. Li (1990), 'A Lagrange multiplier test for the error components model with incomplete panel', *Econometric Reviews*, **9** (1), 103–07.

Breusch, T. and A. Pagan (1980), 'The Lagrange multiplier test and its applications to model specification in econometrics', *Review of Economic Studies*, **47** (1), 239–53.

Breusch, T., G. Mizon and P. Schmidt (1989), 'Efficient estimation using panel data', *Econometrica*, **57** (3), 695–700.
Carrère, C. (2002), 'Impact des Accords Régionaux Africains sur le Commerce Extérieur: Evaluation à l'aide d'un modèle de gravité en panel', Centre d'Etudes et de Recherches sur le Développement International, mimeo.
Egger, P. and M. Pfaffermayr (2003), 'The proper econometric specification of the gravity equation: a three-way model with bilateral interaction effects', *Empirical Economics*, **26** (3), 571–80.
Guillotin, Y. and P. Sevestre (1994), 'Estimations de fonctions de gains sur données de panel: endogénéité du capital et effets de la sélection', *Economie et Prévision*, **116** (5), 119–35.
Hausman, J. (1978), 'Specification tests in econometrics', *Econometrica*, **46** (6), 1251–71.
Hausman, J. and W. Taylor (1981), 'Panel data and unobservable individual effects', *Econometrica*, **49** (6), 1377–98.
Head, K. and T. Mayer (2000), 'Non-Europe: the magnitude and causes of market fragmentation in the EU', *Weltwirtschaftliches Archiv*, **136** (2), 284–314.
Head, K. and T. Mayer (2002), 'Effet frontière, intégration économique et "Forteresse Europe"', *Economie et Prévision*, 152–3, 71–92.
Helliwell, J.F. (1996), 'Do national borders matter for Quebec's trade?', *Canadian Journal of Economics*, **29** (3), 507–22.
Helliwell, J.F. (1997), 'National borders, trade and migration', *Pacific Economic Review*, **2** (3), 165–85.
Helliwell, J.F. (ed.) (1998), *How Much Do National Borders Matter?*, Washington, DC: Brookings Institution Press.
Martinez-Espineira, R. (2002), 'Residential water demand in the northwest of Spain', *Environmental and Resource Economics*, **21** (2), 161–87.
McCallum, J. (1995), 'National borders matter: Canada–U.S. regional trade patterns', *American Economic Review*, **85** (3), 615–23.
Nitsch, V. (2000), 'National borders and international trade: evidence from the European Union', *Canadian Journal of Economics*, **33** (4), 1091–105.
Taglioni, D. (2002), 'Exchange rate volatility as a barrier to trade: new methodologies and recent evidence', *Économie internationale*, **89–90**, 227–59.
Wei, S.-J. (1996), 'Intra-national versus international trade: how stubborn are nations in global integration', National Bureau of Economic Research, Working Paper 5531.
White, H. (1980), 'A heteroskedasticity – consistent covariance matrix estimator and a direct test for heteroskedasticity', *Econometrica*, **48** (4), 817–38.
Wolf, H.C. (1997), 'Patterns of intra- and inter-state trade', National Bureau of Economic Research, Working Paper 5939.

4. North–south integration and multinationals: the case of the automobile industry in Mexico

Sylvie Montout and Habib Zitouna

4.1 INTRODUCTION

In December 1992, Canada, Mexico and the USA signed the North American Free Trade Agreement (NAFTA), which came into effect on 1 January 1994. It is the first formal regional integration agreement involving both developed and developing countries. This regional integration implies the reduction and the elimination of tariff and non-tariff barriers, as well as a general deregulation and strengthening of competition. Restrictions on foreign direct investment (FDI) were eased and the financial sector reformed. This new environment and, in particular, the increased exposure to foreign competition on the home market and abroad provided an important stimulus for foreign direct investment. Indeed, the bringing into force of NAFTA seems to have a positive incidence on the American investment flows inwards in Mexico (Stevens, 1998).

The existing theoretical literature on economic integration and FDI deals with the question of whether regional integration agreements (RIAs), by eliminating trade barriers, promote FDI flows. Regional integration creates a larger market which allows some firms to grow larger and stronger than would have been possible in individual national markets. The main benefits of integration is to make the region more attractive towards location, which should stimulate intra-regional FDI as well as inflows from the rest of the world.

Norman and Motta (1996) found that increased market accessability prompts outside firms to invest in the regional block, reducing product prices, profits of intra-block firms and increasing total surplus. Integrating economies are more likely to gain from improving intra-regional market accessability than from tougher external trade policy, and may wish to offer investment incentives to encourage FDI by outside firms. Norman and Motta (1993) analysed the effects of the creation of a free trade area (FTA) between Eastern European countries on external firms' strategies in supplying these markets. They showed that both market growth and improved market accessability lead the external firms to switch from exporting to FDI.

Most theoretical papers deal with effects on FDI of regional integration between countries at the same stage of development. In this context, Montout and Zitouna (2002) developed a theoretical model based on FDI motives described in Neary (2002). The stress was put on north–south FTAs characteristics, notably wage differences and the possibility of FDI by firms originating from the area. Results suggest:

- A traditional result in multinational firms strategies models: the tariff-jumping motive to FDI holds if transaction costs (including transport and trade barriers) are important relative to additional fixed costs associated to investing abroad.
- Export platform strategy holds if foreign firms choose to locate in the low wage country in order to re-export. This motive depends on wage and trade barriers differences. The more important these differences are, the more likely foreign firms are to use this strategy when intra-regional trade costs fall (countries becoming more and more integrated).
- When analysing the influences of domestic firms' strategies on foreign ones, an eviction effect may exist. It results from insiders relocation in the low wages country which reduces the market accessibility advantages of investing there for outsiders.

Empirical studies found a positive incidence of regional integration on FDIs. Yannopoulos (1990) highlighted the significant growth of intra-regional FDI flows in the European Union. Moreover, Dunning (1997) demonstrated the positive incidence of the EU on the inter- and intracapital flows. In addition, a sectoral analysis on the England agro-food industry by Morgan and Wakelin (2001) emphasized the increase of foreign and domestic investment in this sector. Girma (2002) examines the determinants of FDI location choices in the UK using disaggregated data for manufacturing industry between 1981 and 1991. He concluded that opportunities created by regional integration deepening have changed the FDI flows determinants.

Furthermore, Blonigen and Feenstra (1996) underlined the crucial role of protectionist threat and the existence of tariff barriers. The FDI inflows from outsiders into the region could obviously go up if the average level of protection increases as a result of the free trade area. Moreover, the rise in fears about future protection implies the same outcome. In the same way, Barrell and Pain (1999) found that Japanese investment flows in European countries were influenced by trade barriers.

Blomström and Kokko (1997) analysed in detail the incidence of north American integration on FDIs. They consider that 'the stronger the environmental change connected with regional integration and the stronger locational advantages of the individual country or industry, the more likely it is that integration agreement will lead to inflows of FDI from the outside as well as from the rest of the integrating region' (ibid., p. 31). They highlight differences in structures of regional blocs by distinguishing north–north (Canada and the USA) and north–south regional integration (the inclusion of Mexico). On the one hand, the former agreement had a negligible impact on FDI flows. On the other hand, the latter had a significant incidence on inward foreign investment flows in Mexico.

In this chapter, our aim is twofold: first, we study the determinants of automobile production in Mexico. We find a significant positive (negative) impact of Mexican demand (costs). United States variables have nuanced effects. Moreover, we find positive (negative) impact of Mexican relative demand (costs) on the Mexican production share – regarding Mexican and US ones. Second, we examine the effects of the creation of NAFTA on firms operating in the automobile sector. We find a positive impact on the production of outsiders in Mexico and no significant impact on insiders. Furthermore, it affected positively the Mexican share of the production of either insiders and outsiders, suggesting that, all else equal, it promoted relocation of automobile production in Mexico. Finally, we found that NAFTA affected firms' strategies in 1991 for insiders and 1992 for outsiders.

The reminder of the chapter proceeds as follows: section 4.2 describes the policy framework governing the automotive sector in the NAFTA; in section 4.3, we develop some stylized facts on the automobile industry in NAFTA; and we present the econometric study and results in section 4.4. Finally, section 4.5 concludes.

4.2 THE AUTOMOTIVE REGIME IN THE NAFTA AREA

Until the late 1980s, Mexico used Auto Decrees, foreign investment regulations, and tariffs to keep the industries segmented along the Rio Grande, the border with the USA.

Gradually NAFTA eliminates tariffs and trade balancing requirements on vehicles, and sets up local content requirements. Mexican tariffs on cars and light trucks from the USA or Canada were reduced from 20 to 10 per cent on 1 January 1994. The passenger's car tariff was subsequently reduced by 1.2 per cent in 1995 and by 1.1 per cent per year, and was totally removed on 1 January 2003. For light trucks, the tariff was reduced by 2.5 per cent per year in order to attain zero on 1 January 2003.

The rules of origin establish procedures for determining whether products traded within NAFTA are originating within the member countries and, therefore, are eligible to enjoy the benefits of NAFTA tariff reductions. These rules have been formulated to encourage production in North America and to avoid the establishment of export platforms by non-regionally based firms in any member country of NAFTA. This policy framework was certainly influenced by the predominant presence of affiliates of multinational firms in the production structure of this sector. For example, from 1994 to 1997, a minimum of 50 per cent of a light vehicle's net cost was required to come from North America. From 1998 to 2001, this value has increased to 56 per cent, and it reached 62.5 per cent in 2002. All others vehicles had to meet 50 per cent between 1994 and 1997, 55 per cent between 1998 and 2001, and 60 per cent thereafter.

The local content requirements have encouraged the final automakers to be directly involved in the domestic production of auto parts and to develop suppliers networks regionally.

In addition, the NAFTA substantially liberalizes the North American investment regimes. The agreement establishes a clear, rules-based framework for the impartial treatment of FDI and places strict limit upon the use of performance requirements. The national treatment provisions constitute the conceptual cornerstone of NAFTA. Several provisions of the agreement, however, move beyond national treatment either by establishing common norms for the treatment of FDI among the three signatories, or through the adoption of measures based upon reciprocity. The new environment characterized by security, stability and by a drastic reduction of tariffs on regionally originating goods may influence the location strategies of firms. As a matter of fact, US transnational corporations will be encouraged to rationalize the organization of their north American operations and to increase foreign direct investment in Mexico. Nevertheless, some industries, such as automobiles will be protected from the import competition by strict rules of origin. The principal aims of NAFTA investment provisions are to create an integrated north American market.

4.3 STYLIZED FACTS

Since the beginning of the 1980s, the automobile production in Mexico experienced a significant and continuous increase (see Figure 4.1). Moreover, the production of foreign companies excluding American firms

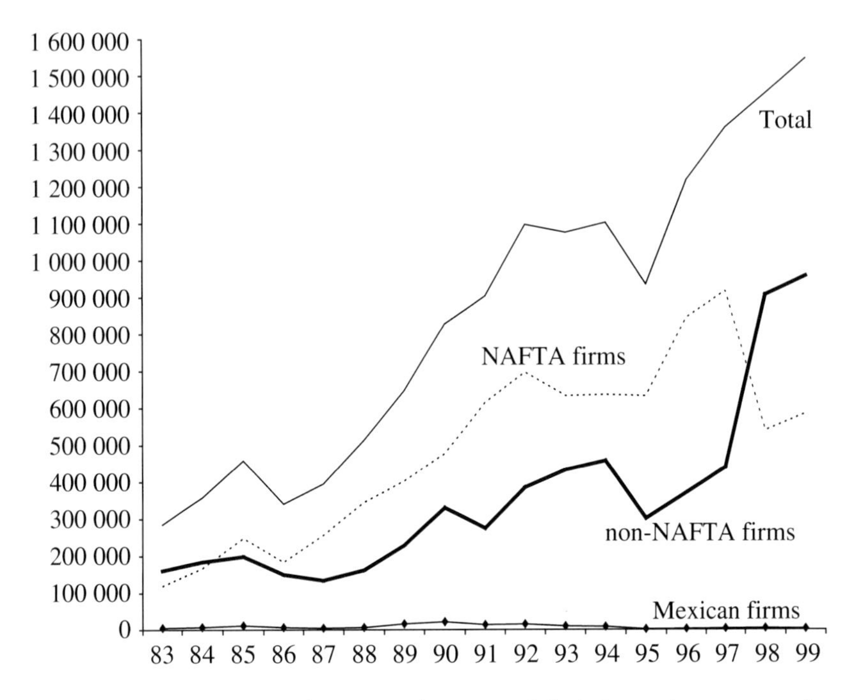

Figure 4.1 Mexican production in the automobile industry by country of origin of firms

knew an important growth and notably since 1997, which represents the date of takeover of Chrysler by Benz, a German firm. This takeover explains the asymmetric evolution of US and outsider companies' production between 1997 and 1998.

The main automobile constructors are Volkswagen, Chrysler, General Motors, Ford and Nissan. In fact, these multinational firms dominate for all the considered period with more than 95 per cent of the production (see Table 4.1). Moreover, the data illustrate the predominant presence of US firms in Mexico until 1997. During this period, they realize, in mean, more than 60 per cent of total production. The substantial modifications in this industry result mainly from investments engaged by Chrysler, Ford and General Motors.

Figure 4.2 illustrates the evolution of Mexican exports from 1983 to 1999. It translates the important role of the US market in addition to the Mexican one. At the end of the period, about 90 per cent of the production is sold in the north American market (USA and Mexico). Indeed, 60 per cent of the production is intended for local consumption and about 35 per cent is exported to the US market. Trade relations between Mexico and

Table 4.1 Production shares (% of total production) of the five largest automobile constructors in Mexico

	1990	1991	1992	1993	1994	1995	1996	1997	1998	1999
Total (in units)	820558	989373	1083091	1086621	1127515	935159	1219424	1359588	1455360	1493666
Chrysler*	20.41	19.62	21.68	21.02	21.61	21.98	29.62	26.18	24.70	21.38
Ford	2.08	22.49	23.75	19.27	20.18	24.31	17.51	18.19	14.67	15.42
GM	20.41	19.46	18.50	17.70	14.29	21.26	21.96	22.13	21.71	21.66
Nissan	16.63	12.37	15.93	17.11	17.17	11.42	11.12	12.71	13.04	12.01
Volkswagen	23.54	22.31	18.65	22.00	22.73	20.47	18.95	18.93	23.29	26.56
Total (shares)	83.07	96.25	98.50	97.09	95.99	99.45	99.16	98.14	97.42	97.02

Note: * From 1997, Chrysler-Benz.

Source: Authors' calculations from French Comity of Automobile Constructors data.

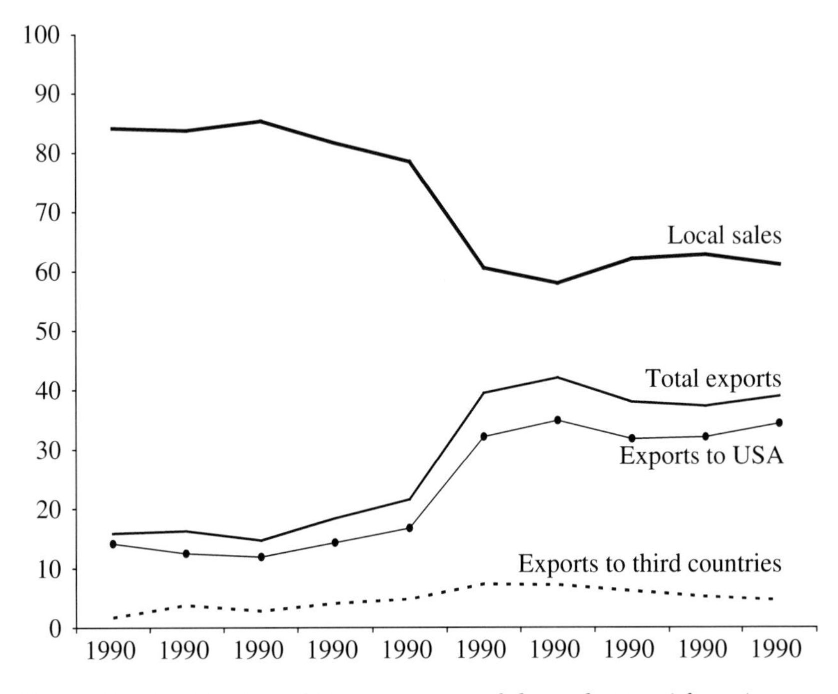

Figure 4.2 Destination of Mexican automobile production (shares)

Canada in this industry are negligible. In fact, in the 1990s, about 95 per cent of Mexican trade in the automobile industry in NAFTA is done with USA.[1] That is why we do not take into account Canadian production, demand and production costs.

Thus, the location of firms in Mexico seems to be motivated by the proximity to the USA in addition to the advantages of Mexico in terms of labour costs. Therefore, this automobile production is essentially influenced by the strategies of multinationals benefiting from Mexican low wage costs, Mexican market size and proximity to the US market.

4.4 ECONOMETRIC STUDY

The North American Free Trade Agreement, being a north–south regional integration, may affect the production and the location strategies of multinational firms (MNFs). Moreover, the outcome could be different depending on the origin of the firm: insider or outsider to the trade area.

In our econometric model, our objectives are:

- We test whether automobile production in Mexico is affected by production costs differential between Mexico and the USA. Do Mexican and US costs affect automobile production in Mexico? In fact, firms may be incited to locate in the low wages country in order to export to the largest market.
- Does Mexican or/and US sectoral demand play a role in determining output of automobile producers in Mexico? It permits us to evaluate the importance of Mexican demand relative to the US one in determining automobile production in Mexico.
- We see if NAFTA contributed to the increase (decrease) of the production of foreign (local) firms. By foreign firms, we mean outsiders.
- We check if NAFTA affected the location choice of MNFs production between the USA and Mexico. Is there a substitution between both alternative locations?

Data and Variables

In order better to explain firm strategies, we use firm data on automobiles produced in Mexico and the USA between 1983 and 1999: 40 firms produce automobiles in Mexico and/or at least for two years in the considered period. Demand, production costs and regional integration variables are integrated in the econometric model to explain production and location strategies of MNFs (see Table 4.2 for a description of variables and data sources).

Endogenous variable

As a dependant variable, we take the volume and the share of production per firm in Mexico. We have information only on final goods. To our knowledge, no data is available on parts and components production in Mexico.

Explanatory variables

Mexican output volume is supposed to be partially explained by the production of the same firm in the USA (P_{US}). In fact, in addition to demand and costs considerations, the production of the same firm in the USA gives us information about the evolution and the strategy of the multinational firm as a whole. If they are positively correlated, it may illustrate its whole situation: if a firm is declining (growing), it decreases (increases) its production in all locations, then reduces (raises) its production in Mexico abstracting from all other considerations. A positive sign may also explain the strategy of 'diversification' of the firm. Firms can specialize in the production of one variety in the USA and another one in Mexico. On the other hand, if production in the USA negatively affects

Table 4.2 Variables used in regressions (sources in parentheses)

Dependent variable	
$Prod_{Mex}$	Automobile production in Mexico (per firm) (French Comity of Automobile Constructors, 1983–99)
$Share_{Mex}$	Mexican share of Automobile production (per firm) (French Comity of Automobile Constructors, 1983–99)
Independent variables	
P_{US}	Automobile production in USA (per firm) (French Comity of Automobile Constructors, 1983–99)
Demand	
$dreg_{Mex}$	differential in registration sales in Mexico relative to previous year (World Automotive market and The Society of Motors Manufacturers and Traders Ltd, 1983–97)
$dreg_{US}$	differential in registration sales in USA relative to previous year (The Society of Motors Manufacturers and Traders Ltd, 1983–99)
$Share_{dreg}$	Share in Mexican new registration regarding US ones $= \frac{dreg_{Mex}}{dreg_{US}}$
Production costs	
$wages_{mex}$	Mexican wages corrected by Productivity per Mexican employee in the automobile sector $= \frac{Mex\ wages}{Mex\ productivity}$ (calculations made by authors from STAN OECD, 1983–99)
$wages_{US}$	US wages corrected by Productivity per US employee in the automobile sector $= \frac{US\ wages}{US\ productivity}$ (calculations made by authors from STAN OECD, 1983–99)
$Share_{wages}$	Share in Mexican wages regarding US ones in the automobile sector $= \frac{wages_{Mex}}{wages_{US}}$ (calculations made by authors from STAN OECD, 1983–99)
Regional integration	
$NAFTA_{loc}$	A dummy for regional integration for NAFTA firms = 1 for NAFTA firms after NAFTA
$NAFTA_{for}$	A dummy for regional integration for non-NAFTA firms = 1 for non-NAFTA firms after NAFTA

the Mexican production of the same firm, it illustrates a substitution of the two locations. In this case, firms favour one location which explains the export platform strategy. For example, until 1987 Volkswagen produced 45 per cent of its north American output in Mexico. Since 1988, it produces only in Mexico.

We assume that individual production in Mexico and the Mexican share of the north American output are influenced by both demand variables and production costs.

Demand The American and Mexican market size may affect positively the automobile production in Mexico. We approximate the Mexican and US demand by a sectoral variable (*dregMex* and *dregUS*): differences between registrations in the considered year with registrations in the previous year. However, if there is substitution relation between Mexican and US locations, an increase in the US demand may have no effect on the production in Mexico. Besides, in the second regression taking Mexican production share as endogenous variable, a positive effect of Mexican (US) demand would mean that a marginal increase in the Mexican (US) demand affects more Mexican production than the US one.

Costs Previous empirical analysis concerning FDI inward in developing countries put the stress on differential in wage costs between the developing and developed economies (Woodward and Rolfe, 1993). The low wage costs represent a considerable advantage for attracting foreign investors (Klayman, 1994). In the same way, Feenstra and Hanson (1997) show the positive correlation between wage costs of home countries of MNFs located in Mexico and investment flows at the benefit of *maquiladoras* (assembly plants). Thus, large wage differentials between developing and developed countries involved in a regional trade agreement incite foreign firms to locate in the former (Thomas and Grosse, 2001). Therefore the incidences of US wages in addition to Mexican ones seem to be a relevant analysis.

We consider US ($wages_{US}$) and Mexican wages ($wages_{Mex}$) at the sectoral level. The former (latter) is expected to have a positive (negative) effect on the Mexican production: an increase in wage differences incites the firms to produce relatively more in Mexico. In order to take into account the differences in qualifications, we correct nominal wages by incorporating Mexican and US productivity per employee. The productivity is measured as production per worker in the automobile sector.

Regional integration Regional integration is approximated by dummy variables because of the non-availability of data about trade barriers. We distinguish the incidence of the creation of NAFTA on domestic ($NAFTA_{loc}$) and foreign firms ($NAFTA_{for}$) located in Mexico. It equals one for local (foreign) firm from the date of the creation of NAFTA, and zero otherwise.

Regressions

In our database, for almost 50 per cent of observations, there is no production in Mexico. This information is important since it illustrates location strategies of firms: producing in Mexico and/or in the USA. That is why we use a Tobit model. This model takes into account the values equal to zero in the dependent variable.

In the first regressions (Table 4.3), we run a Tobit without any panel analysis. In the first model, the dependent variable is the volume of automobile production in Mexico (per firm), In the second, we took the Mexican share – regarding US and Mexican ones – of automobile production (per firm).

Table 4.3 Regressions (OLS)

Model Dependent variable	(1) $Prod_{Mex}$	(2) $Share_{Mex}$
$ln(P_{US})$	0.414***	
	(0.102)	
$ln(dreg_{Mex})$	0.259	
	(0.470)	
$ln(dreg_{US})$	−0.960	
	(2.486)	
$ln(wages_{Mex})$	0.308	
	(0.710)	
$ln(wages_{US})$	−1.481	
	(2.627)	
$ln(Share_{dreg})$		0.234
		(0.235)
$ln(Share_{wages})$		0.244
		(0.483)
$NAFTA_{loc}$	5.995*	4.140*
	(2.337)	(1.466)
$NAFTA_{for}$	−1.526	−0.797*
	(2.249)	(1.415)
Constant	7.825	−10.064*
	(36.910)	(1.107)
N	349	407
LR chi(2)	28.79	13.86
Prob>chi(2)	0.0002	0.0078
Pseudo R2	0.0230	0.0100

Note: Standard errors in parenthesis with *, ** and *** denoting significance at the 1 per cent, 5 per cent and 10 per cent levels.

In the first model, the sign associated with the US production is positive and significant, which illustrates a positive and dependent correlation between the US and Mexican output in this industry. Demand variables are not significant. Neither Mexican nor US demand had an effect on the production of automobiles in Mexico. On the cost side, neither Mexican nor US wages are significant. Finally, it seems that NAFTA had an impact on local firms' production only. Thus, regional integration contributed to the growth of insiders' output and had no effect on outsiders' output.

The results of demand, costs and NAFTA variables have qualitatively similar effects on production in Mexico and the distribution of production between the USA and Mexico (model 2 in Table 4.3).

We have to be cautious with these results because of the existence of a strong heterogeneity between firms. That is why we include firms' fixed effects in next regressions (Table 4.4).

In the first model (volume of Mexican production as a dependent variable), the volume of US production has no more significant effect. Giving the dualistic productive structure between largest constructors which concentrate more than 90 per cent of production and the others, representing small productive units, the equation without fixed effects biased the results. In fact, production in Mexico is not affected by the production of the same firm in the USA.

The Mexican demand variable has a positive and significant effect. This result sheds light on the importance of the Mexican market in determining the volume of automobile production in Mexico. However, US demand has no significant effect. Cost variables are both significant. As expected, Mexican (US) wages have a negative (positive) incidence. Thus, the higher the wages differential is, the more firms are incited to produce in Mexico. Recall that, if we do not correct wages by the productivity, results will be different. In fact, by doing so, we found a positive effect of Mexican wages which reflects an increase in productivity per employee and obviously not an increase in costs for firms.

Turning to the effects of NAFTA on insiders and outsiders, we found a positive impact on the latter meaning that, all else being equal, the creation of this regional integration attracted foreign investors in this industry, whereas, there is no incidence on the production of insiders.

The aim of the second model is to emphasize the location choices between Mexico and the USA. Mexican relative demand regarding the US demand seems to affect positively the share of automobile production in Mexico relative to the production in the USA and Mexico. On the cost side, Mexican relative costs regarding the US costs have a negative effect on the Mexican share of output. This result illustrates the important role of differences in production costs in determining the location of automobiles firms.

Table 4.4 Regressions (Tobit)

Model Dependent variable	(1) $Prod_{Mex}$	(2) $Share_{Mex}$	(3) $Share_{Mex}$
$ln(P_{US})$	−0.075		
	(0.081)		
$ln(dreg_{Mex})$	0.173***		
	(0.104)		
$ln(dreg_{US})$	−0.401		
	(0.541)		
$ln(wages_{Mex})$	−0.275***		
	(0.159)		
$In(wages_{US})$	1.075***		
	(0.589)		
$ln(Share_{dreg})$		0.239*	0.189**
		(0.088)	(0.096)
$ln(Share_{wages})$		−0.375**	−0.442**
		(0.187)	(0.208)
$NAFTA_{loc}$	−0.401	1.567*	1.092***
	(0.533)	(0.555)	(0.618)
$NAFTA_{for}$	3.043*	1.440*	1.192***
	(0.623)	(0.602)	(0.655)
Constant	7.677	−8.446*	−8.408*
	(8.050)	(0.659)	(0.741)
N	349	407	407
LR chi(2)	709.77	606.78	601.05
Prob>chi(2)	0.0000	0.0000	0.0000
Pseudo R2	0.5681	0.4381	0.4339

Note: Standard errors in parenthesis with *, ** and *** denoting significance at the 1 per cent, 5 per cent and 10 per cent levels.

Finally, NAFTA had a significant and positive impact on both local and foreign firms' Mexican shares. So, abstracting for demand and cost considerations, NAFTA modified the production structure of both insiders and outsiders. In fact, NAFTA increased Mexican production relatively more than US production in the automobile industry.

Now, we try to see in which year NAFTA really had an impact on the distribution of automobile production between Mexico and the USA. By doing so, we cheek whether firms anticipated gains resulting from improved market accessability. In fact, in model 2, we chose 1993 as a reference year. We ran different models and found that, for insiders, 1991 is the first year for which NAFTA had a significant and positive impact, whereas for outsiders it is 1992 (model 3).

4.5 CONCLUSION

In this chapter, we employ Tobit estimates in order to study the determinants of automobile production in Mexico. Moreover, we assess the effects of the creation of the North American Free Trade Agreement on the strategies of MNFs by distinguishing insiders and outsiders to the area.

We find a significant positive (negative) impact of Mexican demand (costs). United States variables have nuanced effects. Moreover, we find a positive (negative) impact of Mexican relative demand (costs) on the Mexican production share – regarding Mexican and US ones.

By examining the effects of the creation of NAFTA on firms operating in the automobile sector, we find a positive impact on the production of outsiders in Mexico and no significant impact on insiders.

Furthermore, NAFTA affected positively the Mexican share of the production of both insiders and outsiders, suggesting that, all else being equal, it promoted relocation of automobile production in Mexico.

Finally, we found that NAFTA affected firms' strategies in 1991 for insiders and 1992 for outsiders, meaning that firms anticipate trade policies.

ACKNOWLEDGEMENTS

We wish to thank Matthieu Crozet, Sebastien Jean, Daniel Mirza and all participants at 2002 GDR EFI, EARIE, AFSE and ETSG conferences for valuable suggestions. We are also grateful to Massimo Geloso-grosso for helpful comments.

NOTE

1. Calculations made by the authors from Foreign Trade Statistics (FTS) database, OECD.

REFERENCES

Barrell, R. and N. Pain (1999), 'Trade restraints and Japanese direct investment flows', *European Economic Review*, **43** (1), 29–45.

Blomström, M. and A. Kokko (1997), 'Regional integration and foreign direct investment', *National Bureau of Economic Research, Working Paper 6019*.

Blonigen, B.A. and R.C. Feenstra (1996), 'Protectionist threats and foreign direct investment', *National Bureau of Economic Research, Working Paper 5475*.

Dunning, J. (1997), 'The European internal market programme and inbound foreign direct investment: part II', *Journal of Common Market Studies*, **35** (2), 189–223.

Feenstra, R.C. and G.H. Hanson (1997), 'Foreign direct investment and relative wages: evidence from Mexico's maquiladoras', *Journal of International Economics*, **42** (3–4), 371–393.

Girma, S. (2002), 'The process of European integration and the determinants of entry by non EU multinationals in UK manufacturing', *The Manchester School*, **70**, 315–35.

Klayman, L. (1994), 'Prudent advice', *World Trade*, **7** (7), 72–4.

Montout, S. and H. Zitouna (2002), 'Does north–south integration affect multinationals' strategies?', ETSG Working Paper.

Morgan, C. and K. Walkelin (2001), 'The impact of European integration on FDI: the UK food industry in the 1990s', in J.H. Dunning and J.L. Mucchielli (eds), *Multinational Firms: The Global and Local Dilemma*, London and New York: Routledge.

Neary, P. (2002), 'Foreign direct investment and the single market, *The Manchester School*, **70** (3), 291– 314.

Norman, G. and M. Motta (1993), 'Eastern European economic integration and foreign direct investment', *Journal of Economics and Management Strategy*, **2** (4), 483–507.

Norman, G. and M. Motta (1996), 'Does economic integration cause foreign direct investment', *International Economic Review*, **37** (4), 757–83.

Stevens, G. (1998), 'US direct investment to Mexico: politics, economics, and NAFTA', *Contemporary Economic Policy*, **16** (2), 197–210.

Thomas, D.E. and R. Grosse (2001), 'Country-of-origin determinants of foreign direct investment in an emerging market: the case of Mexico', *Journal of International Management*, **7** (1), 59–79.

Woodward, D. and R. Rolfe (1993), 'The location of export oriented foreign direct investment in the Caribbean Basin', *Journal of International Business Studies*, **24** (1), 121–44.

Yannopoulos, G. (1990), 'Foreign direct investment and European integration: the evidence from the formative years of the European Community', *Journal of Common Market Studies*, **28** (3), 235–59.

5. Trade liberalization and the internal geography of countries

Matthieu Crozet and Pamina Koenig-Soubeyran

5.1 INTRODUCTION

The need to restructure a large number of European policies before launching the final part of the enlargement of the European Union (EU) gathers consensus among European policy-makers. One of the areas of European action to which particular attention will be directed is that of the European regional policies, and two new sources of European funding have already been created specifically for these countries in order to finance regional development.

In this context, it appears relevant to go one step further and to analyse the link between the economic integration of the Central and Eastern European countries (CEECs) with the EU and the economic geography of these countries: how does trade liberalization have an impact on regional development patterns within countries?

The relation between trade and the location of production inside countries has been explicitly studied by recent models of the new economic geography literature, based on the original model of Krugman (1991). Indeed, Krugman and Livas (1996), in a two-country three-region framework, suggest that a decrease in international transaction costs between two countries may foster the dispersion of economic activity inside the home country. Conversely, Alonso-Villar (2001), Monfort and Nicolini (2000) and Paluzie (2001), respectively in a three-country, two-country four-region, and in a two-country three-region framework, show that trade liberalization is more likely to enhance agglomeration of economic activity inside the country opening to trade.

Some empirical work on the topic validate Krugman and Livas's result: Ades and Glaeser (1995) study an 85 countries sample and find a negative relationship between trade and urban concentration. Hanson (2001) analyses the consequences of the North American integration process on the location of activity inside Mexico. He finds a decreasing urban concentration: industries leave Mexico City to locate closer to the American border.

However, Henderson (1996, p. 33), in commenting on Krugman and Livas's model, suggests bringing one more element into the framework. He emphasizes that the impact of an increase in trade depends on the internal geography of the country: 'The impact of trade on national space is situation-specific, depending on the precise geography of the country. . . . In thinking about urban concentration, we may want a more generic or general framework' (ibid.). Our focus in this chapter is twofold: first, using the original new economic geography framework (Krugman, 1991), we develop a theoretical model containing two countries and three regions (domestic regions 1 and 2, and foreign region 0). We analyse the impact of trade liberalization on the internal geography of the domestic country, using a domestic country in which both regions are equidistant from the border. We observe that, in a model in which both the dispersion and agglomeration of economic activity are driven by endogenous elements, trade liberalization leads to the concentration of activity inside the domestic country. Note that Paluzie (2001) already went through these steps. In her model, the predicted outcome is agglomeration, but she does not study thoroughly the reasons for which her result differs from Krugman and Livas's result. In contrast, section 5.4 of this chapter is devoted to putting side by side our model and that of Krugman and Livas, in order to evaluate the origins of the difference in outcomes.

Our second focus in this chapter concerns the configuration in which both domestic regions do not have the same access to the foreign market. Coming up to Henderson's expectations, we generalize the model exposed in sections 5.2 and 5.3 to look at how the result is altered by having a heterogeneous domestic country opening to trade: in this case, we show that trade liberalization is likely to favour the development of border regions.

5.2 THE MODEL

This section exposes a model previewed by Paluzie (2001), which is a simple extension of Krugman's (1991) model of a two-country framework: a domestic country, containing two regions, opens to trade with an exogenous foreign country. We want to focus on the evolution of the economic geography inside the domestic country during the process of trade liberalization.

Consider two countries: a domestic country, containing two regions, labelled 1 and 2, and a foreign country, labelled 0. There are two sectors: one is a monopolistically competitive manufacturing sector, which produces a differentiated good and stands for all increasing to scale production activities in the economy. The other is the constant return to scale, perfectly competitive sector, which produces a homogeneous good. We will assimilate it to the agricultural sector. Factors are specific to each sector. The agricultural and the manufacturing goods are traded both interregionally and internationally.

The foreign country is totally exogenous: it contains L_{A0} agricultural workers and L_0 manufacturing workers, which are all immobile. In the domestic country, regional supply of A labour is fixed: the two domestic regions contain respectively L_{A1}, and L_{A2} workers, which are immobile. In the domestic manufacturing sector, only the total amount of manufacturing labour is fixed: the country has L manufacturing workers, distributed among regions: $L - L_1 + L_2$. The interregional distribution of industrial workers is endogenous: workers are mobile and migrate between the regions 1 and 2 according to the interregional real wage difference. For the rest of the chapter, we normalize the total number of industrial workers in the domestic country: $L = 1$. We set the share of industrial workers in region 1 equal to λ: $L_1 = \lambda$, $L_2 = 1 - \lambda$.

The spatial framework of the model is introduced through the use of a transaction cost variable, representing distance between cities and barriers to trade. As in similar models, a variety produced in region r is sold by the firm at mill price and the entire transaction cost is borne by the consumer. We use an 'iceberg'-type transaction cost variable, which means that a fraction of the shipped good melts away during the journey. When 1 unit is shipped, priced p, only $1/T$ actually arrives at destination. Therefore, in order for 1 unit to arrive, T units have to be shipped, increasing the price of the unit received to pT. Trade in the industrial good bears transaction costs, which differ across regions: T_{12} is the internal transaction cost, which applies to interregional domestic trade (with $T_{12} = T_{21}$). T_{01} and T_{02} are respectively the external transaction costs applying to each domestic region's trade with the foreign country. We assume the agricultural good's trade is costless, both interregionally and internationally. Therefore, its price equalizes everywhere: $p_{A1} = p_{A2} = p_{A0}$. The agricultural good is produced under perfect competition, and we choose technical coefficients equal to 1. As a result in each region $p_A = w_A$. Finally, we use the agricultural good as a numéraire, therefore $w_A = 1$ in each region.

Consumers and Price Indices

Every consumer has the same Cobb-Douglas utility function:

$$U = M^{\mu} A^{1-\mu}, \text{ with } 0 < \mu < 1 \tag{5.1}$$

M is a composite index of the consumption of the manufactured good, A is the consumption of the agricultural good. A share μ of expenditures goes to manufactured goods, and $1-\mu$ to the agricultural good. The composite index M is the following CES function:

$$M=\left[\sum_{i=1}^{n} c_i^{\frac{\sigma-1}{\sigma}}\right]^{\frac{\sigma}{\sigma-1}} \tag{5.2}$$

where c_i represents the consumption of a variety i of the manufactured good, and σ, is the elasticity of substitution between two varieties ($\sigma>1$). Given income Y, each consumer maximizes his utility under the budget constraint $Y=p_A A+\sum_{i=1}^{n} c_i p_i$. We get the following demand function, representing demand emanating from consumers of region s, addressed to a producer i located in region r:

$$c_{i,rs}=\frac{p_{irs}^{-\sigma}}{\sum_{r=0}^{R}\sum_{i=1}^{n_r}(p_{irs})^{1-\sigma}}\mu Y_s,\ r,s=0,1,2 \tag{5.3}$$

Equation (5.3) contains the spatial framework: there are R regions, each of them producing n_r varieties of the manufacturing good. The iceberg transport technology implies that the price of each variety i produced in r and sold in s contains the mill price and the transaction cost: $P_{irs}=P_r T_{rs}$ (because of the symmetry of all varieties produced in the same region, from now on we omit the variety index). We use T_{rs} as a general expression which represents either T_{12}, T_{01}, or T_{02}, assuming that $T_{rr}=1$ and (until section 5.5) that $T_{01}=T_{02}>T_{12}$. Using (5.2) and (5.3), we are thus able to derive the following industrial price index for each region s:

$$G_s=\left[\sum_{r=0}^{R} n_r(p_r T_{rs})^{1-\sigma}\right]^{\frac{1}{1-\sigma}} \tag{5.4}$$

Individual demand (5.3) can now be written

$$c_{rs}=\frac{(p_r T_{rs})^{-\sigma}}{G_s^{1-\sigma}}\mu Y_s,\ r,s=0,1,2 \tag{5.5}$$

Producers

Manufactured goods are produced in a monopolistically competitive industry, following the Dixit and Stiglitz (1977) framework. Each producer has the same production function, expressed in terms of manufacturing labour: $l=\alpha+\beta q$, where l is the total cost, in terms of labour, of producing q varieties. It contains a fixed cost α and a marginal cost β per additional unit produced. Each producer maximizes his profits. As usual in the Dixit and Stiglitz (1977) model, we obtain constant mark-up equations:

$$p_r = \left(\frac{\sigma}{\sigma - 1}\right) w_r \beta \tag{5.6}$$

where p_r is the price of a variety produced in r and w_r is the manufacturing wage in region r. The equilibrium output of a firm producing in region r is derived from the free entry condition:

$$q_r^* = \frac{\alpha(\sigma - 1)}{\beta} \tag{5.7}$$

and the equilibrium on each region's labour market allows us to obtain the equilibrium number of firms in each region:

$$n_r = \frac{L_r}{\alpha\sigma} \tag{5.8}$$

where L_r is the total number of manufacturing workers in region r.

Short-Term Equilibrium

We now want to fully determine the short-term equilibrium. We derive, for a given distribution of labour between regions 1 and 2, the value of w_r that verifies equations (5.5), (5.6), (5.7), (5.8) and the equilibrium condition on the goods' market. The manufacturing wage equation for each region r is thus:

$$w_r = \frac{1}{\beta}\left(\frac{\sigma - 1}{\sigma}\right)\left[\frac{\mu\beta}{\alpha(\sigma - 1)}\left(\sum_{j=0}^{R} Y_j G_j^{\sigma-1} T_{jr}^{1-\sigma}\right)\right]^{1/\sigma} \tag{5.9}$$

with $Y_r = w_r L_r + w_{Ar} L_{Ar}$, and w_{Ar} equal to 1 because we chose it as a numéraire. Equation (5.9) is a typical wage equation in new economic geography models (see Fujita, Krugman and Venables, 1999). It explains that the larger the number of consumers and the lower the number of competitors in regions with low transaction costs to r, the higher will be the nominal wage that a firm producing in r can pay: indeed, the nominal wage in region r tends to be higher if incomes in other regions with low transaction costs to r are high. On the other hand, it tends to be lower if other regions with low transaction costs to r contain a large number of firms (the region's industrial price index $G_j^{\sigma-1}$ may be regarded as an index of concentration).

We are now able to characterize entirely the equilibrium variables in our two-country, three-region setting, for a given spatial distribution of workers. Regional incomes are:

$$Y_1 = w_1 \lambda + L_{A1} \tag{5.10}$$

$$Y_2 = w_2(1-\lambda) + L_{A2} \tag{5.11}$$

$$Y_0 = w_0 L_0 + L_{A0} \tag{5.12}$$

Nominal wages are the solution of the following system, where G and Y have to be substituted for as functions of wages using (5.4), (5.6), (5.8) and $Y_r = w_r L_r + L_{Ar} w_{Ar}$ (see the appendix to this chapter):[1]

$$w_1 = \frac{1}{\beta}\left(\frac{\sigma-1}{\sigma}\right)\left[\frac{\mu\beta}{\alpha(\sigma-1)}(Y_0 G_0^{\sigma-1} T_0^{1-\sigma} + Y_1 G_1^{\sigma-1} + Y_2 G_2^{\sigma-1} T_{12}^{1-\sigma})\right]^{1/\sigma} \tag{5.13}$$

$$w_2 = \frac{1}{\beta}\left(\frac{\sigma-1}{\sigma}\right)\left[\frac{\mu\beta}{\alpha(\sigma-1)}(Y_0 G_0^{\sigma-1} T_0^{1-\sigma} + Y_1 G_1^{\sigma-1} T_{12}^{1-\sigma} + Y_2 G_2^{\sigma-1})\right]^{1/\sigma} \tag{5.14}$$

$$w_0 = \frac{1}{\beta}\left(\frac{\sigma-1}{\sigma}\right)\left[\frac{\mu\beta}{\alpha(\sigma-1)}(Y_0 G_0^{\sigma-1} + Y_1 G_1^{\sigma-1} T_0^{1-\sigma} + Y_2 G_2^{\sigma-1} T_0^{1-\sigma})\right]^{1/\sigma} \tag{5.15}$$

The industrial price indices are then given by:

$$G_1 = \left(\frac{\sigma\beta}{\sigma-1}\right)\left(\frac{1}{\alpha\sigma}\right)^{1/1-\sigma}[L_0(w_0T_0)^{1-\sigma} + \lambda w_1^{1-\sigma} + (1-\lambda)(w_2T_{12})^{1-\sigma}]^{1/1-\sigma} \tag{5.16}$$

$$G_2 = \left(\frac{\sigma\beta}{\sigma-1}\right)\left(\frac{1}{\alpha\sigma}\right)^{1/1-\sigma}[L_0(w_0T_0)^{1-\sigma} + \lambda (w_1T_{12})^{1-\sigma} + (1-\lambda)w_2^{1-\sigma}]^{1/1-\sigma} \tag{5.17}$$

$$G_0 = \left(\frac{\sigma\beta}{\sigma-1}\right)\left(\frac{1}{\alpha\sigma}\right)^{1/1-\sigma}[L_0 w_0^{1-\sigma} + \lambda (w_1T_0)^{1-\sigma} + (1-\lambda)(w_2T_0)^{1-\sigma}]^{1/1-\sigma} \tag{5.18}$$

We finally derive the real wage of each domestic region, which is made of the nominal wage deflated by the price index:

$$\omega_1 = \frac{w_1}{G_1^{\mu}}$$

$$\omega_2 = \frac{w_2}{G_2^{\mu}} \tag{5.19}$$

Long-Term Equilibrium

One can see that if $\lambda = 1/2$ (and if $L_{A1} = L_{A2}$), $\omega_1 = \omega_2$: when the industrial workforce is equally distributed between domestic regions, the real wages are equalized and there is no incentive for workers to move. But what happens if we move one worker from region 2 to region 1? This move will create a real wage differential that may either incite more people to move, or it may lower the real wage in the destination region, in which case the equally distributed configuration would be a stable equilibrium. We assume that industrial workers move between the two regions according to the following migration dynamics:

$$\frac{d\lambda}{dt} = \omega_1 - \omega_2 \tag{5.20}$$

We want to study the relationship between the real wage differential and the fraction of industrial workers living in region 1. We want to identify the spatial equilibria of the model, thus the distributions of workers for which no worker may get a higher real wage by changing location. The equilibrium distributions of the workforce thus consist of the values of $(\lambda, 1-\lambda)$ for which either $\omega_1 - \omega_2 = 0$ and $\lambda \in (0, 1)$, or $\omega_1 - \omega_2 \geq 0$ and $\lambda = 1$, or $\omega_1 - \omega_2 \leq 0$ and $\lambda = 0$.

Unfortunately, as typically in new economic geography models based on the original Krugman (1991) framework, $\omega_1 - \omega_2$ is not a simple function of λ: we are unable to tell precisely for what values of the parameters of the model the spatial equilibria are reached. In the next section we will thus use numerical simulations in order to look at the shape of the real wage differential function.

The evolution of the real wage differential $\omega_1 - \omega_2$ and the equilibrium spatial distribution inside the domestic country depend on the interaction of agglomeration and dispersion forces appearing in the equations we derived above. On the one side, agglomeration forces express the fact that firms and consumers are interested in locating in the same region, because of cost and demand externalities: in equations (5.13) and (5.14), the demand externality emphasizes that a large number of consumers in a region r represents high local expenditure, allowing firms to pay higher wages and thus attracting more firms. The cost externality appears in equations (5.16), (5.17) and (5.18): a high number of firms implies a lot of locally produced varieties, thus a lower price index and more consumers.

On the other side, the dispersion force emanates from the high competition on the good and the factor markets when industrial activity is concentrated in one location: equations (5.13) and (5.14) point that the nominal wage of a region diminishes with the increase in competition, and this leads firms to delocate towards the remote market in order to benefit from lower competition on that market.

Which equilibrium configuration is finally reached depends on the parameters of the models, and specifically on the level of interregional and international transaction costs. In the next section we will consider an economic integration between the domestic and the foreign country, illustrated through a decrease of T_{01}, and T_{02}. We will focus on determining how the presence of a foreign country impacts the internal geography of the domestic country.

5.3 TRADE LIBERALIZATION

This section considers the effect of lowering the international transaction cost on the spatial distribution of activity, in the case of a homogeneous country: the two domestic regions have the same access to foreign markets (T_{01} and T_{02} are set equal to T_0). We explain how we draw the real wage differential curves. For a given value[2] of T_0, we numerically solve ω_1 and ω_2 for a range of values of $\lambda \in (0, 1)$. We then substitute the obtained ω_1 and ω_2 into $\omega_1 - \omega_2$ in order to plot one of the curves below. As shown in Figure 5.1, this is done for three different values of T_0.

Let us analyse Figure 5.1 by starting where workers are symmetrically distributed among regions: $\lambda = 0.5$. This configuration is an equilibrium,

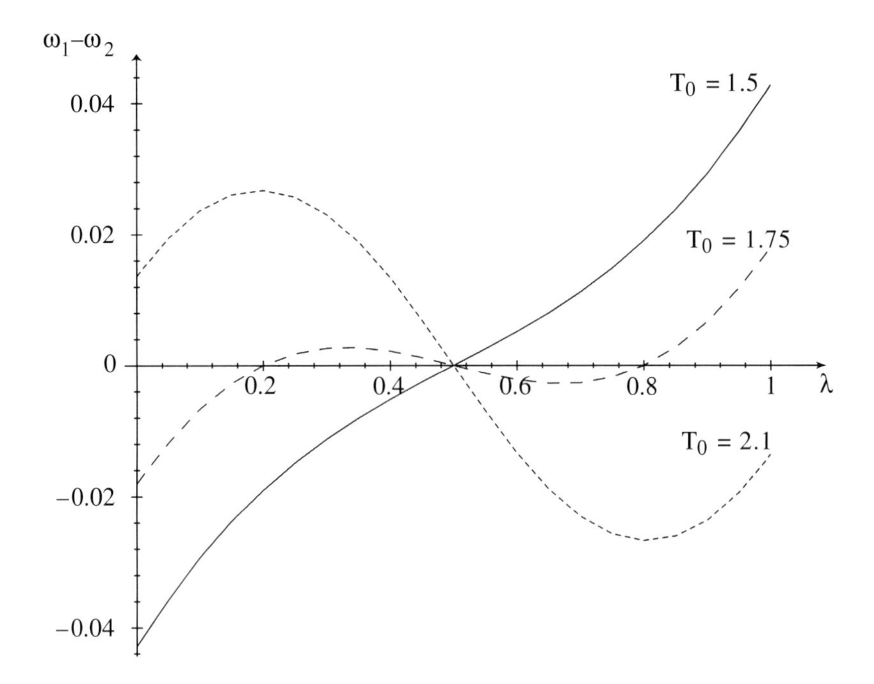

Figure 5.1 Real wage difference for three different external transaction costs

but it will only be stable if, for a marginal increase in λ, the real wage difference becomes negative. The migration of workers will then bring the distribution of workers back to the symmetrical configuration.

The situation in which the domestic country is closest to autarky is illustrated by the dotted curve, drawn for $T_0 = 2.1$ (which means that only 1/2.1 = 0.47 of the shipped quantity arrives at the final destination, corresponding to a transaction cost of 53 per cent). For this level of transaction costs, the dispersed configuration is the only stable equilibrium.[3] The dashed curve illustrates the situation when the economy opens slightly. There are now five equilibria, of which three are stable and two are unstable. While the symmetric equilibrium is still stable, the agglomerated configuration (in either region) has become stable as well. Finally, the more trade barriers are decreased, the more the curve turns upwards; when it comes to cross the x axis with a positive slope (the level $T_0 = 1.5$ corresponds to a transaction cost of 40 per cent), the only stable outcomes are the two agglomerated configurations. We thus highlight this interesting result: according to our simulations, an economic integration is most likely to lead the domestic industrial sector to be spatially concentrated.

Figure 5.2 summarizes how the types of equilibria vary with external transaction costs (solid lines indicate stable equilibria, broken lines

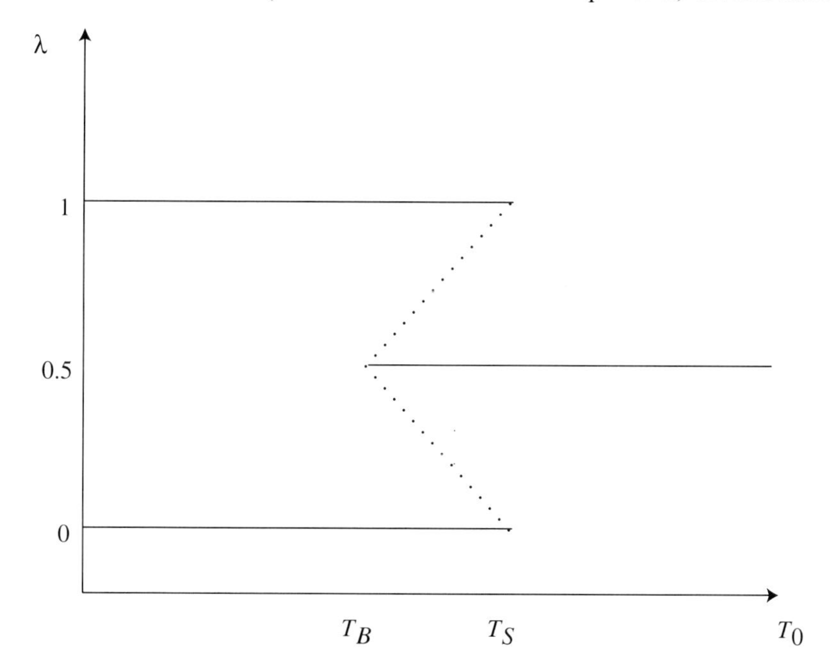

Figure 5.2 Bifurcation diagram

unstable): for sufficiently high T_0, there is a unique stable equilibrium in which the economy is evenly divided between the regions. When T_0 decreases below some threshold value (T_S, the sustain point), new stable equilibria appear in which all manufacturing is concentrated in one of the regions. When a second threshold value (T_B, the break point) is attained by lowering T_0, the symmetric equilibrium becomes unstable, leaving the agglomerated configurations as the only stable outcomes.

Note that simulations' results show that the values of the sustain and break point are influenced by the parameters of the model. First, the lower is σ, the higher is the value of the sustain and break points. Indeed, a low value of σ, indicates a high degree of product differentiation: in other words, the more products are differentiated, the more firms are incited to concentrate production, even if transaction costs are high. Second, the values of the sustain and break points increase with the value of μ, the share of expenditure going to manufactured goods. The larger the share of manufacturing goods, the stronger are cost and demand externalities which lead firms to concentrate production.

The Forces at Stake

What mechanisms explain this outcome? The decrease of the external transaction cost allows two additional elements to impact on the domestic economy: foreign demand and foreign supply. On the one hand, having an access to a large exterior market lowers the incentive for domestic firms to locate near domestic consumers, which represent a smaller share of their sales. Thus the domestic demand externality is weakened by the presence of the foreign demand (in equations 5.13 and 5.14, income from the foreign country becomes a more important part of total demand). For similar reasons, the domestic cost externality is weakened by the presence of the foreign supply: the foreign firms now represent a much more important share of the total supply available to domestic consumers (in equations 5.16, 5.17 and 5.18, the presence of the foreign firms now constitutes the main element that drives the price indices down).

On the other hand, trade liberalization also affects the competition effects within the domestic country. The competition exerted by foreign firms on the domestic market is large compared to the competition of other domestic firms. Therefore, the presence of the foreign supply lowers the need for domestic firms to locate far from domestic competitors, and thus lowers the need to disperse economic activity (in equations 5.16, 5.17 and 5.18, as stated before, the presence of foreign firms lowers both price indices, which then diminish ω_1 and ω_2).

It finally appears that while foreign demand and foreign supply decrease both the agglomeration and the dispersion forces, the simulations show that in the end, a strong economic integration has more effect on the dispersion force: as a result the domestic economy becomes concentrated in only one location.

5.4 COMPARISONS

Differences under Autarky

The purpose of this chapter is to investigate the relation between trade liberalization and the reshaping of the internal geography of countries, using the original model of the new economic geography. Krugman and Livas (1996) analysed the same problematic in a similar framework. However, their result differs from ours as to the evolution of the domestic spatial equilibrium configuration. While we observe agglomeration as a final outcome, their model concludes with the dispersion of economic activity.

The reason why we obtain such differing results lies in the hypotheses driving the dispersion of the industrial sector. In Krugman and Livas's modelling (henceforth KL96), there is no local immobile market to provide an incentive for firms to delocate to the peripheral region. Instead, an exogenous congestion force leads firms to move to the remote region when the cost of being agglomerated is too high. The crucial point remains in the fact that KL96's congestion force does not depend on transaction costs. Hence, the decrease of external transaction costs may only have an impact on the incentives of firms and consumers to locate near each other, that is, on the agglomeration force. The impact of trade liberalization is thus very different in both models. Economic integration, through the increase of exports (foreign demand) and imports (foreign supply), lowers agglomeration forces inside the country. While it also lowers dispersion forces in our model, in KL96's model the dispersion force has no impact at all.

As a result, in KL96 the only stable equilibrium after trade liberalization is a dispersed distribution of the industrial sector. In contrast, the framework we propose in this chapter is based on the same forces as those of new economic geography models of the Krugman (1991) type (henceforth K91). Therefore, the final outcome bears the characteristic of being the result of the interaction of two endogenous forces, and in this sense it is a more general framework.

Note that this difference is visible when comparing both models in their autarkic two-region version (by setting the external transaction cost to $+\infty$). While K91 concludes that a decrease in internal transaction costs will lead to more agglomeration, in KL96 the autarkic country will see its economic activity getting more dispersed. Two features of the KL96 model explain this difference in outcomes: KL96 contains only one sector, which exhibits increasing returns-to-scale, and it comprises only mobile workers. Thus, without the presence of the urban congestion cost, the economy would be concentrated in one of the regions for all values of the internal transaction cost.

To illustrate this characteristic, let us look at the configuration of the domestic economy, in both models, according to the value of the *internal* transaction cost. We want to identify the threshold value of T_{12} at which the agglomerated equilibrium switches from unstable to stable (the *sustain* point of the economy according to T_{12}). We thus set the domestic economy in an agglomerated configuration (for example in region 1), and determine the conditions under which region 1 real wage (ω_1) is higher than region 2 (ω_2): for all values of T_{12} for which $\omega_1 \geq \omega_2$, the agglomerated pattern is sustainable, because industrial workers will not migrate to region 2. Figure 5.3 portrays the sustain point in both models according to T_{12}. The U-shape of the ω_2/ω_1 curve in K91 represents the agglomeration–dispersion pattern. When the internal transport cost T_{12} equals 1, space plays no role and real wages are identical. At the right of this point, the curve is downwards-sloping: a slight increase in T_{12} augments both agglomeration and dispersion forces, but not in the same measure. Demand and cost externalities have more influence on the economy and foster a strong asymmetric configuration, until the relative strength of the forces inverses. The upward-sloping part of the curve depicts a relatively more important increase in the dispersion forces, which finally make the asymmetric pattern unstable. To the right of the sustain point, industrial activity is symmetrically distributed among regions.

The ω_2/ω_1 curve in KL96 has two distinct features. First, it does not bear the upward-sloping part of the K91 U-shaped curve, which means that there is no dispersion of the economy for high values of T_{12}. Second, at low values of T_{12}, concentration of industrial activity is not a stable equilibrium anymore (numerical investigations similar to those exposed in Figure 5.1 indicate that low values of T_{12} lead to the dispersion of industrial activity). As explained above, the presence of the urban congestion cost discourages firms and consumers to support the cost of agglomeration when the internal transaction costs are very low. Hence, the reasons why we obtain, using a K91 setting, opposite results to those obtained by KL96 are already present in the basic hypotheses of the models and in the autarkic two-region settings.

Robustness to Internal Spatial Configurations

An important question arising after comparing the two models concerns the validity of our results for other values of parameters, and specifically

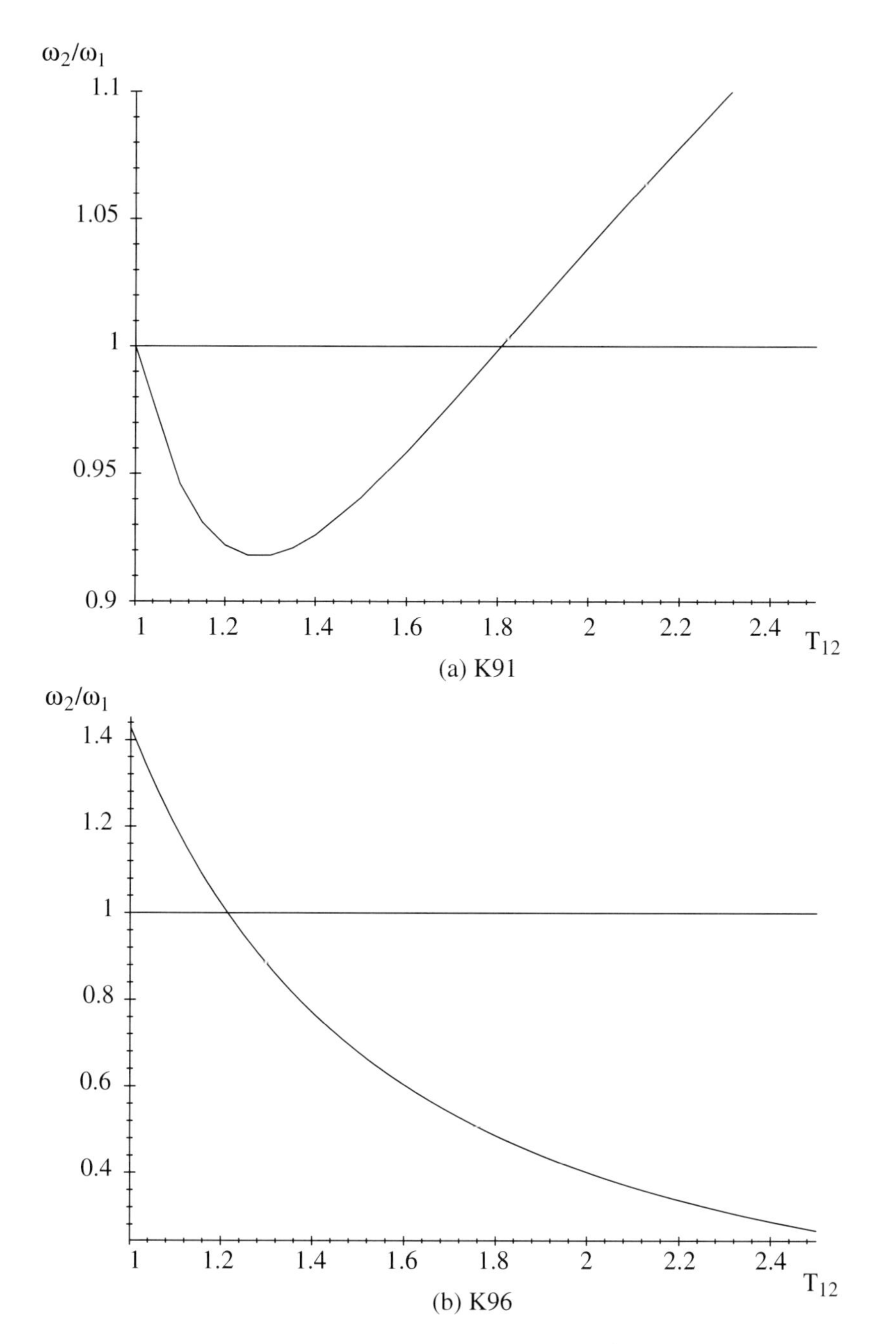

Figure 5.3 Sustain point for K91 and KL96

for other values of the internal transaction cost. To answer this question, let us look again at the configuration of the domestic economy according to the value of the *internal* transaction cost. We want to analyse how the threshold value of T_{12} at the sustain point of the economy varies with T_0.

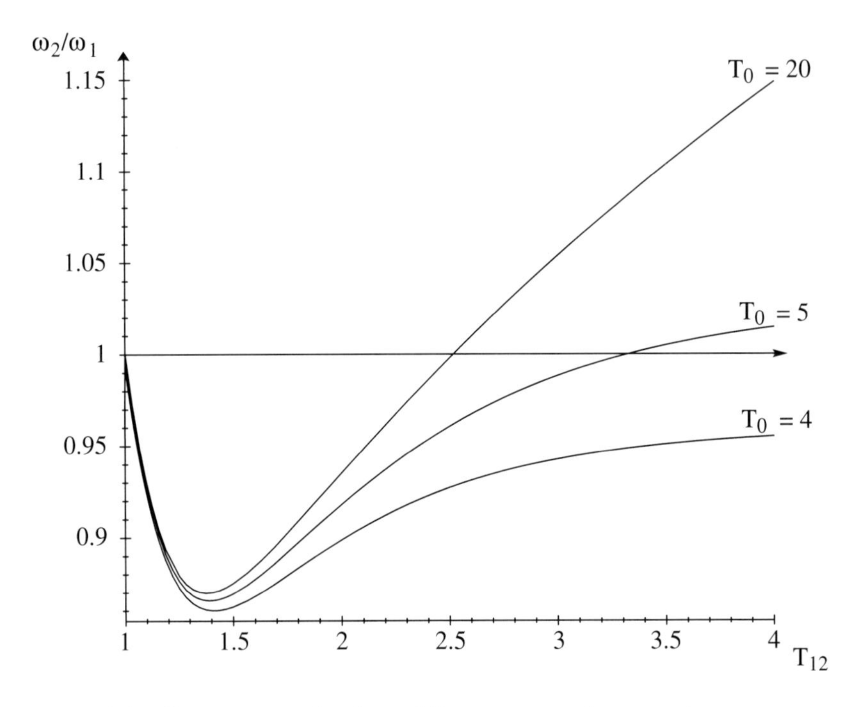

Figure 5.4 Sustain point for three different external transaction costs

Unfortunately, the three-region framework introduces analytical difficulties that are not present in the two-region or in the four-region case. Therefore we are not able to present an analytical proof. We will instead use numerical simulations to investigate how the sustain point of the economy varies with the evolution of the external transaction cost. Figure 5.4 illustrates ω_2/ω_1, as a function of the internal transport cost T_{12}, and this for three different values of T_0. The first curve is drawn for a very high value of T_0, assimilated to very important barriers to trade. As explained above, ω_2/ω_1 is U-shaped. The second curve illustrates the same phenomenon for a lower value of T_0. The visible impact of the economic integration is to lower the right part of the precedent U-shaped curve. According to the description of the curve in the preceding sub-section, the decrease in T_0 specifically impacts the dispersion forces, because the sustain point shifts to the right of the figure. Trade openness augments the range of values of T_{12} for which the economy is agglomerated, that is, the effect of the domestic competition (lower price index) is weakened. This is even more apparent when trade openness accentuates, to the point that the curve doesn't display a sustain point any more: on the last curve, ω_2 never becomes higher than ω_1.

According to the simulations, our theoretical result appears to be robust to the spatial configuration of the domestic economy. Whatever the value of the internal transaction cost, trade liberalization is most likely to foster an economic geography concentrated in one of the two domestic locations. Note that Paluzie (2001), who previewed the theoretical result, did not investigate how international transaction costs affect the sustain point of the economy.

Our result is strengthened by Monfort and Nicolini (2000), who come to identical conclusions in a four regions' setting. They extend a Krugman (1991) framework to a two-country, four-region model and show that international integration, thus the decrease of external transaction costs, is likely to enhance agglomeration in each of the national economies. The four region setting is useful because it allows simplifications and lead to analytical solutions. However, we prefer considering a three-region model. It seems more appropriate because our main focus is centred on the economic geography of the domestic country and it allows us to make direct comparisons between our result and that of Krugman and Livas. Moreover, expanding the original Krugman (1991) two-region framework to a three-region framework allows us to get closer to the modelling of different and richer configurations such as the hub-city case (see Krugman, 1993). This will be particularly apparent in the next section when analysing the case of a country containing a border region.

5.5 BORDER REGIONS

We now ask the same question, but in a slightly different framework: by letting the two external transaction costs differ, we suppose that one of the domestic cities has a better access to the foreign market (region 2 for example). We specify a functional form for T_{rs}. T_{rs} represents all the transaction costs and consists of a cost related to distance and, for international trade, an *ad valorem* tariff. In this section we also adopt a specific and simplified representation of space *à la* Hotelling in which country 0 and region 1 are located at both extremes. Region 2 is the border region. The segment thus has a length equal to d_{01}, and the distance between 1 and 2 is $d_{01} - d_{02}$. We assume that transaction costs are a linear function of distance: $T_{12} = 1 + (d_{01} - d_{02})$ and $T_{01}, = (1 + \text{tariff})\ d_{01}$.

In order to understand how the economic geography of the country evolves with trade openness, as in section 5.3 we use numerical simulations to display the shape of the interregional real wage difference as a function of the workers distribution λ.

Theoretically, the forces impacting on the domestic economy are modified since the country now contains two heterogeneous regions. Two changes are noticeable: first, as observed in section 5.3, foreign demand lowers the domestic agglomeration force. However, an additional effect appears, because domestic firms may now choose to locate in the location closest to the foreign market, which is region 2. We thus highlight one of the potential effects of trade liberalization, which is to *pull* domestic firms towards the border in order for them to benefit from the best access to foreign demand. Then, foreign supply lowers the domestic dispersion force. There is also an additional effect due to the heterogeneity of the regions: region 1, at the end of the segment, allows firms to locate as far as possible from the foreign competitors. Hence, trade liberalization may *push* domestic firms towards the remote regions, as a reaction of protection against the large foreign competition.

Figure 5.5, which is drawn in a similar way as Figure 5.1, illustrates the impact of these forces according to the degree of trade liberalization. As observed in section 5.3, the symmetric distribution of workers is a stable equilibrium for high values of T_0. When T_0 decreases, the curve comes to cross the x axis with a positive slope, meaning that only agglomerated configurations are stable equilibria. However, the curves are not symmetric anymore with respect to the value $\lambda = 0.5$. The push effect of firms towards the interior region is to be seen through the shift of the dotted curve to the right: when the domestic economy is still relatively closed, the increase of the degree of competition driven by foreign supply dominates the pull effect. Economic activities are dispersed but there is an asymmetry leading to the location of more than 50 per cent of the industries in region 1.

The pull effect of firms to the border region is illustrated by the shift of the dark curve to the right. When T_0 is low, the increase of demand emanating from the foreign country dominates the competition effect driven by foreign firms, and the country's economic activity is attracted to the border region. The agglomeration is the only stable equilibrium, but it has more chances to occur in the closest region to the foreign market. Figure 5.5 shows that the concentration of the industry will only occur in region 1 if the latter contains more than 80 per cent of the industrial activity of the country.

The main outcome arising in this section helps to modulate our previous results. The model shows that trade liberalization may foster two effects: a pull effect towards border regions and a push effect inside remote regions. The strength of these phenomena will be shaped by the various

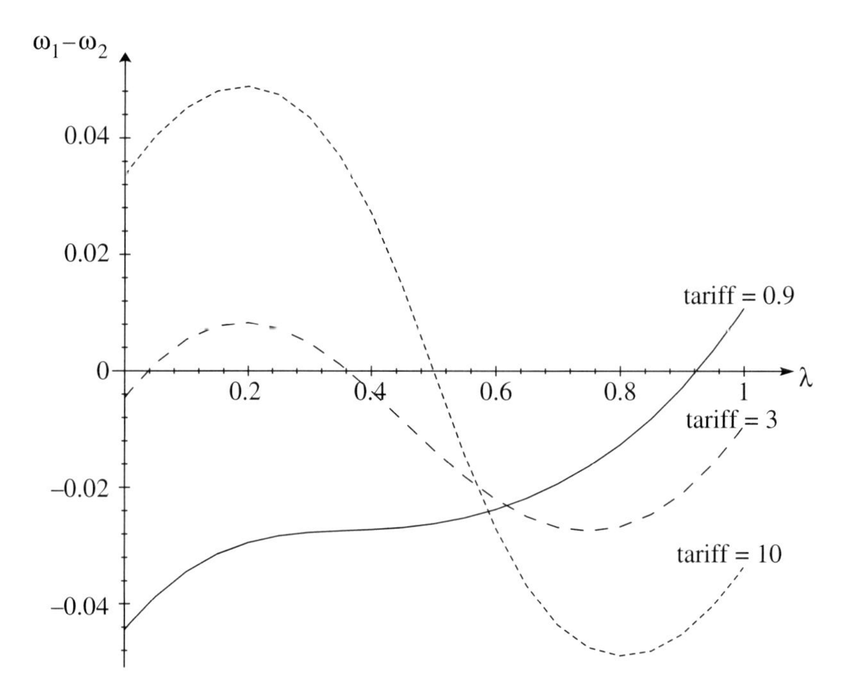

Figure 5.5 Real wage difference when the two regions have different external transaction costs

elements of the model: a large foreign demand for domestic product will increase the pull of the domestic industrial sector towards low-cost access regions. Conversely, a large amount of foreign firms exporting to the domestic market may favour the development of better protected internal regions.

5.6 CONCLUSION

According to Henderson (1996, p. 33), 'The impact of trade on national space is situation-specific, depending on the precise geography of the country. . . . In thinking about urban concentration, we may want a more generic or general framework'. In this chapter we proposed pursuing the analysis of the relation between trade liberalization and the location of production inside countries, by deepening two aspects of the issue. First, we generalized a simple extension of a Krugman (1991) model to a two countries three-region framework. In a setting in which both the agglomeration and the dispersion forces are endogenous, trade liberalization fosters spatial concentration. Second, we studied the same issue in a spatially heterogeneous country. We show that when the domestic country contains a border region and a remote region, trade liberalization generally favours the development of the border region, when competition pressure from international markets is not too high.

APPENDIX SHORT-TERM EQUILIBRIUM: SOLVING NUMERICALLY FOR w_1, AND w_2

The appendix intends to provide more details about the numerical solving procedure of the short-term equilibrium mentioned in section 5.2.

We incorporate equations 5.6 and 5.7 into 5.4 and then substitute 5.4, 5.10, 5.11 and 5.12 into 5.13 and 5.14. We obtain the following two equations. In spite of their complicated aspect, equations 5.21 and 5.22 allow to derive, for a given a distribution of the industrial workforce (λ, $1-\lambda$), the nominal wages w_1, and w_2. Indeed, with numerical values for the parameters σ, μ, for the exogenous foreign variables (w_0, L_0, L_{A0}) and for the domestic agricultural workers (L_{A1}, and L_{A2}), equations 5.21 and 5.22 contain only two unknowns:

$$w_1^{\sigma} = \mu\left[\frac{(w_0 L_0 + L_{A0})T_0^{1-\sigma}}{L_0 w_0^{1-\sigma} + \lambda(w_1 T_0)^{1-\sigma} + (1-\lambda)(w_2 T_0)^{1-\sigma}}\right.$$

$$+\frac{(w_1\lambda + L_{A1})}{L_0(w_0 T_0)^{1-\sigma} + \lambda w_1^{1-\sigma} + (1-\lambda)(w_2 T_{12})^{1-\sigma}} \tag{5.21}$$

$$\left.+\frac{(w_2(1-\lambda) + L_{A2})T_{12}^{1-\sigma}}{L_0(w_0 T_0)^{1-\sigma} + \lambda(w_1 T_{12})^{1-\sigma} + (1-\lambda)w_2^{1-\sigma}}\right]$$

$$w_2^{\sigma} = \mu\left[\frac{(w_0 L_0 + L_{A0})T_0^{1-\sigma}}{L_0 w_0^{1-\sigma} + \lambda(w_1 T_0)^{1-\sigma} + (1-\lambda)(w_2 T_0)^{1-\sigma}}\right.$$

$$+\frac{(w_1\lambda + L_{A1})T_{12}^{1-\sigma}}{L_0(w_0 T_0)^{1-\sigma} + \lambda w_1^{1-\sigma} + (1-\lambda)(w_2 T_{12})^{1-\sigma}} \tag{5.22}$$

$$\left.+\frac{(w_2(1-\lambda) + L_{A2}}{L_0(w_0 T_0)^{1-\sigma} + \lambda(w_1 T_{12})^{1-\sigma} + (1-\lambda)w_2^{1-\sigma}}\right]$$

NOTES

1. The question of the unicity of the solution is difficult to solve when there is more than one equation involved, and we leave it aside for the moment. We explain the procedure for solving numerically for w_1 and w_2 in the appendix to this chapter.
2. The values of the other parameters are: $\sigma = 6$, $\beta = 4/5$, $\mu = 0.4$, $\alpha = 0.4/5$, $T_{12} = 1.75$, $L_0/L = 10$.
3. Figure 5.1 is drawn for a value of T_{12} for which industry is dispersed in autarky ($T_0 \rightarrow \infty$). Similar results are obtained for lower values of T_{12}, but they are not showed here. The results are not as visible because the economy is already agglomerated.

REFERENCES

Ades, A. and E. Glaeser (1995), 'Trade circuses: explaining urban giants', *Quarterly Journal of Economics*, **110** (1), 195–227.

Alonso-Villar, O. (2001), 'Large metropolises in the third world: an explanation', *Urban Studies*, **38** (8), 1359–71.

Dixit, A. and J. Stiglitz (1977), 'Monopolistic competition and optimum product diversity', *American Economic Review*, **67** (3), 297–308.

Fujita, M., P. Krugman and A. Venables (eds) (1999), *The Spatial Economy*, Cambridge: MIT Press.

Hanson, G. (2001), 'US–Mexico integration and regional economies: evidence from border-city pairs', *Journal of Urban Economics*, **50** (2), 259–87.

Henderson, V. (1996), 'Ways to think about urban concentration: neoclassical urban systems versus the New Economic Geography', *International Regional Science Review*, **19** (1&2), 31–6.

Krugman, P.R. (1991), 'Increasing returns and economic geography', *Journal of Political Economy*, **99** (3), 483–99.

Krugman, P.R. (1993), 'The Hub effect: or threeness in international trade', in W.J. Ethier, E. Helpman and J.P. Neary (eds), *Theory, Policy and Dynamics in International Trade*, Cambridge: Cambridge University Press.

Krugman, P.R. (1996), 'Urban concentration: the role of increasing returns and transport costs', *International Regional Science Review*, **19** (1&2), 5–30.

Krugman, P.R. and R. Livas Elizondo (1996), 'Trade policy and third world metropolis', *Journal of Development Economics*, **49** (1), 137–50.

Monfort, P. and R. Nicolini (2000), 'Regional convergence and international integration', *Journal of Urban Economics*, **48** (2), 286–306.

Paluzie, E. (2001), 'Trade policies and regional inequalities', *Papers in Regional Science*, **80**, 67–85.

PART II

Home Market Effects, Market Size and Location Strategies

6. Market size and agglomeration

Keith Head, Thierry Mayer and John Ries

6.1 INTRODUCTION

Positive spillovers between firms and factor cost advantages may explain the observed geographic concentration of industry. Recent research on the influence of demand on production introduces a third reason for concentration. Specifically, the so-called 'home market effect' implies that locations with high demand will host a disproportionate share of industry. Thus, positive spillovers, low factor costs and the home market effect serve as forces that can result in the agglomeration of industry. Proximity has its costs, however. If locations are equally attractive, imperfect competition causes firms producing in the same location to earn lower profits than they would earn if they were to differentiate geographically. Thus, the competition effect serves as a force leading to the geographic dispersion of industry.

This chapter measures geographic concentration of Japanese investment in the USA and Europe and tests for the source of observed concentration. We begin by employing Ellison and Glaeser's (1997) measure of concentration to see if the concentration of Japanese FDI is greater or less than that predicted by our formulation of their random model of investment. Next, we use conditional logit estimation to explore whether, after controlling for market size, the presence of rivals in a foreign location is associated with a higher or lower likelihood of investment in that location. A negative coefficient supports home market effects models whereas a positive coefficient is consistent with positive spillovers between firms. Finally, we relate a region's share of investment to its share of demand to test explicitly for home market effects.

Whether or not observed concentration reflects positive spillovers between firms operating in proximity (agglomeration economies) is an important question because theoretical models of agglomeration economies predict self-reinforcing concentration. These forces enable historical events to determine the geography of an industry, leading to a pattern of 'have' and 'have not' areas that find it difficult to use policy to alter their status. A first step towards determining the strength and pervasiveness of agglomeration economies is to measure the extent that geographic concentration of industries exceeds a sensible benchmark. Measuring geographic concentration is useful since its absence would be sufficient evidence to reject the existence of strong agglomeration economies.

Economists have used two main methods to estimate the significance of industry concentration. The first focuses on outcomes and measures geographic concentration at a point in time. A prominent example is Krugman's (1991) calculation of Gini indexes for three-digit US manufacturing industries. In that study the benchmark for expected activity in a state is its share of total manufacturing employment. Krugman found that most industries were fairly concentrated. Ellison and Glaeser (1997) pointed out that 'lumpiness' – a small number of establishments accounting for a large share of an industry's total employment – and randomness can combine to result in seemingly concentrated outcomes. They proposed a method to calculate concentration in excess of what would occur in a random choice model that accounts for lumpiness. A second approach, initiated by Carlton (1983), examines the process of agglomeration itself. Using a sample of new entrants, this approach estimates a conditional logit regression in which the existing amount of industry activity in a state is an explanatory variable along with a set of controls describing the attractiveness of the state.

Positive findings of concentration – the norm in most empirical work – admit multiple interpretations. Ellison and Glaeser emphasize that their findings of excess concentration are consistent with a model in which *spillovers* cause industries to cluster as well as a model in which certain locations possess *natural advantages* that attract firms in a given industry. To use their examples, we may think of Silicon Valley's information technology cluster as a likely example of the former and Napa Valley's concentration of wineries as a consequence of the latter. In a recent contribution (Ellison and Glaeser, 1999), those same authors show that about 20 per cent of observed geographic concentration can be explained by a small set of natural advantages variables. They consequently 'conjecture that at least half of observed geographic concentration is due to natural advantages' (ibid., p. 316) and attribute the remaining concentration to be explained to spillovers.

Our focus is discriminating between spillovers and a third source of excess concentration: market size. A recent trade literature shows that large demand in a country can translate into a disproportionate share of production. Krugman (1980) first established the result for differentiated goods industries characterized by free entry and increasing returns to scale where consumers have Dixit-Stiglitz preferences. Feenstra, Markusen and Rose (2001) extend this result to a Cournot, segmented markets (CSM) framework with homogeneous goods, free entry, and consumers with Cobb-Douglas utility. Head, Mayer and Ries (2002) employ a location choice framework to show that three models of imperfect competition – the Krugman model, a homogeneous good, Cournot model with linear demand, and the monopolistic competition model of Ottaviano, Tabuchi and Thisse (2002) – yield common predictions about the relationship between a country's share of consumers and its share of firms as well as a country's share of consumers and its net exports.

Our empirical work examines the location decisions of over 1400 manufacturing investments that Japanese firms made in the USA and the European Union since 1970. Several considerations motivated the selection of this sample. First, to compare concentration outcomes with the process that generated them, one requires information on the establishment dates for each of the plants existing at the time concentration is measured. While this seems impractical in the case of indigenous manufacturers, Japanese firms had virtually no presence in the USA or EU prior to 1970. Hence, we can observe location patterns during a compact period of time. A second feature of this sample is that relatively small numbers of investments in each industry cause the lumpiness problem that Ellison and Glaeser designed their index to solve. In contrast, there were so many establishments in US manufacturing that the raw and corrected concentration indexes ended up being about the same in all but a handful of industries. Finally, governments in the USA and EU have devoted substantial resources towards attracting Japanese investment. The wisdom of such outlays depends in part on the strength and pervasiveness of agglomeration effects.

Section 6.2 employs a location choice framework to derive empirical tests that help discriminate between the spillover and home market effect explanations of clustering. We show that the spillover model generates concentration in excess of what would be expected in the Ellison and Glaeser random choice model. However, home market effect models may generate excess concentration or excess dispersion relative to the random choice model. In the empirical section that follows, we use Ellison and Glaeser's index to measure concentration of Japanese FDI by industry and region (the USA and Europe). We show that about a third of the manufacturing industries in our sample exhibit excess concentration. Then we proceed to test for the source of this excess concentration. First, our conditional logit estimates reveal that after controlling for demand, firms are attracted to locations where there exists a high share of Japanese firms, a result consistent with agglomeration and inconsistent with the imperfect competition models. Next we relate the share of firms in a location to that location's share of demand. We find that a disproportionate response (coefficient greater than one) occasionally occurs for investment in the USA but not in Europe. Thus, we get only mixed support for the home market effect. We summarize the results in the final section.

6.2 THEORY

Head, Mayer and Ries (2002) develop three models of imperfect competition in the context of the plant-location decision of N firms. The framework is a two-country model where single-product firms choose to locate a single plant in one country which will serve consumers in both markets. That paper shows that each model generates a similar set of equations. The *difference in profits equation* expresses the difference in the profitability of locating in two alternative production locations in terms of the distribution of demand and the existing distribution of firms. The *share equation* relates a country's equilibrium share of firms as a function of its share of consumers. Here, we will summarize the results for these imperfect competition models and derive a corresponding set of equations for a second model – a spillover model – that we will show generates somewhat different predictions for the coefficients of these equations. In addition, we will compare the level of concentration predicted by the imperfect competition and spillover models to what would obtain under our formulation of the random choice model introduced by Ellison and Glaeser (1997). We begin by describing the models and proceed to derive contrasting predictions that we can test with FDI data.

The three models of imperfect competition analysed in Head, Mayer and Ries (2002) are: the Krugman model as formulated in Helpman and Krugman (1985); the monopolistic competition model of Ottaviano, Tabuchi and Thisse (2002); and the Cournot, segmented markets model analysed in Brander and Krugman (1983). Each of the models incorporate alternative assumptions on the nature of demand, product market competition, and trade costs. In the Helpman-Krugman model, firms produce a single differentiated product and there is a constant elasticity of substitution between goods. Since the authors assume a large number of firms, when choosing prices firms ignore the effect their pricing decision has on the overall price level. Trade costs take the iceberg form whereas they are per unit in the other two models. Firms also produce unique varieties in the Ottaviano-Tabuchi-Thisse model. Quadratic utility yields individual linear demand functions. As in the Helpman-Krugman model, firms choose prices to maximize their profits while neglecting the effect of individual price changes on the price index. The Brander-Krugman model depicts trade in homogeneous goods. Head, Mayer and Ries (2002) derive results for this model based on linear demand. All three models predict that the large country's share of output exceeds its share of firms, a result Helpman and Krugman (1985) call a home market effect.[1] Accordingly, we refer to the three models as home market effects (HME) models.

The spillover model we consider simply posits the profitability of investing in a country is a linear function of the number of firms already established there:

$$\pi_i = a + bn_i \tag{6.1}$$

where n_i is the number of firms locating in country i. The profit function is a reduced form expression. One interpretation is that the presence of firms in a country reduces the production costs of subsequent investors, thereby allowing them to produce greater output and gain higher profits.

The Difference in Profits Equation

Head, Mayer and Ries (2002) posit the *difference in profits equation* showing the difference in profits associated with investing in country 1 versus 2 in terms of 1's share of consumers (x) and its share of firms (s) as

$$\Delta\pi(s, x) \equiv \pi_1(s, x) - \pi_2(s, x) = cs + dx + e \tag{6.2}$$

Coefficient d is the demand effect which is positive: A country's attractiveness is increasing in its share of consumers. Coefficient c is the competition effect which is negative. When marginal costs are equal in the two countries, this equation is linear for the Ottaviano-Tabuchi-Thisse and Brander-Krugman models but nonlinear for the Helpman-Krugman model.

The difference in profit equation for the spillover model is

$$\Delta\pi(s) = bN(2s - 1) \tag{6.3}$$

In contrast to the HME models, this equation is an increasing function of s and independent of x. Thus, these contrasting predictions can be a basis for discriminating between the models.

Suppose that firms choose location sequentially and myopically that is they take the existing value allocation of firms in their industry, s, as given and do not attempt to influence the subsequent locations of other firms. Suppose further that the firms perceive the difference in profits between two locations to be equal to the true (modelled) difference plus a random error term, denoted u. In that case, the probability a firm will choose country 1 is given by

$$\Pr(\pi_1 - \pi_2 = cs + dx + e > -u) \tag{6.4}$$

We assume u is given by the logistic distribution and estimate the probability of choosing country 1 as a function of s and x.

The HME models predict $c<0$ and $d>0$ whereas the spillover model predicts $c>0$ and $d=0$.

The Share Equation

We solve for the equilibrium distribution of firms, s, by setting the difference in profits equation equal to zero. This yields the share equation which is linear for all three HME models and can be expressed as

$$s = g + hx \tag{6.5}$$

where $h = d/(-c) > 1$ and $g = e/(-c) < 0$ when marginal costs are equal in the two countries. The equation generates a greater than one-to-one relationship between a country's share of firms and its share of output. Since a country's share of firms cannot exceed one or be less than zero, the following piecewise function describes s:

$$s = \begin{cases} 0 & \text{if } x < -g/h \\ 1 & \text{if } x > (1-g)/h \\ g + hx & \text{otherwise} \end{cases} \tag{6.6}$$

In the case of the spillover model, setting the difference in profits equation equal to zero and solving for s yields the obvious result that profits are equal when there is an equal number of firms in each country. However, this distribution is not an equilibrium as firms could increase profits by moving to the other country. Thus, the two equilibria are all firms located in country 1 or all firms located in country 2.

The share equation provides a second means for discriminating empirically between the HME models and the spillover model. We can estimate

$$s = g + hx + \epsilon \tag{6.7}$$

where ϵ is an error term. In the HME models, $g<0$ and $h>1$. In contrast, s is independent of x in the spillover model. Instead firms tend to completely concentrate in one country or the other. In the empirical implementation, there are nine locations. With nine locations, the spillover model predicts that the intercept will reflect the average location share, therefore implying $g = 1/9$.

Concentration Relative to the Dartboard

In the remainder of this section, we compare concentration predicted by the home market effect and spillover models to that of the dartboard model introduced by Ellison and Glaeser (1997). They envision an investment as a dart and the host regions as areas on a dartboard. In our formulation, regions with larger demand are represented by larger areas and, therefore, are expected to receive larger shares of darts.[2] The dartboard model is a sensible 'baseline' that can be compared to observed investment concentration.

Ellison and Glaeser consider a measure of concentration, G, calculated as the sum of squared differences between each host region's share of industry-level and aggregate economic activity. If x_i is the share of area i in 'all' activity (demand in our formulation) and S_i is location i's share of activity in a particular industry, the G equals $G=\sum(S_i-x_i)^2$, for possible location choices $i=1 \ldots M$. With a large number of darts, the dartboard model predicts $G=0$. In this case, investment in a region is distributed in proportion to the size of demand. Values above zero reflect geographic concentration.

This index can create a false impression of concentration when investment is 'lumpy,' that is when a small set of investors accounts for most of the amount invested. A simple example illustrates this case. Consider two investments into two equal-sized countries. The dartboard model predicts that half the time both investments will land in the same country and half the time in opposite countries. Thus, $G=0$ half the time and is positive ($G=.5$) half the time. Lumpiness (only two investments) and random location imply the expected value of G will be .25.[3] It would be mistaken to interpret a positive value of G in such cases as concentration due to agglomeration economies, the home market effect, or other economic mechanisms. Thus, we will consider an industry to have excess concentrated when G exceeds its *expected* level under the dartboard. Likewise, excess dispersion occurs when G is less than the dartboard model prediction.

We begin by evaluating the HME models. In the two-country case considered in Head, Mayer and Ries (2002), the G index can be re-expressed as

$$G=2(S-x)^2 \tag{6.8}$$

where in our formulation S is country 1's share of output and x is its share of consumers. We have already established the distribution of firms, s, as a function of the distribution of demand, x. In the Helpman-Krugman model, each firm produces the same output thus $S=s$ for all x. In the Brander-Krugman and Ottaviano-Tabuchi-Thisse models, output per firm varies with x. The appendix shows that in the absence of costs differences, these models predict that output per firm is greater for firms in the large market. This means that $S>s$ when $x>1/2$ and $S<s$ when $x<1/2$. Thus, the large country produces a disproportionate share of output relative to its share of consumers. Figure 6.1 displays the plots of S and s against x for the

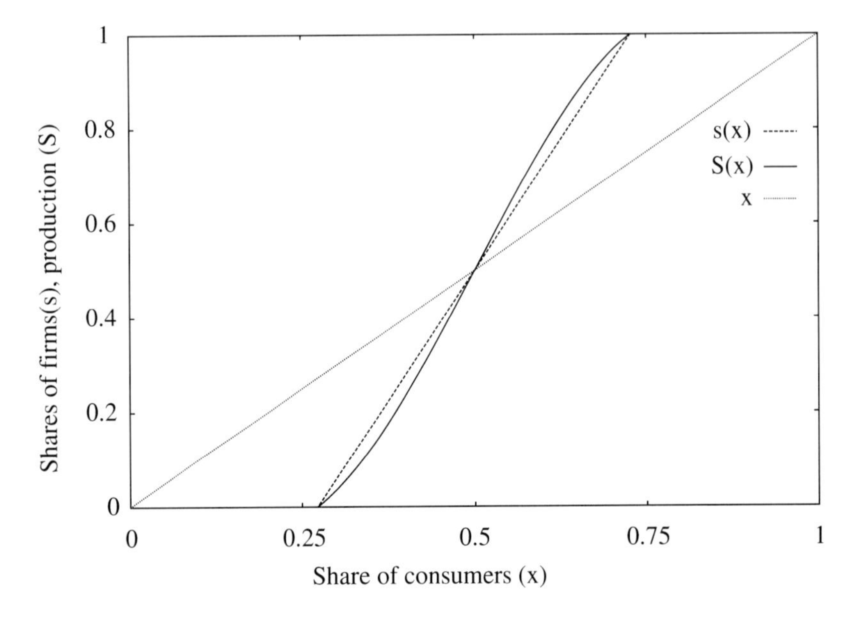

Figure 6.1 Shares of demand, firms and employment

case of equal marginal costs of production. The 45-degree line in Figure 6.1 indicates the values for which the location of the industry mimics the international location of demand. The dotted line represents equilibrium s for the three HME models. It also represents S in the case of the Helpman-Krugman model. The solid line characterizes equilibrium S for the Ottaviano- Tabuchi-Thisse and the Brander-Krugman models. The share of firms grows linearly with the share of consumers with a slope greater than one. The share of production exhibits a 'S' shape around this line, with production being even more clustered than firms. Intuitively, when $x > 1/2$ there are more firms in country 2 and each of these firms produces more than the firms in country 1 because the transport gives firms in country 2 greater access to the larger pool of consumers than firms located in country 1.

Figure 6.1 also provides an indication of the behaviour of G in equilibrium. Recall that G equals $2(S-x)^2$ in the two-country case and thus is an increasing function of the difference between S and x. It equals zero at $x=0$, $x=1/2$ and $x=1$, and reaches two peaks between these points.

We are interested in contrasting the values of G in our model for different ranges of the distribution of demand with those expected in the dartboard model developed in Ellison and Glaeser (1997). The important insight of Ellison and Glaeser is that G in the dartboard model will be greater than zero when a small number of establishments accounts for a large share of total employment in a region. As discussed earlier, the example of two darts thrown at a target with two equal-sized areas will only generate an area's share of investment matching its share of the overall target half the time. Thus, expected G in this case will exceed zero. Ellison and Glaeser determine the expected concentration exhibited by a dartboard model to be

$$\mathrm{E}[G] = DH \tag{6.9}$$

where $H \equiv \sum z_k^2$ is the Herfindahl for the plant-level concentration of activity in the industry (z_k is plant k's share of total output in the industry) and $D \equiv 1 - \sum x_i^2$ is a measure of the dispersion of economic activity across locations. To gain intuition on the terms D and H, consider the case of M identical countries and N identical firms. This implies $H = 1/N$ and $D = 1 - 1/M$. Expected concentration, $\mathrm{E}[G]$, only approaches zero as N becomes large. In the case of the empirical work that follows, this condition will not normally be met so we expect $G > 0$ even if location choice is random as depicted by the dartboard model.

Figure 6.2 characterizes the relationship between G and DH. We generate the figure using the Brander-Krugman model and the appendix establishes that the qualitative results are the same in the other two models.[4] DH has a parabolic shape with a peak at $x = 1/2$ in the three HME models. G

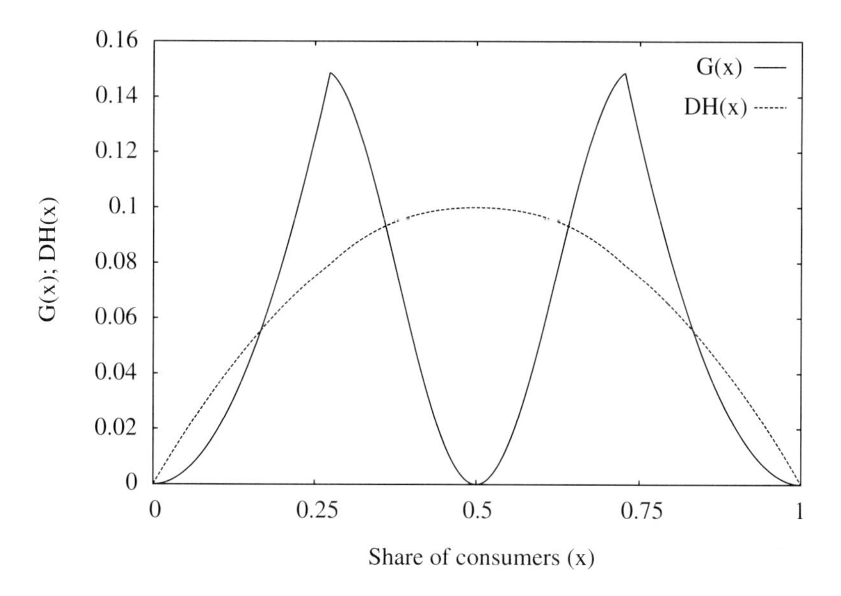

Figure 6.2 Predicted values of the raw concentration index (G)

has two peaks on either side of $x=1/2$. The figure shows that G can be either higher or lower than $E[G]=DH$. $G<DH$ when countries are equal sized ($x=.5$) or nearly equal sized. This result is due to competition effects that encourage firms to differentiate geographically. When market size considerations are absent, firms will never locate in the same country and we would observe complete dispersion of investment. In the dartboard model, however, random chance causes firms to cluster with some positive probability.

As x deviates from .5, however, market size considerations induce firms to cluster and the large country's share of output will exceed its share of demand. This leads to equilibrium concentration in excess of what is expected under the dartboard model ($G>DH$). The decline in G in the outer portions of the graph is related to the corner solutions that occur in our model where all firms locate in the large country ($s=1$ or $s=0$). This decline in G in the outer portions of the graph creates additional regions where $G<DH$. In the range of x where $s=1$ or $s=0$, all firms in the industry are located in the same country. Nevertheless, G changes with the x since it is a function of that variable. G equals zero when the complete concentration of industry mimics the complete concentration of demand.

With regard to the spillover model, the analysis is much simpler. The equilibria consist of all firms located in country 1 ($s=1$) or country 2 ($s=0$). In the two-country case, the G index equals $2(S-x)^2$. Consequently, half the time $G=2(1-x)^2$ and half the time $G=2x^2$. Thus, on average $G=x^2+(1-x)^2$. Recall that expected concentration, $E[G]$, equals DH where H is the plant-level Herfindahl index and $D=1-[x^2+(1-x)^2]$. Thus,

$$G-E[G]=G-DH=[x^2+(1-x)^2](1+H)-H \qquad (6.10)$$

The positive first term is at its minimum value for $x\equiv 1/2$. Setting $x=1/2$ yields

$$G-DH=1/2(1-H) \qquad (6.11)$$

This expression is strictly positive as long as the number of firms exceeds one implying $H<1$. Thus, the spillover model predicts concentration in excess of the baseline dartboard prediction.

Table 6.1 summarizes the competing predictions of the models in regard to the Ellison and Glaeser concentration measure, conditional logit estimation of the probability of choosing a location and OLS estimates of the share equation.

Table 6.1 Discriminating hypotheses

Methodology	Estimate	Predictions	
		Pure spillovers	HME
Ellison and Glaeser (1997)	G, DH	$G > DH$	any
Conditional logit	$P_i = \frac{e^{cs_i + dx_i}}{\sum_j e^{cs_j + dx_j}}$	$c > 0, d = 0$	$c < 0, d > -c$
Share regression	$s_i = g + hx_i$	$g = 1/9, h = 0$	$g < 0, h > 1$

6.3 EMPIRICS

We start by looking at the G indexes to see if some industries exhibit significantly negative $G - DH$. We then estimate a conditional logit on the location choices of Japanese firms in the USA and in Europe to identify demand effects, competition effects and spillovers. Finally, we estimate the relationship between a country's share of demand and its share of FDI industry by industry as a test for home market effects. All of the empirical tests are conducted at the industry level. In the body of this section we provide tables summarizing the results for the set of industries. The appendix lists results for individual industries.

We use two samples of Japanese FDI in the two major host areas of overseas investment: the USA and the European Union. The observations come from a survey of the Japan External Trade Organization (JETRO, 1996) for investments in the EU and from a survey by the JEI (Japan Economic Institute, 1990) for FDI in the USA. We restrict the period covered to be 1970–92 for the US case and 1970–95 for the European one, periods covering the vast majority of investments. To be able to compare across samples, we first classify the investments in the same industry classification (namely three-digit US SIC). We also use the nine US regions as the choice set of Japanese investors in the USA instead of the US states, because the number of regions precisely corresponds to the number of European countries we are considering. We also drop acquisitions for Japanese FDI in the United States (JETRO does not give any indication on the greenfield/acquisition nature of FDI in Europe but states that an important share of FDI is greenfield[5]). Our sample for Japanese FDI in the USA covers 888 investments, while we have 572 investments in nine European countries (France, Germany, the UK, Spain, Italy, Ireland, Belgium, the Netherlands and Portugal).

Table 6.2 Summary statistics on G

	Mean H	Mean G	$G<DH$		$G>DH$	
			$--$	$-$	$+$	$++$
Japanese FDI in the USA	0.33	0.38	0%	36%	30%	34%
	0.33	0.37	0%	31%	41%	28%
Japanese FDI in the EU	0.35	0.39	0%	29%	38%	33%
	0.35	0.36	0%	38%	37%	25%
All US mnfg. est.	N/A	N/A	0%	3%	N/A	N/A
	0.03	0.07	0%	3%	17%	80%

Note: The signs $-$ and $+$ respectively design that $G-DH$ is negative or positive with an absolute value inferior to two standard deviations. Conversely, $--$ and $++$ repectively design that $G-DH$ is negative or positive with an absolute value superior to two standard deviations.

Table 6.2 gives the summary statistics of G and its expectation under the dartboard model E[G] for our two samples: Japanese investments in the nine US regions and in the nine European countries. The formulas for G and its dartboard expectation shown in the theory section are:

$$G=\sum(S_i-x_i)^2, \quad \mathrm{E}[G]=DH \tag{6.12}$$

where $H\equiv\sum z_k^2$ is the Herfindahl index of industry plant sizes that is z_k is plant or affiliate k's share of total employment in the industry. $D\equiv 1-\sum x_i^2$ measures the dispersion of economic activity across locations. We consider two ways of defining x_i, the aggregate economic activity in an area. Our primary measure will be location i's share of Japanese total affiliate employment in the considered zone (the USA or the EU). This follow's Ellison and Glaeser's (1997) use of total manufacturing employment. Since the theoretical model interprets x_i as representing country i's share of demand, we also calculate x_i using GDPs of European countries and the population of American regions. We use the figures corresponding to the end of the sample, that is 1995 GDP for European nations and 1992 population of American regions.

For investment into the USA and Europe, the first line reports results for our demand measure of x_i (GDP or population). The second line reports the results for x defined as the total employment of manufacturing affiliates. This latter interpretation of x was emphasized by Ellison and Glaeser (1997). To permit comparison with their results, we report the results for the comprehensive sample of plants in the USA used by Ellison and Glaeser. Their study used states, rather than our nine regions, as the geographic unit.

To obtain an idea of how large the deviation of the concentration index G from the dartboard DH is, we use the variance of G defined by Ellison and Glaeser (1997) as:

$$\mathrm{Var}[G] = 2\left\{ H^2\left[\sum x_i^2 - 2\sum x_i^3 + \left(\sum x_i^2\right)^2\right] - \sum_j z_j^4\left[\sum x_i^2 - 4\sum x_i^3 + 3\left(\sum x_i^2\right)^2\right] \right\} \quad (6.13)$$

We consider FDI in an industry to be geographically clustered when the absolute value of $G - DH$ is larger than two standard deviations of G.

For each host region, the mean values of the Herfindhal index as well as the index of raw concentration G is given as well as the percentage of industries exhibiting concentration lower or greater than the dartboard expectation. It should first be emphasized that the two samples exhibit striking similarities in terms of average levels of both industry and geographical concentration. As could have been expected, the Herfindhal indexes and raw geographic concentration indexes of Japanese affiliates are much higher than the corresponding figures for the sample of American firms. This latter result is a consequence of the much larger number of plants used by Ellison and Glaeser.

Our first noteworthy result is that no industry in either host area is characterized by a G less than DH by more than two standard deviations. As emphasized in the beginning of this section, industries with an observed clustering measure substantially *under* the dartboard would have been discriminating in favour of the HME models. However, the table reveals that FDI in no industries in either the USA or Europe exhibit significant excess dispersion. Instead, roughly 70 per cent of the industries are not substantially more or less concentrated than the dartboard and the remaining 30 per cent exhibit excess concentration.

The next two empirical exercises generate industry-specific estimates of coefficients for the model specifying the probability of a country/region receiving investment (conditional logit) and relating the share of FDI to the share of demand in a country/region. An important point to keep in mind is that each industry regression for the share equation contains nine observations (the number of regions/countries). Thus, we have limited information to assess the statistical significance of reported relationships.

Table 6.3 summarizes the results of conditional logit estimations by industry of the location choices of Japanese firms in Europe and in the USA. For each area, Table 6.3 reports the number of industries for which the estimation of the conditional logit was possible, the average value of G, and the distribution of estimated coefficients on variable s, the share of firms in the region. There are two rows for each area. The first row gives results for the unrestricted sample, the second row gives results only for the industries for which $G-DH$ was greater in absolute value to two standard deviations of G.

Table 6.3 Summary statistics on conditional logit

			Negative c coef.		Positive c coef.		
	# of industries	Mean G	10%	not sig.	not sig.	10%	5%
USA	57	0.32	0%	18%	44%	5%	33%
	21	0.45	0%	0%	33%	5%	62%
EU	38	0.33	3%	24%	34%	10%	29%
	15	0.43	0%	7%	20%	20%	53%

An important feature of the industry by industry logit estimation of location choice is that only one industry exhibits a significantly negative coefficient on s (the Yarn and Thread Industry in the EU (SIC 228). Also about 40 per cent of the industries exhibit a positive and significant (at the 10 per cent level) influence of rivals' location on a firm's location choice independently of the location zone. This figure is dramatically increased when one considers the sub-sample of industries that are substantially concentrated according to the $G-DH$ index. Around 70 per cent of industries which are much more concentrated than the dartboard also exhibit a significant positive coefficient on s in the conditional logit estimation. Together, those features leave little support for the HME models of location choice presented in the theory section which predict a negative coefficient on s and indicates that the spillovers explanation to clustering may be relevant in a great number of industries. Of course, the negative influence of product market interactions may exist but it could be outweighed by positive influences. One positive factor is positive spillovers between firms. Moreover, s may be reflecting positive attributes of regions/countries attracting investments that are not accounted for in our model.

Our last empirical exercise tests for the home market effect by estimating equation 6.5 for each of our industries. The HME models yield a more than proportional relation between the equilibrium share of firms and the share of demand in the location. The HME models also predict a negative intercept as a result of the home market effect. We thus calculate the share of Japanese investments in each American region (European nation) at the end of the sample period and regress it against the share of demand, that is the share of population (share of GDP) for the same year. The estimation method is a tobit regression intended to account for the fact that many industry/location combinations did not get any Japanese investment. Table 6.4 gives summary results of these market size effect estimations. It states in particular how the coefficient on the demand ratio significantly differs from one, an indication of the home market effect.

For each area, the first row reports results for the whole sample of industries and the second row reports the intercept when the coefficient on demand is significantly greater than one. Although the number of industries exhibiting a coefficient significantly greater than unity on demand is not very large (nine for Japanese FDI in the USA, two for Japanese FDI in the EU), those sectors show a consistent home market effect as they are generally ones for which the intercept is significantly negative.[6] It is noteworthy that the proportion of industries exhibiting a coefficient on the share of demand superior to unity is greater in the case of investment in the USA relative to investment in the EU (the mean value of the coefficient is 6.04 for FDI in the USA and 1.27 for EU as a hosting zone). This is consistent with HME model predictions in which the coefficient h in equation 6.5 is strictly decreasing in the trade cost τ. That is, making the reasonable assumption that trade costs are generally significantly higher inside the EU than inside the USA, our model predicts that the steepness of the s curve in Figure 6.1 should be closer to the 45-degree line in the EU case, resulting in a lower estimate of the coefficient on x for this sample.

This section has assessed whether the pattern of Japanese FDI in the USA and Europe is consistent with the predictions of the HME models or pure spillovers model. We have employed three discriminating tests: the difference between concentration measure G against the dartboard prediction DH, conditional logit regressions relating the probability of investment to a location's existing share of investment and its share of demand, and the share regression relating a location's share of industry investment to its share of demand. Now we identify the industries that seem to be most consistent with one model or the other. Recall that Table 6.1 displays the parameter predictions of the models in terms of the three empirical methods. We consider that an industry 'passes' the discriminating test of a particular model if the estimated coefficient or statistic is consistent with the prediction shown in Table 6.1.

In general, we consider a parameter estimate to be consistent with a model if it passes a significance test. In the case of the Ellison-Glaeser measure of economic concentration, the criterion is whether G is two standard deviations away from DH. With regard to conditional logit regressions, directly estimated parameters are considered consistent with a model when the t-test is significant at the 10 per cent level with two exceptions. The prediction of

Table 6.4 *Summary statistics on home market effects*

	# of industries	Coefficient on demand (h)						Intercept (g)				
		− − −	− −	−	+	+ +	+ + +	− − −	− −	−	+	+ + +
USA	70	0%	0%	19%	69%	3%	10%	7%	6%	79%	9%	0%
	9							56%	33%	11%	0%	0%
EU	49	6%	6%	39%	45%	4%	0%	0%	2%	73%	18%	6%
	2							0%	50%	50%	0%	0%

Note: Three positive or negative signs denote significance at the 5 per cent level, two signs denote significance at the 10 per cent level and a unique sign denotes the sign of the insignificant t-stat. The significance is calculated with respect to 1 for the demand variable and with respect to 0 for the intercept. Regressions run using tobit.

the HME models that $d > -c$ is not subject to a significance test. In the case of the share regressions, parameter estimates are evaluated based on a 10 per cent significance level.

Table 6.5 places industries listed by three-digit SIC numbers into cells indicating the industry estimates are in accordance with model predictions. The appendix provides the industry name for each industry number. The figures in boldface identify industries which correspond to the whole set of predictions of the model they are classified in.

Table 6.5 Results on discriminating hypotheses

	Explaining model	
Hosting area	Pure spillovers	Home market effects
USA	372, **205**, **209**, **253**, **282**, **323**, **344**, **345**, **346**, **369**, **371**	289, 331, 347, 363, 375, 382, 386, 394
EU	356, **285**, **358**, **366**, **371**, **394**	352

Note: Industries in normal font pass two out of three tests in Table 6.1; industries in bold face pass all three tests.

For instance, industry 371 is characterized by a concentration index greater than the dartboard by more than two standard deviations. It also has a positive and significant coefficient c and a coefficient d not significantly different from zero in the conditional logit. For this industry, we also find that coefficients g and h are respectively not significantly different from 1/9 and 0. Thus this industry passes all three tests of the spillover model. However, some industries only pass some of the discriminating tests and we show industries in normal font that pass tests of two (out of the three) methods. For instance, there are nine industries characterized by home market effects in the share equation but c is not significantly negative in the conditional logit. These industries trivially pass the Ellison-Glaeser test since the HME models do not restrict how G deviates from DH. We put these industries in normal font in the HME column as they pass only two of the tests. Correspondingly, normal font industries in the pure spillovers column are those that pass two tests of this model.

As can be seen in the table, only a minority of industries that we examine appear to be consistent with a particular model. Of those that are, most are consistent with the spillover model. Two points should be kept in mind when assessing these results. First, we have limited information to conduct statistical tests: There are a relatively small number of investments in each industry and nine locations. Second, it is possible that the two competing models may have some relevance for a particular industry, thereby making it impossible to satisfy all requirements of any single 'pure' model (there may be both home market effects and spillovers present).

While the number of industries characterized by spillovers is not very large, the specific industries turn out to represent a very important share of Japanese overall investment, particularly in the USA. The three-digit SIC industry 371 corresponds to motor vehicles assembly and parts and represents 27 per cent of all Japanese employment in the US sample. Together, the spillovers industries represent about 41 per cent of total Japanese affiliates employment in the USA. The equivalent figure is around 17 per cent for Japanese FDI in the EU with motor vehicles representing 15 per cent alone. However, we add a caution about the interpretation of these results as suggesting spillovers characterizes a large share of Japanese investment. If spillovers exist in an industry, it should be evident in both host areas. However, only motor vehicles (371) obtains results that are consistent with spillovers for both US and EU regressions.

6.4 CONCLUSION

Industry agglomeration may occur for a number of reasons. Firms in the same industry may be attracted to locations with favourable factor conditions. They may locate near similar firms to access positive spillovers. The home market effect is a third reason to observe concentration of industry.

The starting point to investigating the sources of industry concentration is identification of agglomeration itself. This can be accomplished by comparing observed concentration against a sensible benchmark. The benchmark we employ is a random choice model of investment where investment mirrors the distribution of demand subject to random variation. This baseline model is a particular formulation of the one used in Ellison and Glaeser (1997). We find significant excess concentration for over one-quarter of our industries. No industries exhibit significant excess dispersion.

Our HME models all predict a linear and more than proportional relationship between the share of firms and the share of local demand in an industry, which can result in excess concentration. The models give rise to two empirical tests. First, the probability of a location receiving investment is a positive function of its share of demand and a negative function of the share of firms already there. Second, the line relating an location's share of investment and its share of demand should have a negative intercept and a slope exceeding one. We contrast these predictions with those expected under pure spillover model.

We employ regression analysis at the industry level to test the models. The probability and share relations are estimated with conditional logit and tobit estimation, respectively. The parameter estimates from these regressions are the basis to evaluate the consistency of the data with each model. The power of these tests are limited by the small number of observations in the regressions. We find that many industries are consistent with the spillover model although the same industries do not emerge in the separate analysis of the two host areas. There is also partial support for the HME models. Overall, we find that no single model among the ones we consider explains the pattern of Japanese FDI across industries. Thus, FDI concentration appears to arise from a number of sources.

APPENDIX 6.1 GEOGRAPHIC CONCENTRATION BY INDUSTRY

Table 6.6 gives summary results by SIC three-digit industry of the three empirical methods used in this paper. For each of the two host regions, the USA and European Union, are given the G_i index, the coefficient c on the share of previous investments (s) in the conditional logit and the coefficient on x (h_i) in the share equation. Those three coefficients are indexed by $i = eu, us$ denoting the hosting zone. The G figures are given a sign superscript indicating whether G is less or greater than the dartboard expectation DH. A star additionally indicates the industries for which the deviation from the dartboard is superior to 2 standard deviations.

For coefficients c_i and h_i, * and † indicate respectively significance at the 5 and 10 per cent levels. Statistical significance is calculated with respect to 0 for c_i and with respect to 1 for h_i.

APPENDIX 6.2 DATA SOURCES AND CONSTRUCTION

The data used in this chapter came from four sources:

Japan Economic Institute Greenfield manufacturing investments in the USA from 1970 to 1990 (operation dates, so some investments dated as late as 1992).

Japan External Trade Organization Manufacturing investments in Europe.

Population Estimates Program Population Division, US Bureau of the Census provides annual estimates of population for each state.

Eurostat Regio provide GDP for each European nation.

Table 6.6 Concentration of Japanese FDI in the USA and the EU

SIC	Industry	G_{us}	c_{us}	h_{us}	G_{eu}	c_{eu}	h_{eu}
201	Meat products	$.4^{-}$	4.6	2.97	.	.	.
202	Dairy	.	.	.	$.26^{-}$	−77.16	2.17
203	Fruits, vegetables, soups, etc.	$.3^{+*}$	2.6*	8.33	.	.	.
204	Grain mills	$.66^{+*}$	17.08	.89	$.79^{-}$	.	.
205	Bread, cake etc.	$.67^{+*}$	4.02*	22.71	$.79^{+}$	.	.
206	Sugar & confectionery	$.84^{-}$	.	.	$.45^{+}$	2.9*	1.96
207	Food preparations etc.	$.3^{-}$	.	25.16	1.12^{+}	.	.
208	Beverages	$.81^{+*}$	8.88*	4.02	$.22^{+*}$	$1.94^{\dagger}$	1.95
209	Miscl. food preparations	$.64^{+*}$	3.7*	3.18	$.31^{-}$	−67.62	.89
211	Cigarettes	.	.	.	$.9^{+}$	.	.
221	Cotton broad woven fabrics	$.78^{+*}$	.	.	.	.	.
222	Silk & manmade fibre broad woven fabrics	$.78^{-}$	.	.	.	.	.
223	Wool broad woven fabrics & wool blankets	.	.	.	$.9^{+}$	.	.
225	Knit fabrics & hosiery	$.84^{-}$	.	.	.	.	.
227	Floor coverings	$.32^{-}$	1.64	16.36	.	.	.
228	Yarns & thread	$.55^{+*}$	113.06	$47.16^{\dagger}$	$.16^{+}$	$-6.53^{\dagger}$	.22*
229	Textile goods, nspf	$.52^{-}$	−1.74	7.15	$.91^{+}$	.	.
231	Men's suits & coats	.	.	.	$.91^{+*}$	39.58	.
232	Men's shirts, trousers, etc.	.	.	.	$.35^{-}$	.	3.4
233	Women's & infants' outerwear	$.33^{-}$	.	10.73	$.83^{+}$	.	2.1
236	Outerwear, npsf	$.81^{-}$	.	.	.	.	.
238	Wearing apparel, nspf	$.84^{-}$	.	.	$.9^{+}$	.99	5.16
239	Fabricated textile articles, nspf	$.23^{+*}$	.37	.65	.	.	.
242	Lumber	$.15^{+}$	2.66*	16.06	.	.	.

243	Millwork, plywood, & veneer	.81^{-}	.	.	.	.	.
251	Household furniture, nspf	.81^{+}	.	.	.	.	.
253	Public building & related furniture	.48^{+*}	4.11*	−.82	.61^{+}	.	−.04
261	Pulp mill products	.81^{-}	.	.	.	.	.
262	Paper mill products	.81^{-}	.	.	.34^{-}	1.29	1.48
265	Boxes of paper or paperboard	.8^{-}			1.05^{+*}		
267	Converted paper, except boxes	.31^{+}	.13	1.63	.	.	.
271	Newspapers	.81^{-}	.	.	.	.	.
272	Periodicals	.84^{+*}	40.02	.	.	.	.
273	Books & pamphlets	.99^{+}	.	.	.	.	.
275	Printed matter, nspf	.56^{+*}	7.29	12.21	.	.	.
278	Blankbooks, looseleaf binders	.81^{-}	.	.	.	.	.
279	Plates prepared for printing	.28^{+}	2.45	7.51	.	.	.
281	Industrial inorganic chemicals	.22^{-}	−.38	4.6	.13^{+}	.13	.22†
282	Plastics, synthetic resins, rubber, fibres	.36^{+*}	2.48*	.21	.33^{+}	.38	−.04
283	Drugs	.28^{-}	3.74*	4.47	.12^{-}	.6	.48
284	Soaps, detergents, cosmetics	.45^{-}	.	13.16	.11^{-}	1.37	1.89
285	Paints, varnishes, & allied products	.92^{+}	.	.	.32^{+*}	2.96†	−.99†
286	Industrial organic chemicals	.23^{-}	−342.58	3.67	.	.	.
287	Agricultural chemicals, nspf	.45^{-}	.	−.12	.55^{+}	.67	.63
289	Miscellaneous chemical products	.13^{+}	−.14	1.98*	.25^{+}	−1.4	.22*
299	Products of petroleum coal, nspf	.8^{-}	.	.	.	.	.
301	Tyres & inner tubes	.8^{-}	.	.68	.05^{-}	−1.63	1.67
305	Rubber & plastics hose belting	.19^{+}	1.96†	3.46	1.05^{+}	.	.
306	Druggist or medical supplies	.3^{+*}	1.77	1.2	.72^{+*}	1.89	3.56
308	Miscellaneous plastics products	.07^{+}	−.19	1.67	.27^{+*}	3.74*	.08
314	Footwear, except rubber	.78^{-}	.	.	.71^{+}	.	−.04
321	Flat glass	.49^{+}	2.17	2.19	.89^{+*}	1.87	−1.79

Table 6.6 (continued)

SIC	Industry	G_{us}	c_{us}	h_{us}	G_{eu}	c_{eu}	h_{eu}
322	Glass & glassware, pressed or blown	$.78^{-}$	.	.	$.53^{+}$	.	3.46
323	Glass products, made of purchased glass	$.35^{+*}$	2.44*	2.48	.	.	.
325	Structual clay products	$.81^{-}$	.	.	$.48^{+}$	−68.95	−1.12
326	Ceramic sanitary & industrial ware	$.52^{-}$	−13.52	2.97	.	.	.
329	Non-metallic mineral products, npsf	$.58^{+}$	1.73	.32	.	.	.
331	Blast furnace, steel works/mills	$.09^{+}$	1.7	2.23*	.	.	.
332	Iron & steel products	$.8^{-}$	.	.	1.05^{+}	.	.
333	Smelter & refined non-ferrous metals	$.76^{-}$	.	10.73	.	.	.
334	Secondary S&R of non-ferrous metals	$.8^{-}$	.	.	.	.	.
335	Rolled, drawn & extruded non-ferrous metal	$.22^{+*}$	1.24	2.11	$.43^{+}$	$2.11^{\dagger}$	3.96
336	Non-ferrous foundries (castings)	$.8^{+*}$	110.63	.	$.9^{+}$	.	.
339	Primary metal products, nspf	$.8^{+}$	.	.	.	.	.
342	Cutlery, tools	$.23^{-}$	−.18	.4	.	.	.
343	Heating equip.	1.01^{+}	.	.	.	.	.
344	Fabricated structural metal products	$.36^{+*}$	2.81*	1.89	.	.	.
345	Bolts, nuts, screws, etc.	$.52^{+*}$	5.31*	2.11	.	.	.
346	Metal forgings & stampings	$.22^{+*}$	2.12*	2.82	.	.	.
349	Fabricated metal products, nspf	$.11^{+}$	−.48	2	$.31^{+*}$	−.31	$-.06^{\dagger}$
351	Engines & turbines	$.36^{-}$	1.68	−1.71	.	.	.
352	Farm & garden machinery	$.68^{+*}$	.63	3.48	$.13^{-}$	.64	$2.69^{\dagger}$
353	Construction, mining & oil-field machinery	$.07^{-}$	1.48	2.38	$.08^{-}$	−2.12	.34*
354	Metalworking machinery	$.12^{+}$	3.08*	1.67	$.17^{+*}$	.74	1.47
355	Special industry machinery	$.11^{+}$	.95	1.53	$.4^{+*}$	2.28	1.84
356	General industrial machinery	$.21^{+*}$	.81	4.38	$.4^{+*}$	2.55*	.82

357	Office, computing machines	.16^{+}	2.77*	1.45	.63^{+}*	2.78*	.89
358	Refrigeration machinery	.1^{+}	2.28*	2.27	.45^{+}*	2.15†	.22
359	Fluid power pumps	.14^{-}	−.71	1.27	.	.	.
361	Electric distribution equip.	.42^{-}	−70.67	7.5	.	.	.
362	Electrical industrial apparatus	.44^{+}	1.63	2.46	1.05^{+}	.	.
363	Household appliances	.18^{-}	.18	15.36*	.32^{+}	.96	1.25
364	Electric lighting & wiring equip.	.44^{+}*	2.16*	2.59	.15^{-}	−.79	.58
365	Radio & TV receiving equip.	.15^{+}	1.5	2.45	.27^{+}*	2.76*	1.02
366	Communication equip.	.16^{+}	2.53	3.85	.73^{+}*	3.44*	−1.41
367	Electronic components	.1^{+}	3.21*	2.07	.17^{+}	2.91*	.75
369	Electrical machinery, nspf	.3^{+}*	2.09*	.56	.37^{+}	−.32	.63
371	Motor vehicles & parts	.35^{+}*	5.48*	1.74	.3^{+}*	3.9*	.26
372	Aircraft & parts	.81^{+}*	4.76†	.	.	.	.
374	Railroad equip.	.84^{-}	.	.	.	.	.
375	Motorcycles, bicycles	.6^{-}	.	44.28*	.23^{+}	2.73*	1.01
379	Miscl. transp. equip.	.78^{-}	.	.	.	.	.
381	Engineering & research inst.	.99^{+}	.	.	.	.	.
382	Mechanical measuring & controlling inst.	.07^{-}	.52	2.22*	.21^{+}*	3.61*	.83
384	Surgical, medical, & dental inst.	.36^{-}	−.19	1.2	.37^{+}	−.29	.62
385	Opthalmic goods & parts	.43^{-}	.	−.56	.2^{-}	−4.48	1.59
386	Photographic equip. & supplies	.21^{+}	2.65†	5.73*	.14^{+}	−1.13	1.48
387	Watches, clocks	.81^{+}*	.	.	.52^{-}	.	4.58†
393	Musical instruments	.21^{-}	−10.88	1.89	.17^{-}	−74.42	2.55
394	Toys & athletic goods	.26^{+}	1.34	5.62†	.51^{+}*	2.69*	3.47
395	Pens, pencils, etc.	.13^{-}	.94	.7	.36^{-}	.	3.46
396	Costume jewelry, etc.	.76^{-}	.	13.16	.	.	.
399	Miscl. mnfg., nspf	.28^{-}	−149.71	−.69	.	.	.

APPENDIX 6.3 FIRM SIZE DIFFERENCES AND G

This appendix first establishes that in the Brander-Krugman model, firms located in the large country produce greater output than firms located in the small country. Since the large country hosts a disproportionate share of firms, this result implies that the large country will produce a disproportionate share of output. We will then detail the analytics of the Brander-Krugman relationship between $G-DH$ and x which is plotted in the text. Although the results are simpler in the Brander-Krugman case, all qualitative results are similar under the Ottaviano-Tabuchi-Thisse and Helpman-Krugman models for which we only display the same equilibrium $G-DH$ against x plots.

Since firms in a given country are identical in our model, in equilibrium $S=sNz_2$, where z_2 is the individual market share of a firm located in country 2. Market shares for a representative firm operating in country k are

$$z_k=\frac{q_{k1}+q_{k2}}{Q_1+Q_2} \tag{6.14}$$

where q_{ki} is the output of a firm located in country k sold to consumers in country i and Q_i is total output sold to consumers in country i. Inserting equilibrium quantities available in the appendix of Head, Mayer and Ries (2002) in this equation allows us to solve for z_k and evaluate equilibrium S.

Equilibrium quantities when marginal costs are equal in the Brander-Krugman model are

$$q_{22}=\frac{(1-x)M(1-\omega+sN\tau)}{(N+1)},\ q_{21}=\frac{xM(1-\omega-\tau-sN\tau)}{(N+1)}. \tag{6.15}$$

$$q_{11}=\frac{xM(1-\omega+(1-s)N\tau)}{(N+1)}q_{12}=\frac{(1-x)M(1-\omega-\tau-(1-s)N\tau)}{(N+1)}, \tag{6.16}$$

where M is the total number of consumers and ω measures marginal costs. Inserting these quantities into $Q_1=(1-s)Nq_{11}+sNq_{21}$ and $Q_2=(1-s)Nq_{12}+sNq_{22}$, we obtain total quantity consumed and produced on the whole market:

$$Q_1+Q_2=\frac{MN[1-\omega-x\tau-s(\tau(1-2x))]}{N+1} \tag{6.17}$$

Inserting equilibrium quantities into the formula for z_k, we obtain the difference in market shares:

$$z_2 - z_1 = \frac{N+1}{N} \frac{\tau(2x-1)}{1-\omega - x\tau + s[\tau(2x-1)]} \tag{6.18}$$

If $z_2 = z_1$ then both equal $1/N$, so $S = s$. If firms in country 2 are larger than firms in country 1, that is $z_2 - z_1 > 0$, S will exceed s. This will occur when $x < 1/2$.

Equilibrium z_1 and z_2 are used to calculate $H = (1-s)Nz_1^2 + sNz_2^2$. Recalling that $D = 1 - x^2 - (1-x)^2$, we get

$$DH = [1 - x^2 - (1-x)^2] \left\{ \frac{1}{N} + \frac{(N+1)^2(1-s)s\tau^2(1-2x)^2}{N[1-\omega-\tau(x+s(1-2x))]^2} \right\} \tag{6.19}$$

The equilibrium value of $G = (S-x)^2 + (x-S)^2$ requires to solve for the equilibrium share of output S which in turn requires to solve for s as a solution to $\pi_2 - \pi_1 = 0$:

$$s = \frac{2(1-\omega-\tau/2)}{N\tau} x - \frac{1-\omega-((N+1)\tau/2)}{Nt} \tag{6.20}$$

Which finally gives us all the elements to trace G and DH as functions of x in Figure 6.2.

Figure 6.3 plots $G - DH$ for the Helpman-Krugman model. Figure 6.4

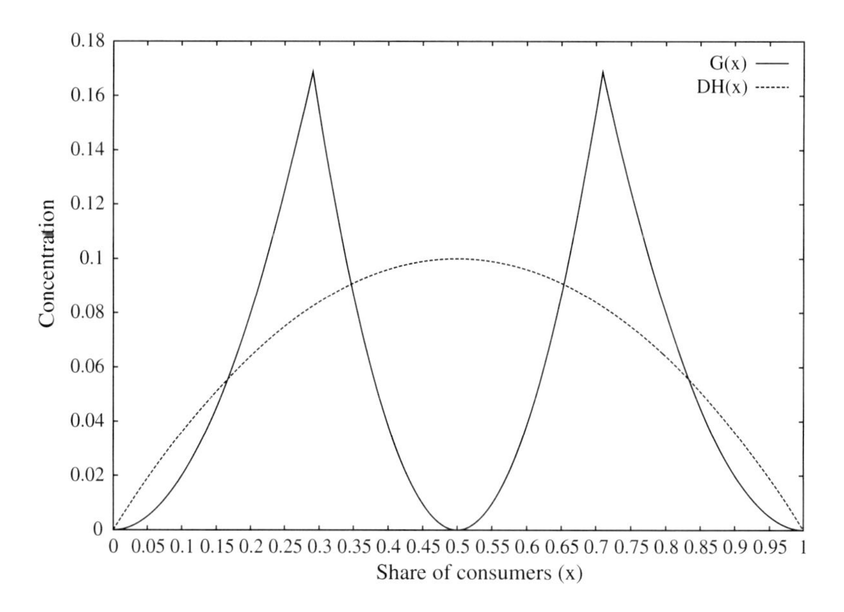

Figure 6.3 G *for the Helpman-Krugman model*

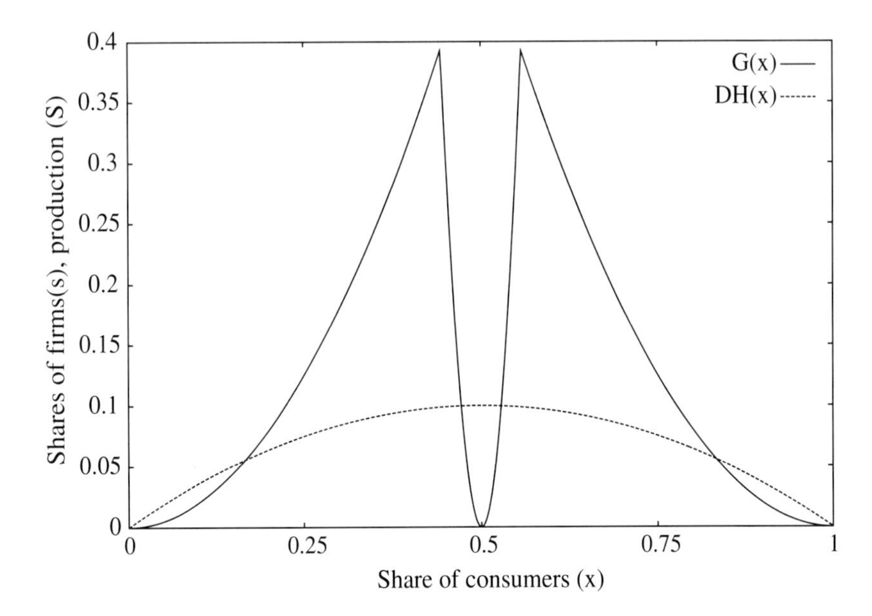

Figure 6.4 G *for the Ottaviano-Tabuchi-Thisse model*

plots $G-DH$ for the Ottaviano-Tabuchi-Thisse model. Like the corresponding figure for the Brander-Krugman model shown in the body of the text, G, DH when country–size asymmetries are small or in regions of x where all production is concentrated in a single country. For intermediate size asymmetries, $G>DH$ and concentration is in excess of that predicted by the dartboard.

NOTES

1. As we are focusing on foreign direct investment here, the term home market might seem slightly misleading. However, we choose to use this terminology because of its widespread use.
2. Ellison and Glaeser mainly consider area sizes to reflect the exogenously given overall distribution of manufacturing. They also show results when income is the size measure.
3. When investment lands in the same country $G=(1-.5)^2+(0-.5)^2=.5$ whereas G equals zero when the investments land in different countries.
4. The figure assumes marginal costs are equal to zero in both countries, trade costs τ equal to 0.1, and a range for N that gives rise to trade in both directions.
5. About 65 per cent of all Japanese FDI in Europe is greenfield. The corresponding figure for the most represented industry in terms of the number of investments (electronics devices and components) is around 80 per cent.
6. The two exceptions, one for Europe and one for the USA, have negative estimates of the intercepts which are not significantly different from zero.

REFERENCES

Brander, J. and P. Krugman (1983), 'A reciprocal dumping model of international trade', *Journal of International Economics*, **23**, 313–21.

Carlton, D. (1983), 'The location and employment choices of new firms: an econometric model with discrete and continuous endogenous variables', *Review of Economics and Statistics*, **65**, 440–49.

Ellison, G. and E.L. Glaeser (1997), 'Geographic concentration in U.S. manufacturing industries: a dartboard approach', *Journal of Political Economy*, **105** (5), 889–927.

Ellison, G. and E.L. Glaeser (1999), 'The geographic concentration of industry: does natural advantage explain agglomeration', *American Economic Review Papers and Proceedings*, **89** (5), 311–16.

Feenstra, R., J. Markusen and A.K. Rose (2001), 'Using the gravity equation to differentiate among alternative theories of trade', *Canadian Journal of Economics*, **34** (2), 430–47.

Head, K., T. Mayer and J. Ries (2002), 'On the pervasiveness of home market effects', *Economica*, **69** (275), 371–90.

Helpman, E. and P.R. Krugman (1985), *Market Structure and Foreign Trade*, Cambridge: MIT Press.

Japan Economic Institute (JEI) (1990), *Japan's Expanding Manufacturing Presence in the United States*, 1990 Updated Survey.

Japan External Trade Organization (JETRO) (1996), *12th Current Survey of Japanese Manufacturing Investment in Europe*, Tokyo: JETRO.

Krugman, P. (1980), 'Scale economies, product differentiation, and the pattern of trade', *American Economic Review*, **70**, 950–59.

Krugman, P.R. (1991), Geography and Trade, Cambridge, MA: MIT Press.

Ottaviano, G., T. Tabuchi and J.-F. Thisse (2002), 'Agglomeration and trade revisited', *International Economic Review*, **43**, 409–36.

7. The home market effect in a Ricardian model with a continuum of goods

Federico Trionfetti

7.1 INTRODUCTION

An interesting new development in the international trade literature has made important advancements in the attempt to distinguish empirically between various models of international specialization and trade. Research in this stream has developed along both a theoretical and an empirical path that are complementary to each other. Theoretically, the task is to identify a testable discriminating criterion; that is, an observable relationship between endogenous and exogenous variables that is compatible with one model and incompatible with the alternative(s). The empirical task is to verify whether such a prediction is observed empirically. If the predicted relation is observed empirically, then the model with which it is compatible is *empirically* the *true* model to the exclusion of all other models. The discriminating criteria so far utilized in the literature are variants of the 'home market' or 'market size' effect. Broadly speaking the market size effect establishes a relation between demand and output: it says that – *ceteris paribus* – a country's share of world demand is reflected more than proportionally on the country's share of world output. Thus, a country with larger than average demand (market) for good X will host a more than proportionally larger than average share of world output of good X. The market size effect is a prediction of models characterized by increasing returns and imperfect competition, while it is typically not a prediction of constant return perfectly competitive models. For this reason the market size effect and its variants have been utilized extensively as a discriminating criterion between these two classes of models. The theoretical explorations have studied the effect of market size on international specialization in various models: Heckscher-Ohlin, Armington, monopolistic competition, Cournot oligopoly with and without product differentiation. The purpose of this chapter is to add a further piece to this mosaic of theoretical explorations by studying the relation between demand and output in the Ricardian model. In particular the chapter explores the effect of market size on international specialization in the Ricardian model with a continuum of goods developed by Dornbush, Fisher and Samuelson (1977).

7.2 RELATIONSHIP TO THE LITERATURE

The comparison between the standard Heckscher-Ohlin model and the monopolistic competition model developed in Krugman (1980) gives us the clear cut result shown in Helpman and Krugman (1985): the market size effect is a prediction of the monopolistic competition model and not of the Heckscher-Ohlin model. This distinction is utilized for the first time by Davis and Weinstein (1999; 2003) as a discriminating criterion to distinguish between the two models. In their seminal contributions they test various empirical specification and find stronger evidence of the market size effect at the regional level (Davis and Weinstein, 1999) than at the international level (Davis and Weinstein, 2003). A different manifestation of the market size effect is found in terms of the export pattern rather than production pattern. This is found in Krugman (1980) who demonstrates that the country with a larger market for a monopolistic competitive good will run a trade surplus in that good. In a theoretical paper Davis (1998) challenges both versions of the market size effect. He shows that imposing trade balance in the monopolistic competitive sector and introducing trade costs in the homogenous goods sector eliminates the market size effect.

In an empirical work Hanson and Xiang (2002) test an export version of the market size effect. They find evidence in support of the market size effect in particular for industries with high transport costs and strong increasing returns; for industries with low transport cost it is neighbourhood market size that matters. In a theoretical paper Weder (1995) considers absolute and relative differences in market size. He finds that, while absolute differences result in the larger country having the higher wage, it is relative differences that determine the patter of specialization and trade. In a later empirical study Weder (2002) finds evidence in support of this hypothesis; he also finds that the relation between home market and exports is stronger for industries with high economies of scale.

Head and Ries (2001) have developed a new discriminating criterion based on the effect of trade costs on the relationship between share of output and share of demand. They consider two models: one is the Krugman (1980) model, the other one is the Armington (1969) model. The latter is characterized by constant returns to scale, perfect competition and product differentiation by country of origin, thereby reflecting Armington's (1969) assumption that consumers perceive national product differently from foreign product. Head and Ries show an important difference between the two models that lies in the effect that trade costs have on the relationship between market size and international specialization. In the Krugman model an increase in trade costs reduces the market size effect. Conversely, in the Armington model, an increase in trade costs increases the effect of market size on output. This difference constitutes a new discriminating criterion that they utilize in the empirical study. Using data for US and Canadian manufacturing they find evidence in support of both models depending on whether within or between variations are considered; most of the evidence, however, is in favour of the Armington model.

Trionfetti (2001) also develops a new discriminating criterion that he derives by introducing a home bias in individuals' preference structure. He shows that a country tends to specialize in the production of the good for which it has a relatively large home-biased demand if the good is produced by an increasing returns monopolistic competitive sector. In contrast this relationship between home-biased demand and specialization does not exists in constant return perfectly competitive sectors. This result constitutes a discriminating criterion. He finds that for ten sectors the share of output is not affected by the share of home-biased demand while for seven sectors the share of output depends positively on the share of home-biased demand. Then the first group of sectors is attributed to the constant returns perfect competitive paradigm, while the second group of sectors is attributed to the increasing returns perfect competitive paradigm. Brülhart and Trionfetti (2002) utilize the same discriminating behaviour but modify the econometric implementation and utilize a more comprehensive data set.

In a comprehensive theoretical investigation Head, Mayer and Ries (2002) have studied the pervasiveness of the market size effect on a number of different models. Besides the Krugman (1980) monopolistic competition model based on Dixit and Stiglitz (1977) they consider the Brander (1981) model which assumes strategic interaction and homogeneous goods, and the Ottaviano, Tabuchi and Thisse (2002) model which assumes product differentiation, linear demand and firms reaction to proximity of competitors. They find that both of these models generate the market size effect. Indeed in the Brander model and in the Ottaviano-Tabuchi-Thisse model the market size effect is even stronger than in the Krugman model. This result is interesting because it shows that the peculiar assumptions of the Dixit-Stiglitz structure are not necessary for the market size effect and can be considered as inconsequential simplifying assumptions. In the same paper Head, Mayer and Ries also consider the model by Markusen and Venables (1988) which assumes an oligopoly where products are differentiated by country of origin. In this model the relationship between share of output and share of demand is less than proportional when the degree of product differentiation is very high, while it is more than proportional when products are homogeneous, in which case the model reverts to the Brander model. A further result which appears in Head, Mayer and Ries (2002) is that whether the relationship between share of output and share of demand is more than proportional or less than proportional almost never depends on relative country size. In the Krugman, Armington, Brander and Ottaviano-Tabuchi-Thisse models the relationship is linear. In the Markusen-Venables model the relationship is non-linear but the degree of proportionality crosses the value of one only for some specific values of parameters.

From this tour of the literature it emerges that the market size effect is quite pervasive and does not depend on the specific assumptions of the Dixit-Stiglitz structure. The only model in which the market size effect surely does not emerge is the pure Heckscher-Ohlin model. The three assumptions of homogeneous goods, constant returns to scale and perfect competition characterizing this model seem suffcient to assure the absence of the market size effect.

The only major theoretical paradigm not yet considered by this literature is the Ricardian model. As is well known, the Ricardian model shares the assumptions of constant returns to scale, homogenous products and perfect competition with the Heckscher-Ohlin model. It is interesting to ask the question as to whether these three assumptions guarantee the absence of home market effect in the Ricardian model. To this purpose I consider the Ricardian model with a continuum of goods as developed by Dornbush, Fisher and Samuelson (1977). Three main conclusions are derived from this analysis. First, the effect of market size on international specialisation is positive even in the absence of trade cost. This effect does not appear in any other model so far studied in the literature. Second, while there is no market size effect when countries are similar in size, there is a market size effect when countries are very different in size. This result contrasts with the independence of the degree of proportionality from country size that is found in all other models.[1] Third, contrary to the Armington model, an increase in trade costs reduces the intensity of the relationship between demand and output. This is also interesting because the Ricardian model shares with the Armington model the assumptions of perfect competition and constant returns to scale.

The remainder of the chapter is as follows: section 7.3 illustrates the model, section 7.4 shows the case of zero transport costs, section 7.5 illustrates the effect of a home-biased demand, section 7.6 discusses the effect of transport costs and section 7.7 concludes the chapter.

7.3 THE MODEL

The structure of the model follows Dornbush, Fisher and Samuelson (1977). We consider a world composed of two countries: Home and Foreign. Following the Ricardian tradition we assume that labour is the only factor of production. Each country is endowed with L and L^* units of labour respectively. The world population is normalized to one so that $L = 1 - L^*$. A continuum of goods indexed by z in the interval [0, 1] is produced in the world economy and the pattern of specialization is determined endogenously. The input requirement per unit of output of commodity z for the home country and the foreign country respectively are denoted with $a(z)$ and $a^*(z)$. Following Dornbush-Fisher-Samuelson (DFS) we rank goods in decreasing order of comparative advantage for the home country. That means we rank goods such that

$$\frac{a^*(z')}{a(z')} > \frac{a^*(z'')}{a(z'')} \tag{7.1}$$

for any $z'' > z' \in [0, 1)$. It is convenient to define $A(z) \equiv a^*(z)/a(z)$ as the relative productivity of the home country. By construction the function $A(z)$ is decreasing in z and we further assume that it is differentiable so that $A'(z) < 0$ everywhere in [0, 1].

The condition of perfect competition drives prices equal to marginal costs, thus in each country we have: $p(z) = a(z)w$, and $p^*(z) = a^*(z)w^*$. We assume from the start that trade my be costly and that trade costs are the same for all goods and the same in each direction. We further assume that trade costs are of the iceberg type: for one unit sent from either country, a fraction $t \in [0, 1]$ arrives at destination; $t = 1$ is free trade while $t = 0$ is a prohibitive trade cost.

The condition of production in Home (of non-export by Foreign) for any good z is: $p(z) \cdot t^{-1}p^*(z)$ which can be rewritten as: $a(z)w \leq 1/t\, a^*(z)w^*$. Similarly the condition of production in Foreign (non export by Home) is: $p(z)t^{-1} \geq p^*(z)$ which can be rewritten as: $a(z)w\, 1/t \geq a^*(z)w^*$. These two conditions can be more conveniently written making use of the function $A(z)$. This is:

$$\frac{w}{w^*} \leq \frac{1}{t}A(z) \tag{7.2}$$

$$\frac{w}{w^*} \geq tA(z) \tag{7.3}$$

For future reference let us denote with $\bar{z}$ the value of z for which equation 7.2 is satisfied with equality. Likewise let us denote with $\bar{z}^*$ the value of z that satisfies equation 7.3 with equality.

Most of the home market effect literature has been able to derive results under the condition of symmetry between countries. For easiness of comparison of the Ricardian model with the other models we conform with this tradition. We then impose some conditions of symmetry in comparative advantage. The first symmetry condition we imposes is that $A(1/2)=1$. That means that the central commodity requires the same input per unit of output in both countries (none of the countries has an absolute advantage in $z=1/2$). This implies that, absent trade costs, if each country produces half of the number of commodities in the world we have $w/w^*=1$. The second symmetric requirement we impose on $A(z)$ is that the comparative advantage of Home (Foreign) be symmetric around $z=1/2$. That means $A(z)-1=1-A(1/2+z)$ for any $z\in[0, 1/2]$. An infinity of functional forms satisfies this requirement. In the sequel we use a simple linear example where $A(z)=1-a\,(z-1/2)$, with $a\in[0, 2]$. The restriction on a is needed if we assume that all goods will be produced in equilibrium.

Preferences are represented by the expenditure shares. We extend the Dornbush-Fisher-Samuelson specification in a way that allows for the presence of a home bias in the preference structure. Thus the expenditure share on each good is function of the bias towards that good. Let us define with $H(h, z)$ and $F(f, z)$ the expenditure share on each commodity z for the Home and Foreign consumers respectively. The parameters h and f represent intensity of the home bias of Home's and Foreign's consumers respectively. Naturally the expenditure shares must meet the requirement that:

$$\int_0^1 H(h, z)dz=1 \tag{7.4}$$

$$\int_0^1 F(f, z)dz=1 \tag{7.5}$$

Goods can be produced anywhere and the pattern of international specialization is not known *ex ante*. Therefore we have to be careful and define the home bias in a way that is independent from the pattern of production that will realize in equilibrium. What does it mean to like home goods in a Ricardian model? We define the home bias as a preference for the goods in which the country has an *ex ante* comparative advantage. Given the symmetry of $A(z)$ this means that the Home's consumers like goods in the interval [0, 1/2) more than the average and like goods in the interval (1/2, 1] less than the average while they like the good $z=1/2$ just as the average. Naturally this preference structure must meet the requirement represented by equations 7.4 and 7.5. In the sequel we use a simple linear example in which the expenditure shares are:

$$H(h, z)=1-h(z-1/2) \tag{7.6}$$

$$F(f, z)=1+f(z-1/2) \tag{7.7}$$

where $h, f \in [0, 2]$ represent the home bias of Home and Foreign respectively. Again the restriction on the value of h and f is necessary if we assume that all goods are consumed. Home (Foreign) is home biased if $h>0$ ($f>0$). In the sequel for the sake of symmetry we will impose that $h=f$ throughout the chapter. The cases $h=f=0$ is the DFS case in which consumers in neither country are home bias. Figure 7.1 represents our specifications of $A(z)$ (solid line), $H(h, z)$ (downward sloping dashed line), and $F(f, z)$ (upward sloping dashed line). The parameters used in Figure 7.1 are: $a=2$, $h=f=1$.

To close the model we need to write the market equilibrium equations or, which is the same, the trade balance equilibrium. Recalling that $\bar{z}$ and $\bar{z}^*$ are

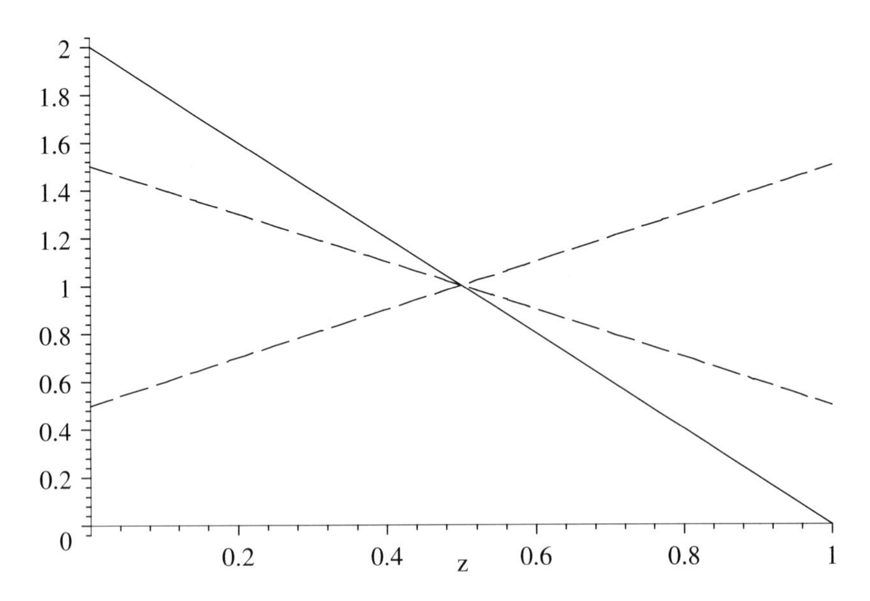

Figure 7.1 Technology and home bias

the marginal commodity produced in Home and Foreign respectively, that is Home produces the set of goods $[0, \bar{z}]$ and foreign produces the set of goods $[\bar{z}^*, 1]$, the market equilibrium equation or the trade balance equation can be written as follows:

$$\frac{w}{w^*} = \frac{\int_0^{\bar{z}^*} F(f,z)}{[1 - \int_0^{\bar{z}} H(h,z)dz]} \frac{L^*}{L} \tag{7.8}$$

Equations 7.2 and 7.3 taken with equality and equation 7.8 determine the relative wages w/w^* and the marginal values $\bar{z}$ and $\bar{z}^*$ as function of h, f, t and L, L^*.

We are now ready to study the effect of country size and home bias on the pattern of international specialization. Let us define the ratio between home and foreign production as $\xi \equiv \bar{z}/(1-\bar{z}^*)$ and the ratio between domestic and foreign labour force as $\lambda \equiv L/L^*$. We want to study the magnitude of the derivative $d\xi/d\lambda$. We modify slightly the terminology normally utilized in the literature. We say that there is a home market effect if the derivative is positive, and we say that there is a magnification effect if the derivative is larger than one. This terminology seems more appropriate. If the derivative is positive, it means that the market size has an effect on output and, therefore, it seems logical to say that there is a market size effect. If this effect is more than proportional then, borrowing from other theorems in trade literature, it seems appropriate to say that there is a magnification effect (of market size on output). We can also study the home market effect in terms of the relationship between share output and share of labour force. Recalling that the world economy produces all goods in [0, 1] and that world endowment of labour is one. The home economy's share in output is z and in size is L. There is a home market effect if $dz/dL > 0$ and there is a magnification effect if $dz/dL > 1$.

We analyse the case of zero transport costs first. We then analyse a case in which countries are (symmetrically) home biased. Finally, we analyse a case where transport costs are positive but there is no home bias.

7.4 ZERO TRANSPORT COSTS AND NO BIAS

We start the analysis with the simplest case of zero transport costs ($t=1$) and no bias in demand ($h=f=0$). Equations 7.2, 7.3 and 7.8 determine $\bar{z}$, $\bar{z}^*$ and w/w^*. However, when trade costs are zero equations 7.2 and 7.3 are identical and, consequently, $\bar{z}=\bar{z}^*$. Further, when demand is not home biased the first ratio on the right-hand-side of equation 7.8 simplifies grandly. Figure 7.2 shows the graphical representation of the equilibrium.

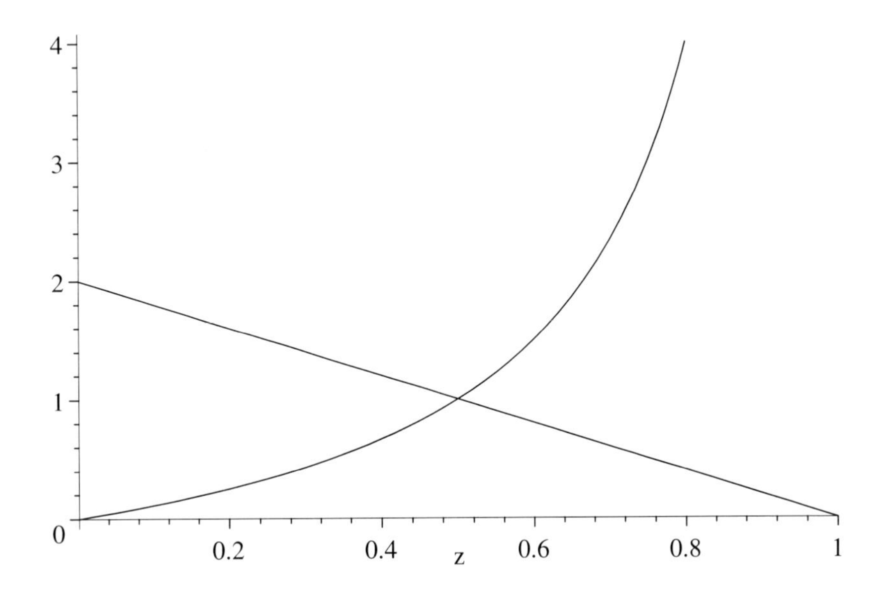

Figure 7.2 Free trade equilibrium

The upward sloping line is the right-hand-side of equation 7.8 and the downward sloping line is any of equations 7.2 or 7.3.

Using equations 7.2, 7.3 and 7.8 we have the explicit solution for $\bar{z}$:

$$\bar{z} = \frac{1}{4aL}(3aL + 2 - \sqrt{(a^2L^2 + 12aL + 4 - 16aL^2)} \tag{7.9}$$

Figure 7.3 plots $\bar{z}$ in the a, L plane.

We note from equation 7.9 that $\bar{z}$ is increasing with L, as it is intuitive, and ranges between [0, 1] . Note also that $\bar{z} = 1/2$ when $L = 1/2$. Also note that as it is intuitive $\lim_{L \to 1} \bar{z} = 1$ and $\lim_{L \to 0} \bar{z} = 0$. Quite clearly there is a market size effect.

We now investigate whether there is a magnification effect. Computing $d\bar{z}/dL$ we have:

$$\frac{d\bar{z}}{dL} = \frac{1}{2}\frac{3aL + 2 - \sqrt{(a^2L^2 + 12aL + 4 - 16aL^2)}}{aL^2\sqrt{(a^2L^2 + 12aL + 4 - 16aL^2)}} > 0 \tag{7.10}$$

The positive sign of the derivative confirms that there is a market size affected. To check for the presence of a magnification effect we should check that there is a set of admissible values of a and L that satisfies the inequality $d\bar{z}/dL > 1$. The explicit solutions of $d\bar{z}/dL > 1$ leads to the cum-

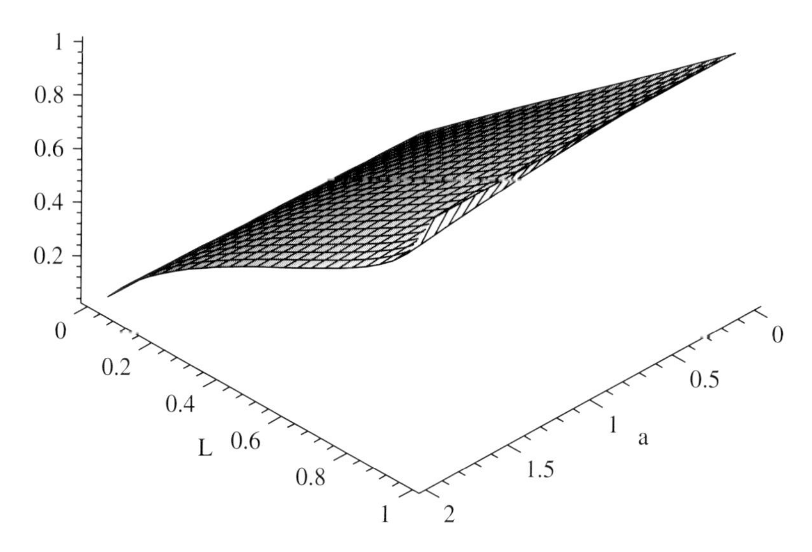

Figure 7.3 Market size and specialization in free trade

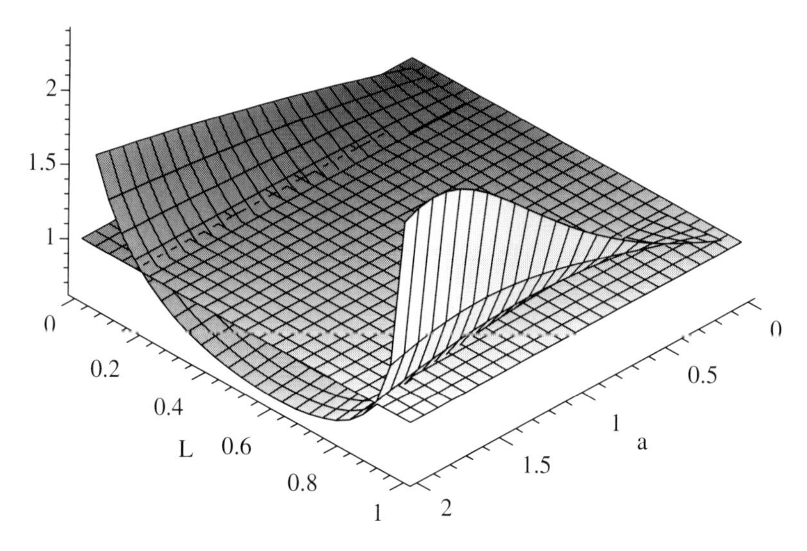

Figure 7.4 Magnification effect in free trade

bersome expression resulting from the Cardano's formula. It is more convenient to plot equation 7.10 in the a, L space to glean the information we want. Figure 7.4 plots $d\bar{z}/dL$ and the plane $z = 1$. It is apparent that for small and large values of L we have $d\bar{z}/dL > 1$.

We conclude that:

Proposition 1 In the Ricardian model with a continuum of goods, with zero transport costs and with no home bias there is a home market effect for any relative country size but there is no magnification effect when countries are fairly similar in size. Conversely when countries are very different in size there is a magnification effect.

This result is interesting because it contrasts with the result that obtains in all other models where, absent trade costs, there is no effect at all of market size on output.

7.5 HOME BIAS

In the previous section we were able to find an explicit solution for $\bar{z}$. In this section we have to confine the analysis at the symmetric equilibrium because of the highly intractable nature of the equations to be solved. We also assume that countries are identically home biased ($h=f$) so that the bias has non-consequences on the equilibrium. We then find $dz/d\lambda$ at the symmetric equilibrium ($\lambda=1$; $z=1/2$) knowing that such equilibrium exists. Differentiating totally around the symmetric equilibrium and using the implicit function theorem we have:

$$\frac{d\xi}{d\lambda}=4\frac{h-4}{ah-4a-16}\in\left[\frac{2}{5},1\right]. \tag{7.11}$$

The derivative is positive but less than one; there is a market size effect but there is not a magnification effect. An increase in Home's relative size results in an increase in the number of goods produced by Home. But this increase is less than proportional to the increase in Home's relative size. The derivative is declining in h. This result tells us that:

Proposition 2 The magnitude of the market size effect is reduced by the presence of a home bias.

Finally, the derivative equals one in the case of no home bias ($h=f=0$) and no comparative advantage ($a=0$). This is consistent with the fact that the limit for $a\rightarrow 0$ of the right-hand-side of equation 7.10 equals one. Also notice that expression 7.11 evaluated at $h=0$ equals equation 7.10 evaluated at $L=1/2$ as it should be. The fact that the lower bound of equation 7.11 is strictly positive is the consequence of the assumption that all goods are consumed and of the linear specification of households preferences.

7.6 TRANSPORT COSTS

We now introduce transport costs but we assume absence of home bias. It is convenient at this stage to set $a=2$ in order to avoid corner solutions. Equations 7.2 and 7.3 at equality together with 7.8 determine $\bar{z}$, $\bar{z}^*$ and w/w^*. Incidentally setting 7.2 = 7.3 gives us $\bar{z}^*$ as function of $\bar{z}$; this is: $\bar{z}^* = z/t^2 - (2+\alpha)(1-t^2)/2at^2$. This allows us to focus on the solution for $\bar{z}$ knowing that the corresponding value of $\bar{z}^*$ can be easily found. Setting $h = f = 0$ and solving equations 7.2, 7.3 and 7.8 gives us:

$$\bar{z} = \frac{1}{4}\frac{4t\dfrac{L}{1-L} + 1 - \sqrt{\left(1 + 8t^3\dfrac{L}{1-L}\right)}}{t\dfrac{L}{1-L}} \in (0, 1) \tag{7.12}$$

It is useful to note some property of this solution. First, $\bar{z}$ ranges between zero and one, and it is increasing with L. Further: $\lim_{t\to 0} \bar{z} = 1$ (in autarky each country produces the entire range of goods); and $\lim_{L\to 1} \bar{z} = 1$ (all goods are produced in Home when the Home economy equals the world economy).[2]

We can now verify whether there is a market size and a magnification effect. Computing the derivative $d\bar{z}/dL$ gives us the following expression:

$$\frac{d\bar{z}}{dL} = -\frac{1}{4}\frac{\sqrt{\left(-\dfrac{-L+1+8t^3L}{L-1}\right)}L + 4t^3L - L + 1 - \sqrt{\left(-\dfrac{-L+1+8t^3L}{L-1}\right)}}{\sqrt{\left(-\dfrac{-L+1+8t^3L}{L-1}\right)}L^2 t(L-1)} \tag{7.13}$$

Once again, plotting the expression against the plane $z=1$ gives us the information we want at a glance. Figure 7.5 plots equation 7.13, it is immediately clear that there is a market size effect except at autarky ($t=0$). Figure 7.5 shows also that there is a magnification effect when Home is very small or very large and if transport costs are suffciently small.

Thus:

Proposition 3 In the Ricardian model with a continuum of goods and transport costs there is a magnification effect when countries are different in size and transport costs are suffciently low.

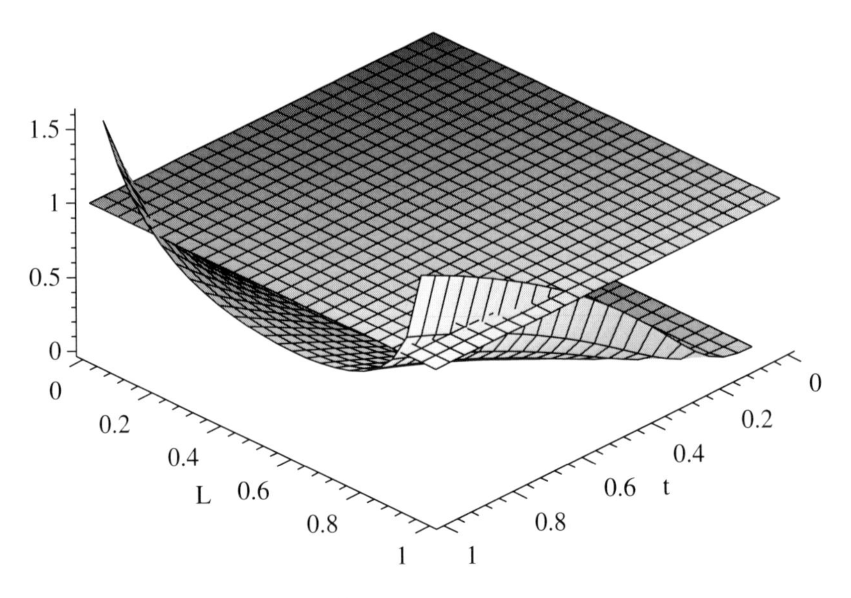

Figure 7.5 Magnification effect with transport costs

The next information we want to obtain concerns the effect of transport costs on the home market effect. We compute the derivative $(d\bar{z}/dL)/dt$ and plot it in Figure 7.6. It is apparent from Figure 7.6 that $(d\bar{z}/dL)/dt > 0$ everywhere. This means that:

> *Proposition 4* In the Ricardian model with a continuum of goods a decline in trade costs increases the home market effect.

This result can be contrasted with the effect of trade costs on the magnitude of the home market effect in the Armington model and in the Krugman model. As shown in Head and Ries (2001), in the Armington model an increase in trade costs increases the home market effect, which reaches its maximum value equal to one in autarky. Conversely in the Krugman model an increase of trade costs reduces the size of the derivative, which reaches its minimum equal to one at autarky. The Ricardian model with a continuum of goods behave similarly to the Krugman model, an increase in transport costs increases the size of the home market effect. This result is interesting because the Ricardian model shares two key features with the Armington and Heckscher-Ohlin paradigms, namely, constant returns to scale and perfect competition. Yet with respect to the effect of trade costs on the magnitude of the market size effect it behaves like the Krugman model. This further complicates the derivation of robust testable hypothesis.

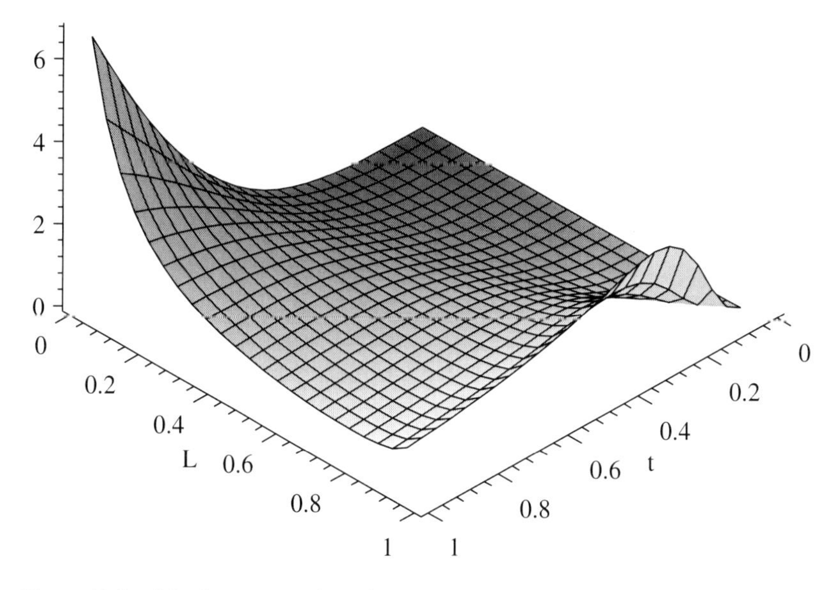

Figure 7.6 Market size and trade costs

7.7 CONCLUSION

The literature on the home market effect has developed very rapidly. Previous works have studied the effect of market size on international specialization in a variety of models: Monopolistic competition *à la* Dixit-Stiglitz, monopolistic competition with firms reaction to proximity of competitors, oligopoly with and without product differentiation, as well as models with constant returns to scale and product differentiation by country of origin. One result that emerges from this literature is that the magnification effect is quite pervasive. Only the assumptions of perfect competitions, constant returns to scale and product homogeneity seemed to guarantee the absence of the magnification effect.

This chapter's contribution to this literature is to study the effect of market size on international specialization in the Ricardian model with a continuum of goods. The study of the Ricardian framework is particularly interesting because this framework reunites the three assumptions that seemed to guarantee the absence of a magnification effect, namely, perfect competition, constant returns to scale and homogeneous products. Interestingly this chapter has shown that these three conditions are not suffcient to exclude the presence of the magnification effect. Propositions 3 and 1 have shown that the magnification effect emerges when countries are very different in size. Further, proposition 1 has shown that the market size effect and the magnification effect can emerge even in the absence of trade costs. In this respect the Ricardian model behaves differently from all other models.[3] Finally, proposition 4 shows an interesting difference between the Ricardian model and the Armington model. The two models share the assumptions of perfect competition and constant returns to scale. Yet in the former an increase in trade costs decreases the magnitude of the market size effect, whereas in the latter an increase in trade costs increases the magnitude of the market size effect (Head and Ries, 2002). This means that, in respect of the effect of trade costs on the magnitude of the market size effect, the Ricardian model behaves like the Krugman model.

As discussed above, when countries are approximately of equal size the magnification effect is not a feature of the Ricardian model. This result combined with the results of the previous literature seems to confirm that the magnification effect emerges only in models characterized by imperfect competition and increasing returns. While increasing returns and imperfect competition are not sufficient, they seem to be necessary conditions for the magnification effect.[4] When countries are very different in size then the assumption of imperfect competition and increasing returns are not necessary condition any longer. This result may bear implications for the empirical studies when very small countries are in the sample.

NOTES

1. Possibly with the exception of specific parametric configuration of the Markusen-Venables model.
2. Note also that $\lim_{L \to 0} \bar{z} = 1 - t^2$, which means that although a country may be very small it may produce a large range of goods (possibly all) if trade costs are very high (in autarky).
3. Trionfetti (2001) has shown that the market size effect at zero trade costs exists in monopolistic competition (but not in the Heckscher-Ohlin model) when demand is home biased.
4. Imperfect competition and increasing returns are not suffcient to generate the magnification effect when demand is home biased (see Trionfetti, 2001; Bülhart and Trionfetti, 2002).

REFERENCES

Armington, P.S. (1969), 'A theory of demand for products distinguished by place of production', *IMF Staff Papers*, **16**, 159–76.

Brander, J. (1981), 'Intra-industry trade in identical commodities', *Journal of International Economics*, **11**, 1–14.

Brülhart, M. and F. Trionfetti (2002), 'A test of trade theories when expenditure is home biased', University of Lausanne, mimeo.

Davis, D.R. (1998), 'The home market, trade and industrial structure', *European Economic Review*, **88**, 1264–76.

Davis, D.R. and D.E. Weinstein (1999), 'Economic geography and regional production structure: an empirical investigation', *European Economic Review*, **43**, 379–407.

Davis, D.R. and D.E. Weinstein (2003), 'Market access, economic geography and comparative advantage: an empirical test', *Journal of International Economics*, **59** (1), 1–23.

Dixit, A. and J.E. Stiglitz (1977), 'Monopolistic competition and optimal product diversity', *American Economic Review*, **67**, 297–308.

Dornbush, R., S. Fisher and P. Samuelson (1977), 'Comparative advantage, trade, and payments in a Ricardian model with a continuum of goods', *American Economic Review*, **67** (5), 823–39.

Hanson, H.G. and C. Xiang (2002), 'The home market effect and bilateral trade patterns', NBER Working Paper No. 9076, July.

Head, K. and J. Ries (2001), 'Increasing returns versus national product differentiation as an explanation for the pattern of US–Canada trade', *American Economic Review*, 91(4), 858–76.

Head, K., T. Mayer and J. Ries (2002), 'On the pervasiveness of the home market effects', *Economica*, **69** (275), 371–90.

Helpman E. and P.R. Krugman (1985), *Market Structure and Foreign Trade*, Cambridge, MA: MIT Press.

Krugman, P.R. (1980), 'Scale economies, product differentiation, and the pattern of trade', *American Economic Review*, **70**, 950–59.

Markusen, J.R. and A.J. Venables (1988), 'Trade policy with increasing returns and imperfect competition: contradictory results from competing assumptions', *Journal of International Economics*, **20**, 225–47.

Ottaviano, G.I.P., T. Tabuchi and J. Thisse (2002), 'Agglomeration and trade revisited', *International Economic Review*, **43** (2), 409–35.

Trionfetti, F. (2001), 'Using home-biased demand to test for trade theories', *Weltwirtschaftliches Archiv*, **137** (3), 404–26.

Weder, R. (1995), 'Linking absolute and comparative advantages to intra-industry trade theory', *Review of International Economics*, **3** (3), 342–54.

Weder, R. (2002), 'Comparative home-market advantage: an empirical analysis of British and American exports', University of Basel, mimeo.

8. Footloose capital, market access and the geography of regional state aid

Gianmarco I.P. Ottaviano

8.1 INTRODUCTION

Market access plays a key role in many recent models of international trade. Such models study the impact of frictions in goods and factors mobility on the location of imperfectly competitive industries in the presence of increasing returns to scale (Helpman and Krugman, 1985). Their central result is the so-called *home market* or *market size effect* (henceforth, HME), according to which, in the case of a two-country economy, the location with larger local demand succeeds in attracting a more than proportionate share of firms in the aforementioned industries. In the case of more than two countries, rather than local demand, what matters is overall market access (Krugman, 1993). For example, a small central country may have better overall market access than a large peripheral one and, thus, despite its local demand disadvantage, may end up attracting a larger share of imperfectly competitive firms.[1] This pattern of demand-driven specialization maps into trade flows and generates the theoretical prediction that large central countries should be net exporters of goods produced under increasing returns and imperfect competition.[2]

From an empirical viewpoint, those predictions seem to find some support in the data. For example, Feenstra, Markusen and Rose (1998; 2001) argue that the HME is crucial to understand the empirical success of gravity equations, which explain bilateral trade flows in terms of incomes and distance between trade partners. Using disaggregated trade data from Statistics Canada World Database, they show that the HME appears to be relevant in both differentiated and homogeneous goods sectors, even though more in the former than in the latter. Using disaggregated data on UK–US trade, Weder (1997) finds that relative demand has a positive relationship with net exports as implied by the HME. Davis and Weinstein (1998; 1999) find evidence of the HME in disaggregated trade data between OECD countries. Based on disaggregated production data from Eurostat, Trionfetti (1998), Midelfart-Knarvik et al. (2000) as well as Brülhart and

Trionfetti (2001) argue that market access is significant in explaining EU industrial specialization. Finally, analysing disaggregated industry data for Canadian and US manufacturing, Head and Mayer (forthcoming) also find supportive evidence for the HME.[3]

From a theoretical viewpoint, the focus is on the two-country case. The underpinnings of the HME are unveiled by Krugman (1980) and Helpman and Krugman (1985) with respect to imperfectly competitive industries characterized by product differentiation and free entry. Helpman (1990) qualifies previous results by stressing the demand conditions under which the HME materializes in those sectors. These conditions require the cross-elasticity between varieties of a differentiated good to be larger than the overall price-elasticity of demand for the differentiated good as a whole. Davis (1998) points out the relevance of the actual incidence of trade costs in all sectors and shows that, when transportation costs on perfectly competitive goods are considered, the HME may disappear altogether because trade cost in those sectors can effectively limit the mobility of firms in differentiated sectors. Feenstra, Markusen and Rose (1998) show that there is nothing crucial in product differentiation and free entry per se in that the HME can be expected even in homogenous-good sectors with restricted entry. All that matters is the presence of positive price–cost margins. Finally, Head, Mayer, and Ries (2000) point out that, when goods are differentiated according to their location in the geographical rather than in product space, the HME might again disappear.

To sum up, the HME seems a robust implication of trade models with imperfect competition even though its actual intensity is likely to vary from sector to sector depending on returns to scale, trade costs, entry barriers and elasticities of demand and substitution.[4] This statement, however, is subject to two main caveats. First, it holds if we focus on a sector insulated from the rest of the economy, that is, the HME is a partial equilibrium phenomenon that might be washed away by general equilibrium interactions as stressed by Helpman (1990) or Davis (1998). Second, it can be defined rigorously only with two countries that differ in nothing but size, which is not the case when technology or factor-abundance driven advantages are present or when products are differentiated according to geographical location as in the counterexample by Head, Mayer and Ries (2000).

Nonetheless, despite its theoretical success and its promising explanatory power, the welfare properties of the HME are still little understood (see, for example, Braunerhjelm et al., 2000). In particular, the literature does not provide any answer to the fundamental question of whether the spatial distribution of economic activities implied by the HME is efficient for the economy as a whole. The aim of the present chapter is to give a first answer to that question and to show how that answer can be used to discuss the desirability of current regional policies that, in most cases, aim at promoting the location of firms in peripheral regions as markets get increasingly integrated.

In particular, the chapter proposes a simple two-country two-factor model with a monopolistically competitive sector. To focus on the implications of the HME and in the light of the two caveats discussed above, the monopolistically competitive market is insulated from all other markets and one country is a scaled-up version of the other. Monopolistic competitive firms are modelled *à la* Ottaviano, Tabuchi and Thisse (2002), but differently from this chapter their location is driven by footloose capital mobility rather than by workers' migration. This allows for the description of a realistic situation in which capital is freely mobile between countries while labour is not. The model reveals an overall tendency of the monopolistically competitive sector to inefficiently cluster in the country that offers better market access. The more so the stronger the market power of firms as well as the intensity of increasing returns to scale and the lower the trade costs. As these features are likely to differ widely across sectors, those results provide theoretical ground to the promotion of regional policies that are both region and sector specific.

The chapter is in six additional sections. Section 8.2 describes regional state aid in the EU as a natural policy background for the theoretical analysis. Section 8.3 presents the model. Section 8.4 shows how the HME arises as a market equilibrium result. Section 8.5 studies the welfare properties of the market equilibrium with respect to the level of trade barriers. After pointing out that also the efficient allocation of firms exhibits a HME, it argues that the market pattern of firms' location is suboptimally biased in favour of the larger ('central') country, the more so the lower trade costs are. Section 8.6 shows that subsidies towards the small ('peripheral') country can be used to restore efficiency. Their amount falls as integration is deepened, but rises with the distance between centre and periphery. Section 8.7 concludes.

8.2 POLICY BACKGROUND: EU REGIONAL INTERVENTION

To define the issues at stake, a natural example is the case of the EU, which devotes staggering amounts of money to regional objectives. For instance, in 1997 the total budget of the European Union consisted of the equivalent of 87.6 billion euros, funded mainly through VAT (42.3 per cent), direct member states' contribution that are proportional to their GDP (40.3 per

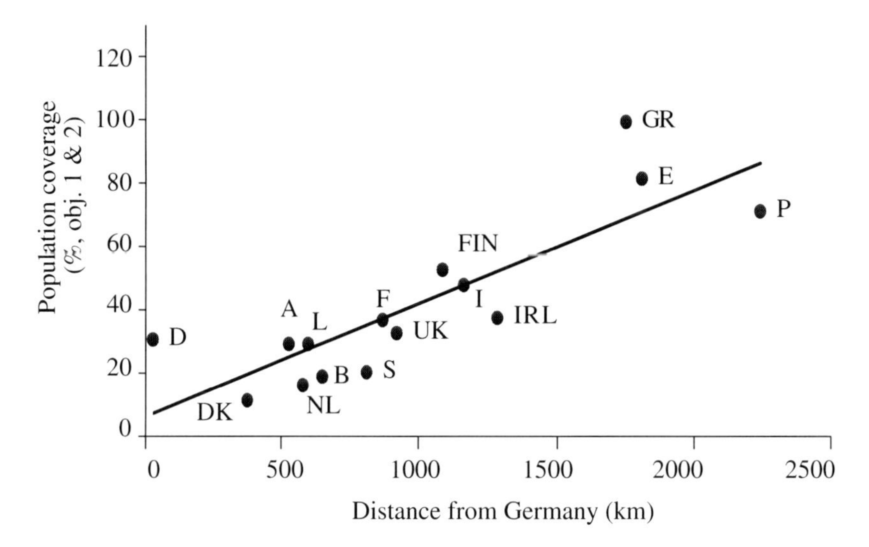

Figure 8.1 *EU structural funds*

cent) and custom duties on imports from outside the EU (16.5 per cent). Most of the budget was devoted to two areas of intervention: 47 per cent to the Common Agricultural Policy (CAP) and 36.3 per cent to Structural Funds (SFs). In relative terms, the total endowment of the SFs corresponds to 1.2 per cent of the joint GNP of EU members states and for the period from 1994 to 1999 it reached almost 154 billion euros (at 1994 prices). As to SFs, two main general categories of expenditures can be identified. *Economic aid* (76.4 per cent) aims at improving the attractiveness of regions to firms both indirectly through the provision of public goods (mainly infrastructures) and directly through the compensation of individual economic enterprises. *Social aid* (9.9 per cent) targets regional unemployment and human-capital accumulation through education and skill upgrading. Since member countries' contributions to the EU budget are proportional to their respective GDPs, the geographical allocation implies a clear pattern of *international redistribution* especially to the advantage of the countries at the EU periphery, namely Ireland, Greece and Portugal, as well as of *interregional redistribution* mainly to the advantage of the less developed peripheral regions of Italy, Spain and Eastern Germany. Such a pattern is clearly visible in Figure 8.1, which plots the SFs coverage of population across countries as a function of an index of geographical peripherality for the planning period 2000–06.[5]

The periphery bias of EU SFs is accompanied by the direct control over members states' regional aid aimed at supporting productive (*initial*) investment and job creation.[6] This is achieved through *state aid caps*, that is, upper (percentage) limits to goverment support to private investments no matter whether the aid comes from local, regional, national or EU sources. As SFs state aid caps follow the logic of spatial concentration and rule out support confined to individual firms or areas of activity. The aim is to foster the development of less-favoured regions by encouraging firms to settle there and, in any case, to reduce the effects of integration on periphery-to-centre relocation. The broad principle is that '[n]o trading relationship will work properly without agreed rules on the granting of subsidies' (European Commission, 1995) and it is implemented by Articles 92–94 of the Treaty of Rome (1957). In particular, as clarified by the European Commission (1995): 'Article 92 specifies that state aids which distort or threaten to distort competition by favouring certain companies or the production of specific goods, and which affect trade between member states, are incompatible with the common market'. Figure 8.2 depicts regional state aid caps across member states as a function of peripherality.[7] It matches Figure 8.1 in showing that, as pointed out by Braunerhjelm et al. (2000), '[t]he overall pattern of EU regional policy spending follows precisely the pattern that might be expected of the Commission, which is trying to achieve regional convergence [a.k.a., *cohesion*] in terms of EU GDP per capita'.[8]

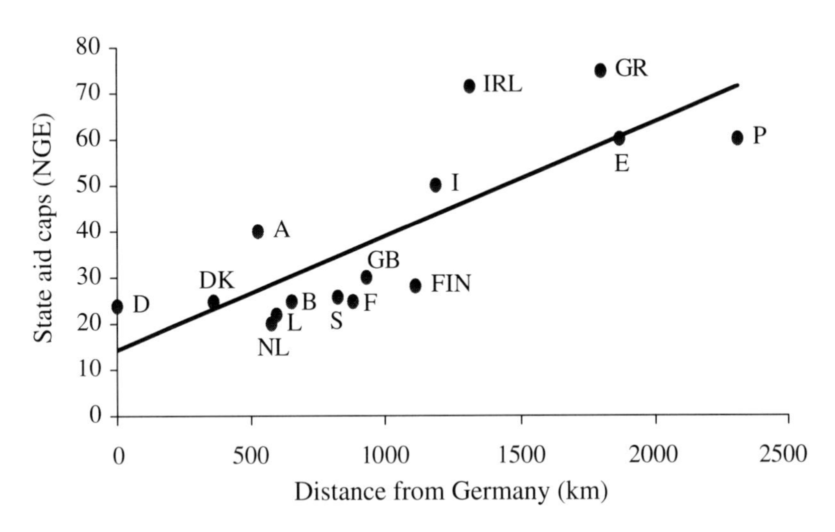

Figure 8.2 EU aid caps

What has trade theory to say about the above pictures? Is the logic of redistribution from centre to periphery sound as the EU faces ongoing economic integration? If so, is it about equity, efficiency, or both?

As a good approximation we can divide the possible answers into two main positions. The first is based on the neoclassical world of constant returns to scale and perfect competitition. In this world countries specialize according to their comparative advantage, and each of them as a whole attains its efficient pattern of production. In other words, trade integration is Pareto improving. Nevertheless, within the same country there may be gainers and losers. If disadvantaged interests are geographically concentrated, then there is a need for interregional transfers based on equity considerations. Notice, however, that the effects of integration (whether positive or negative) should be stronger in central regions that, by definition, are closer to international markets. At the international level, a large domestic market reduces the gains from trade integration so that, again based only on equity considerations, if anything, large countries should be compensated by small ones. Thus, the neoclassical paradigm provides little support to centre-to-periphery redistribution both on equity and efficiency grounds.

The second position considers the world of increasing returns to scale and imperfect competition. As discussed in the introduction, this is the realm of the HME, that is, (imperfect) trade integration makes firms relocate from peripheral to central regions. This affects negatively the former and positively the latter. The reason is that firms have market power and command rents in terms of prices set above marginal costs. These rents are extracted by firms from consumers and reduce the welfare of a country when the firms and the consumers involved belong to that same country. However, when firms and consumers are in different countries, those rents increase the welfare of the country to which firms belong. As a result, countries benefit from the expansion of their imperfectly competitive export sectors (*direct rent shifting*) as well as from an inflow of formerly foreign firms in those sectors in so far as rents are not entirely repatriated (*indirect rent shifting*) and the inflow lowers domestic consumer prices (Brander and Spencer, 1984; Helpman and Krugman, 1989; Brander, 1995). Thus, with imperfect competition, centre-to-periphery relocation implies indeed that trade integration favours central countries more than peripheral ones, which may even lose. This provides equity-based support to centre-to-periphery redistribution.

Compared with the foregoing results this chapter moves one step further and identifies precise *sectoral* conditions under which centre-to-periphery redistribution is desirable not only on equity, but also on efficiency grounds. When such conditions are met, deeper trade integration enhances spatial inefficiency, thus increasing the need for redistribution. At the same time, however, it reduces the intensity of redistribution required. While these insights support the EU approach to regional intervention, at the same time they stress its incompleteness. Indeed, in so far as industry-specific characteristics are likely to determine the practical relevance of spatial inefficiency, regional policies should be not only region specific, as they currently are in the EU, but also sector specific.

8.3 THE MODEL

The analytical framework is based on the monopolistically competitive model put forth by Ottaviano and Thisse (2002) as well as Ottaviano, Tabuchi and Thisse (2002).[9] The economy consists of two countries, H and F, which are endowed with two factors, capital K and labour L. To fit the European situation, capital and labour differ in terms of international mobility. In particular, labour is assumed to be geographically immobile. Its total stock equals L, and it is evenly distributed so that a δL workers reside and work in country H. On the contrary, capital is assumed to be perfectly mobile, it is owned by workers, its total stock equals K, and it is distributed so that σK units are owned by country H residents (with $\sigma \in (0, 1)$) while γK units are used in country H production (with $\gamma \in [0, 1]$). Hence, $(\gamma - \sigma)K > 0$ (< 0) measures capital inflows to (outflows from) country H from (to) country F. Since the focus of the analysis is on the HME, we are interested in situations in which one 'central' country (say H) is *proportionately* larger than the other 'peripheral' one (say F). This requires to set $\delta = \sigma > 1/2$.

In the economy there are two sectors, modern and traditional. The modern sector is capital intensive and supplies a horizontally differentiated good under increasing returns to scale and monopolistic competition. In particular, there is an endogenous mass of firms N, each producing a single variety of the differentiated good by means of a fixed amount ϕ of capital K. The traditional sector produces a homogeneous good under constant returns to scale and perfect competition. It uses labour L as the only input with one unit of L required to produce one unit of output. This good is freely traded and is chosen as the numeraire. On the contrary, the varieties of the modern sector are traded at a cost of τ units of the numeraire per unit shipped between the two countries.

Preferences are identical across individuals and described by the following quasi-linear indirect utility function which is symmetric in all varieties:

$$V(y; p(i), i \in [0, N]) = -a \int_0^N p(i)di + \frac{b + cN}{2} \int_0^N [p(i)]^2 di$$

$$-\frac{c}{2}\left[\int_0^N p(i)di\right]^2+y+\bar{q}_0 \tag{8.1}$$

where $p(i)$ is the price of variety $i \in [0, N]$, y the consumer's income, and $\bar{q}_0$ her initial endowment of the numeraire. In equation 8.1, $a>0$ expresses the intensity of preferences for the differentiated product with respect to the numeraire; $b>0$ means that the representative consumer is biased toward a dispersed consumption of varieties, thus reflecting a love for variety; $c>0$ expresses the substitutability between varieties so that the higher c, the closer substitutes the varieties. Finally, the initial endowment $\bar{q}_0$ in the numeraire is assumed to be large enough for the consumption of the numeraire to be strictly positive at the market equilibrium and optimal solutions.

Market clearing implies that the number n_H of firms belonging to the modern sector and located in country H is equal to:

$$n_H=\gamma K/\phi \tag{8.2}$$

so that the number of firms in F is

$$n_F=(1-\gamma)K/\phi \tag{8.3}$$

Consequently, the total number of firms (varieties) in the economy is fixed by endowments and technology and equal to $N=K/\phi$.

Entry and exit are free so that profits are zero in equilibrium. Hence, equations 8.2 and 8.3 imply that any change in the number of firms located in one country originates from a corresponding change in the locally employed stock of capital. By equations 8.2 and 8.3, the demand and supply of capital in each country are equal. As a result, the corresponding equilibrium returns to capital are determined by a bidding process among firms which ends when no firm can earn a strictly positive profit at the equilibrium market prices.

Firms are assumed to take advantage of positive trade costs to segment markets, that is, each firm sets a price specific to the market in which its product is sold. This assumption follows from empirical work showing that, even within a unified economic area, firms succeed to price discriminate between spatially separated markets (McCallum, 1995; Head and Mayer, 2000). As shown below, in equilibrium arbitrage is not profitable to third parties.

In what follows, we focus on country H. Things pertaining to country F can be derived by symmetry. Using the assumption of symmetry between varieties and Roy's identity, individual demands for a representative firm in H are given by:

$$q_{HH} = a - (b + cN)\, p_{HH} + cP_H \tag{8.4}$$

and

$$q_{HF} = a - (b + cN) p_{HF} + cP_F \tag{8.5}$$

where $p_{HH}(p_{HF})$ is the price set in $H(F)$ by a firm located in H and

$$P_H \equiv n_H p_{HH} + n_F p_{FH} \tag{8.6}$$

$$P_F \equiv n_H p_{HF} + n_F p_{FF} \tag{8.7}$$

Clearly, P_H/N and P_F/N can be interpreted as the price indices prevailing in countries H and F.

A representative firm in H maximizes its profits, which, after using (8.4) and (8.5), are defined by:

$$\Pi_H = p_{HH}[a - (b + cN)p_{HH} + cP_H]\, \sigma L + (p_{HF} - \tau)\, [a - (b + cN)p_{HF} + cP_F]\, (1 - \sigma)L - \phi r_H \tag{8.8}$$

where r_H is the return to capital prevailing in H.

Market prices are obtained by maximizing profits while capital returns are determined as described above by equating the resulting profits to zero. Since we have a continuum of firms, each one is negligible in the sense that its action has no impact on the market. Hence, when choosing its prices, a firm in H accurately neglects the impact of its decision over the two price indices P_H and P_F. In addition, because firms sell differentiated varieties, each one has some monopoly power in that it faces a demand function with finite elasticity. On the other hand, since the price index enters the demand function as an additive term (see equations 8.4 and 8.5), a firm must account for the distribution of the firms' prices through some aggregate statistics, given here by the average market price, in order to find its equilibrium price. As a consequence, the market solution is given by a Nash equilibrium with a continuum of players in which prices are interdependent: each firm neglects its impact on the market but is aware that the market as a whole has a non-negligible impact on its behaviour.

Since profit functions are concave in own prices, solving the first order conditions for profit maximization with respect to prices yields the equilibrium prices:

$$p_{HH} = \frac{1}{2}\frac{2a + \tau cN(1 - \gamma)}{2b + cN} \tag{8.9}$$

$$p_{FF} = \frac{1}{2} \frac{2a + \tau c N \gamma}{2b + cN} \tag{8.10}$$

$$p_{HF} = p_{FF} + \frac{\tau}{2} \tag{8.11}$$

$$p_{FH} = p_{HH} + \frac{\tau}{2} \tag{8.12}$$

which depend on the total number of active firms as well as on their distribution between the two countries.

Substracting τ from equations 8.11 and 8.12, we see that firms' prices net of trade costs are positive regardless of their spatial distribution if and only if

$$\tau < \tau_{trade} \equiv \frac{2a\phi}{2b\phi + cK} \tag{8.13}$$

The same condition must hold for consumers in $F(H)$ to buy from firms in $H(F)$, that is, for the demand in 8.5 evaluated at the prices in equations 8.10 and 8.11 to be positive for all γ. From now on, equation 8.13 is assumed to hold. Consequently, we consider a setting in which there is a priori intra-industry trade.

Using equation 8.13 we observe that more firms in the economy lead to lower market prices for the same spatial distribution (γ; $1 - \gamma$) because there is more competition in each local market. Similarly, both the prices charged by local and foreign firms fall when the mass of local firms increases because competition is fiercer. Equilibrium prices also rise when the degree of product differentiation, inversely measured by c, increases provided that equation 8.13 holds. Moreover, it can be easily checked that $p_{HF} - p_{HH} < \tau$ (that is, there is *dumping*) so that the prohibition of arbitrage associated with the assumption of segmented markets is not binding.

Finally, local sales rise with τ because of the higher protection enjoyed by the local firms but exports fall for the same reason. By using equations 8.8, 8.9 and 8.11, it is easy to check that the equilibrium operating profits earned by a firm established in H on each separated market are as follows:

$$\Pi_{HH} = (b + cN)\, p_{HH}^2 \sigma L \tag{8.14}$$

where Π_{HH} denotes the profits earned in H while the profits made from selling in F are

$$\Pi_{HF} = (b + cN)\, (p_{HF} - \tau)^2 (1 - \sigma) L \tag{8.15}$$

Thus, an increase in the number of firms in one country decreases the operating profits of local sales due to tougher local competition: the equilibrium price falls as well as the quantity of each variety bought by each consumer.

The individual consumer surplus S_H in country H associated with the equilibrium prices in equations 8.9 and 8.12 is then as follows (a symmetric expression holds in country F):

$$S_H(\gamma) = -a[\gamma p_{HH} + (1-\gamma)p_{FH}]N$$
$$+\frac{b+cN}{2}[\gamma p_{HH}^2 + (1-\gamma)p_{FH}^2]N - \frac{c}{2}[\gamma p_{HH} + (1-\gamma)p_{FH}]^2 N^2 \tag{8.16}$$

which can be shown to be quadratic in γ. Differentiating twice this expression with respect to γ shows that $S_H(\gamma)$ is concave. Furthermore, equation 8.13 implies that $S_H(\gamma)$ is always increasing in λ over the interval [0, 1]. Hence, as more firms enter in H, the surplus of residents rises because local competition becomes fiercer; however, this effect gets weaker and weaker as the number of local firms increases.

The equilibrium return to capital prevailing in country H can be obtained by evaluating $r_H(\gamma) = (\Pi_{HH} + \Pi_{HF})/\phi$, thus yielding the following expression:

$$r_H(\gamma) = \frac{b\phi + cK}{4(2b\phi + cK)^2\phi^2}\{[2a\phi + \tau cK(1-\gamma)]^2\sigma L$$
$$+ [2a\phi - 2\tau b\phi - \tau cK(1-\gamma\}^2(1-\sigma)L\} \tag{8.17}$$

which is also quadratic in γ. Standard, but cumbersome, investigations reveal that $r_H(\gamma)$ is convex and decreasing in γ. In other words, the equilibrium return to capital wage falls with the local number of firms so that, while $S_H(\gamma)$ rises, $r_H(\gamma)$ decreases with γ. This effect gets weaker and weaker as the number of local firms increases because the larger their number, the weaker the marginal impact of a new entrant on the intensity of local competition. Moreover, inspection of the square bracketed terms reveals that operating profits per unit sold are larger on domestic than on distant sales, and the more so the smaller the fraction of domestic firms.

8.4 THE MARKET OUTCOME

We are now ready to determine the equilibrium location of firms as the result of the international allocation of capital. Since it is capital flows that determine the location of firms, an equilibrium arises when no capital owner can earn strictly higher returns by changing the country serviced by her capital endowment. This happens for $0<\gamma<1$ whenever capital returns are equalized in the two countries:

$$r_H(\gamma)=r_F(\gamma) \tag{8.18}$$

and for $\gamma=1$ [$\gamma=0$] whenever $r_H(1)\geq r_F(1)$ [$r_F(0)\geq r_H(0)$].[10] In these latter cases the modern sector is clustered in one country only, with the other country completely specialized in the production of the traditional good.

Using equation 8.17 as well as the corresponding expression for country F in equation 8.18, the differential return on capital can be expressed as:

$$r_H(\gamma)-r_F(\gamma)=C\{\tau[4a\phi-\tau(2b\phi+cK)](\sigma-1/2)-\tau^2cK(\gamma-\sigma)\} \tag{8.19}$$

with $C\equiv[(b\phi+cK)K]/[2\phi^2(2b\phi+cK)]>0$. The differential is, thus, a decreasing linear function of γ.

The right hand side of equation 8.19 shows that the equilibrium spatial allocation of capital is determined by the interaction of the two terms inside the curly bracket. The first term depends on the spatial distribution of consumers (σ) while it is independent from the location of firms (γ). Since the coefficient of $(\sigma-1/2)$ is positive in so far as equation 8.13 holds, that term measures a *market access* advantage due to trade costs saving: were the overall spatial distribution of firms to mirror the distribution of consumers ($\gamma=\sigma$), it would nonetheless be better to be located in the larger country because, as mentioned above, operating profits per unit sold are larger on domestic than on distant sales. This is not necessarily true when there is a more than proportionate presence of firms in the larger country ($\gamma>\sigma$). In that case, the second term in equation 8.19 points out that there is a *market crowding* penalty, which derives from the fact that, as the fraction of firms in the larger market grows, operating profits per unit sold fall on domestic sales and rise on distant ones (see equation 8.17). This increases the incentive to export and the associated trade cost burden. Indeed, if no country offered better market access than the other ($\sigma=1/2$), then the operating profits maximizing allocation of firms would mirror the spatial distribution of consumers ($\gamma=\sigma$) as that would minimize trade costs.

Equation 8.19 also reveals that the balance is tilted in favour of market access when a and ϕ are large (given 8.13) as well as when b, c and K are small. Under such circumstances, the elasticities of demand and substitution of a typical variety (see equations 8.4 and 8.5) are both small, thus implying that a large component of operating profits is independent from the overall distribution of firms. In particular, as intuition would have it, in the limit case of monopoly ($c=0$) only market access considerations matter since a firm's operating profits are unrelated to other firms' locations. Finally, the balance between market access and crowding is also affected by the level of trade costs in that access considerations dominate for low trade costs, while crowding concerns are crucial for large trade costs. The reason why is that, with lower trade costs, a larger fraction of operating profits is independent from the overall location of firms.

Solving equation 8.19 for γ, we obtain the equilibrium location of firms:

$$\gamma^M = \sigma + \frac{4a\phi - \tau(2b\phi + cK)}{\tau cK}(2\sigma - 1) \tag{8.20}$$

so that γ^M is always larger than σ whenever $\sigma > 1/2$ and less than 1 whenever τ is larger than

$$\tau_{cluster} \equiv \frac{4a\phi(2\sigma - 1)}{2b\phi(2\sigma - 1) + cK} \tag{8.21}$$

When τ falls short of this threshold, the modern sector is clustered inside country H and country F is completely specialized in the production of the traditional good. Therefore, the incomplete specialization of F is compatible with international trade flows only if $\tau_{trade} > \tau_{cluster}$, that is,

$$\sigma < \frac{1}{2} + \frac{cK}{4(b\phi + cK)} \tag{8.22}$$

which shows that the modern sector is more likely to cluster the larger country H (larger σ), the higher the degree of product differentiation (lower c), the more intense the returns to scale (larger ϕ). When equation 8.22 is violated, trade always leads to complete specialization of the smaller country in the production of the traditional good.

The fact that γ^M is always larger than σ (given $\sigma > 1/2$) reveals the existence of a HME: the larger country H attracts a more than proportionate number of modern firms. In particular, we have:

$$\frac{d\gamma^M}{d\sigma} = \frac{2\phi(2a - \tau b)}{\tau cK} \tag{8.23}$$

which is larger than 1 whenever τ is smaller than:

$$\tau_{HME} \equiv \frac{4a\phi}{2b\phi + cK} \tag{8.24}$$

This is indeed the value of τ that erases the market access advantage in equation 8.19.

Therefore, since $\tau_{HME}=2\tau_{trade}>\tau_{trade}$, *trade is always associated with a HME*. Moreover, by comparing equation 8.24 with equation 8.21, it is easy to notice that τ_{HME} is the maximum value of $\tau_{cluster}$ achieved at $\sigma=1$. Therefore, we have also $\tau_{HME}>\tau_{cluster}$.

The equilibrium capital flow from F to H is:

$$CF_{FH}\equiv(\gamma^M-\sigma)K=\frac{(2\sigma-1)[4a\phi-\tau(2b\phi+cK)]}{2\tau c} \tag{8.25}$$

which is positive given equation 8.13. Of course, this is also a measure of relocation defined as $(\gamma^M-\sigma)N=CF_{FH}/\phi$. By equation 8.25, the extent of relocation is a decreasing function of c as well as K and an increasing function of a as well as ϕ for the same reasons discussed above. Moreover, it is also a decreasing function of τ, implying that capital flows grow as trade costs fall. Interestingly enough, since, as it can be easily shown, the total trade volume is also a decreasing function of τ, the model predicts that foreign direct investment and international trade grow together as economic integration deepens. As a result, the larger country H increasingly exchanges the modern good against the services of both factors. In the case of capital the inflow is direct, while in the case of labour it is embodied in traditional imports.

8.5 THE EFFICIENT OUTCOME

In principle the model has two potential sources of inefficiency. On the one side, for a given spatial distribution γ, when pricing above marginal cost, firms do not take into account the social loss in terms of consumer surplus. On the other, for given prices, when choosing location they do not consider the impact of their decisions on competitors' profits and consumers' surpluses. Notice however that, differently from Dixit and Stiglitz (1977), in the present setting the total number of firms N is always efficient since, as a consequence of equations 8.2 and 8.3, that number is determined by the total endowment of K and the technology parameter ϕ.

Consider initially a *first-best planner* who has enough instruments to eliminate all sources of inefficiency. In other words, assume that the planner is able (1) to assign any number of firms to a specific country and (2) to use lump-sum transfers from workers to pay for the loss firms may incur while pricing at marginal cost. The planner chooses γ in order to maximize the following social welfare function (recall that individual utilities are quasi-linear):

$$W(\gamma)=S_H(\gamma)\sigma L+S_F(\gamma)(1-\sigma)L \\ +r_H(\gamma)\gamma K+r_F(\gamma)(1-\gamma)K+\text{constant} \tag{8.26}$$

which is simply the sum of all workers' indirect utilities and where all prices have been set equal to marginal cost:

$$p_{HH}=p_{FF}=0 \quad \text{and} \quad p_{HF}=p_{FH}=\tau \tag{8.27}$$

The planner actually engages in international trade as long as consumers want to buy foreign varieties (q_{HF}, $q_{FH}>0$), which is the case if and only if trade costs are such that:

$$\tau<\tau^{O}_{trade}\equiv\frac{a\phi}{b\phi+cK} \tag{8.28}$$

Since $\tau^{O}_{trade}<\tau_{trade}$, as in Brander and Krugman (1983), there is a range of relatively large but not prohibitive trade costs in which inefficient commerce takes place at the market outcome due to the dumping behaviour of firms.

Up to a positive multiplicative constant, the first order condition of the planner's problem is:

$$\tau[2a\phi-\tau(b\phi+cK)](\sigma-1/2)-\tau^2cK(\gamma-\sigma)=0 \tag{8.29}$$

Straightforward comparison with equation 8.19 shows that the planner gives less weight to market access than the decentralized outcome. This happens for the following reason. Starting with $\gamma=\sigma>1/2$, as γ rises, the local sales of each firm in H go down while its distant sales go up. The opposite happens to firms in F. However, given $\gamma=\sigma>1/2$, the net result is an increase in aggregate shipments and thus in aggregate trade costs. The fact that the planner internalizes this effect explains why the social weight of market access falls short of the private one.[11]

Solving equation 8.29 in γ yields the first best spatial distribution of firms:

$$\gamma^{O}\equiv\sigma+\frac{(2a\phi-\tau(b\phi+cK)}{\tau cK}(2\sigma-1)>\sigma \tag{8.30}$$

which, under equation 8.28, implies that also the planner delivers a HME by allocating a more than proportionate share of firms in the larger country. However, since clearly $\gamma^{O}<\gamma^{M}$, the market outcome has an inefficiently large number of firms in country H. Moreover, such inefficiency is larger the stronger the decentralized HME: $d\gamma^{O}/d\sigma=(1/2)(d\gamma^{M}/d\sigma)>1$.

While the first-best planner is an interesting benchmark, in reality marginal cost pricing is difficult to implement because of the lack of the lump-sum instruments involved. It is therefore useful to consider the choice of a *second-best planner* who is able to assign any number of modern firms to a specific country but is unable to use lump-sum transfers from workers to firms. In this case, the planner chooses γ in order to maximize equation 8.26 evaluated at market prices in equations 8.9 to 8.12 so that she engages in trade if and only if equation 8.13 holds.

The second-best first order condition is:

$$\tau[8a\phi(3b\phi+cK)-3\tau(2b\phi+cK)^2](\sigma-1/2)-\tau^2cK(8b\phi+3cK)(\gamma-\sigma)=0 \tag{8.31}$$

which implies that, relative to market crowding, market access is overweighed with respect to the first best, and underweighed with respect to the decentralized outcome. As the first-best planner, the second-best one internalizes the adverse trade cost surcharge that additional firms in H impose on local incumbents. However, since under monopolistically competitive pricing firms absorb part of the trade costs ($p_{HF}-p_{HH}<\tau$), the surcharge is smaller than under marginal cost pricing.

Solving equations 8.31 in γ yields the second-best spatial distribution of firms:

$$\gamma^S \equiv \sigma + \frac{8a\phi(3b\phi+cK)-3\tau(2b\phi+cK)^2}{2\tau cK(8b\phi+3cK)}(2\sigma-1) \tag{8.32}$$

which, given equation 8.13, implies that also the second-best planner delivers a HME. In particular, we have $d\gamma^S/d\sigma=[(6b\phi+2cK)/(8b\phi+3cK)](d\gamma^M/d\sigma)$ so that $d\gamma^M/d\sigma>d\gamma^S/d\sigma>d\gamma^O/d\sigma>1$.

By simple inspection $\gamma^S<\gamma^M$ with

$$\gamma^M-\gamma^S=\frac{\phi(2a-\tau b)(2b\phi+cK)(2\sigma-1)}{\tau cK(8b\phi+3cK)}>0 \tag{8.33}$$

so that the market outcome leads to too much concentration also with respect to the second-best allocation; the more so the stronger the HME. It is also readily verified that $\gamma^O<\gamma^S$ with:

$$\gamma^S-\gamma^O=\frac{\phi(2a-\tau b)(4b\phi+cK)(2\sigma-1)}{2\tau cK(8b\phi+3cK)}>0 \tag{8.34}$$

This suggests that both sources of inefficiency work in the same direction by supporting a spatial distribution of firms that is too uneven. Notice also that $(\gamma^S - \gamma^O) < (\gamma^M - \gamma^S)$ so that the second best is closer to the first best than to the market outcome. Finally, the discrepancies between γ^M, γ^S, and γ^O grow as τ falls: *economic integration widens the gap between market and efficient outcomes.*

8.6 POLICY IMPLICATIONS

How can a policy-maker implement the efficient spatial distribution of firms? Are EU policies going in the right direction? To answer these questions we have to consider once more the logic of the model. For concreteness, we target the second-best allocation.

Modern firms' location is determined by capital owners decisions on the provision of their services. These decisions are guided by the differential between the returns to capital in the two countries, $[r_H(\gamma^S) - r_F(\gamma^S)]$. Since such differential decreases with γ (see equation 8.17) being zero at γ^M and γ^S is smaller than γ^M, then it must be that $[r_H(\gamma^S) - r_F(\gamma^S)] > 0$, that is, at γ^S there is a positive gap between capital returns in the larger country H and in the smaller country F. Any policy tool that is able to fill in that gap will achieve the second best.

The related gain in terms of overall welfare will be:

$$W(\gamma^S) - W(\gamma^M) = \frac{(2\sigma - 1)^2 (2a - \tau b)^2 (b\phi + cK)L}{8c(8b\phi + 3cK)} \tag{8.35}$$

which increases as the level of trade costs falls. In other words, *economic integration increases the welfare loss due to the inefficient spatial distribution of firms at the market outcome.*

With the practices of the EU in mind, we consider an investment subsidy to the fixed costs of firms in F levied through income taxation.[12] Let s^* be the *optimal investment subsidy* per unit of capital invested in F. Then, s^* is such that $[r_H(\gamma^S) - r_F(\gamma^S) - s^*] = 0$ implying:

$$s^* = \frac{\tau L(2a - \tau b)(b\phi + cK)(2\sigma - 1)}{2\phi(8b\phi + 3cK)} \tag{8.36}$$

This shows that the optimal subsidy is an increasing function of the trade costs τ (since equation 8.13 holds), the total capital stock K, the substitutability between varieties c, while it is a decreasing function of the intensity of returns to scale ϕ. Consequently, as trade costs fall, the optimal subsidy shrinks: *as countries get more integrated*, the overall welfare loss due to the inefficient distribution of modern firms rises but, at the same time, *the amount of international redistribution needed to restore efficiency falls.* The explanation is that, as trade cost falls, firms become increasingly footloose. While, on the one hand, this fosters their inefficient concentration in the larger country, on the other, it makes them more sensitive to any differential in subsidies.[13] The same effects are associated with falling c and rising ϕ.

8.7 CONCLUSION

A distinguishing feature of new trade models is the so-called home market effect, that is, in the case of two countries, the more than proportionate location of imperfectly competitive increasing-return sectors in the larger country. However, despite its centrality and the distortions at its origin, so far the home market effect has attracted surprisingly little attention in terms of its global welfare implications.

This chapter represents a first step in the direction of filling that gap. Using a simple new trade model, it has shown that sectors characterized by increasing returns to scale and imperfect competition tend to be inefficiently over-concentrated in the larger country, the more so the lower trade costs are. This implies that, in the process of integration, the demand for active policy intervention to reduce economic disparities between large ('central') countries and small ('peripheral') ones may stand not only on equity, but also on efficiency grounds. However, industry-specific characteristics are likely to determine the practical relevance of spatial inefficiency. Accordingly, and different from current EU practice, regional policies should be targeted not only to specific peripheral regions but also to specific sectors characterized by steeply increasing returns to scale and strong firms' market power.

Stemming from a first attempt, these results are obviously preliminary and should be qualified by studying more general models of the HME. As discussed in the introduction, in the wake of existing results, such models should be built on two main pillars. First, the HME is essentially a partial equilibrium phenomenon that might be washed away by general equilibrium interactions. Consequently, one should focus on a sector insulated from the rest of the economy. Second, the HME can be defined only when countries differ in nothing but market access. So far, in the absence of a benchmark measure of market access with many countries, one should concentrate on a two-country economy where market access is simply captured by local market size.

APPENDIX

The aim of this appendix is to show that the essence of the reason why the first best planner delivers a HME is trade costs minimization.[14] Accordingly, consider the problem of minimizing aggregate trade costs under marginal cost pricing ($p_{HH}=p_{FF}=0$, $p_{HF}=p_{FH}=\tau$):

$$\min_{\gamma} \tau[q_{FH}(1-\gamma)\sigma + q_{HF}\gamma(1-\sigma)] \tag{A1}$$

where, given equations 8.4 and 8.5, quantities shipped are:

$$q_{FH}=a-(b+cN)p_{FH}+cN[\gamma p_{HH}+(1-\gamma)p_{FH}]=a-(b+cN)\tau+\tau c(1-\gamma)N \tag{A2}$$

$$q_{HF}=a-(b+cN)p_{HF}+cN[\gamma p_{HF}+(1-\gamma)p_{FF}]=a-(b+cN)\tau+\tau c\gamma N \tag{A3}$$

Thus, after substitution of (A2) and (A3), (A1) can be rewritten as:

$$\min_{\gamma} \tau\{[a-\tau(b+cN)][(1-\gamma)\sigma+\gamma(1-\sigma)]+\tau cN[(1-\gamma)^2\sigma+\gamma^2(1-\sigma)]\} \tag{A4}$$

where the first term inside the curly brackets refers to the spatial distribution of the component of individual import demands that is common to all consumers no matter where they reside. The associated trade costs are clearly minimized when all firms are located in the bigger region (whenever trade costs are low enough to allow for trade). As to the second term inside the curly brackets, it concerns the spatial distribution of the component of individual import demands that depends on the location of firms. This is a convex function of γ with a minimum at $\gamma=\sigma$.

The corresponding necessary condition for minimization is:

$$\tau\,[a\phi-\tau(b\phi+cK)](\sigma-1/2)-\tau^2 cK(\gamma-\sigma)=0 \tag{A5}$$

where we have used the fact that $N=K/\phi$. Condition (A5) shows that trade costs minimization gives less weight to market access than the first best outcome. It can be readily solved in γ to yield

$$\gamma^T=\sigma+\frac{[a\phi-\tau(b\phi+cK)]}{2\tau cK}(2\sigma-1)>\sigma \tag{A6}$$

where the inequality is granted by equation 8.28.

Expression (A6) implies the existence of a HME:

$$\frac{d\gamma^T}{d\sigma} = \frac{\phi(a - \tau b)}{\tau c K} > 1 \tag{A7}$$

which is, however, less pronounced than in the first best case ($\gamma^O > \gamma^T$) as it can be readily verified by comparing (A6) with equation 8.3.

Given previous discussions, the HME is entirely driven by the minimization of trade costs associated with the component of individual import demands that is common to all consumers no matter where they reside.

ACKNOWLEDGEMENTS

I am indebted to seminar participants at University of Bologna Centre in Buenos Aires, University of Milan Bicocca, Catholic University Milan, HWWA Hamburg, NHH Bergen, ERWIT2001 London, as well as CEPR/RTN Workshop on 'The Economic Geography of Europe' in Villars for comments on earlier drafts. In particular, I wish to thank Fabrizio Barca, André Sapir and Jacques Thisse for discussions on policy implications, as well as Gabriele Tondl and Thierry Mayer for the provision of relevant data. Financial support from Bocconi University, University of Bologna, HWWA and the European Commission is gratefully acknowledged.

NOTES

1. Notice that, as a consequence, with more than three countries, it is not even clear the benchmark against which to measure the local presence of imperfectly competitive firms. In other words, 'more than proportionate' with respect to what?
2. This implication derives even more strongly from 'new economic geography' models (Fujita, Krugman and Venables, 1999), which show that, in the presence of demand and cost linkages between factors and firms, the HME can be powerful enough to cause catastrophic agglomeration of imperfectly competitive increasing-return sectors once trade costs fall below a certain threshold.
3. While finding supportive evidence for the HME, Head and Mayer (forthcoming) stress the overall better empirical performance of an alternative theoretical explanation grounded on country-based product differentiation (the so-called Armington model). Head, Mayer and Ries (2000) clarify the relation between such model and the HME.
4. See, also, Trionfetti (1998) as well as Head, Mayer and Ries (2000) for recent surveys.
5. In Figure 8.1 the chosen measure of the peripherality of a country is the distance of its capital city from the capital of Germany (the large central country). Such measure is admittedly rough, but more sophisticated indexes would not alter the basic centre-periphery pattern revealed by the picture. Population coverage refers to Objective 1 (regions suffering general underdevelopment as signalled by per capita incomes below 75 per cent of the EU average) plus Objective 2 (regions suffering from a concentration

of declining industries as measured by observable job losses in specific sectors). The source of data is European Commission (2001a).
6. Note that, generally speaking, the European Commission rules out any form of operating aid to firms.
7. The measure of the peripherality is the same as in Figure 8.1. The state aid cap of a country is selected as the highest regional state aid cap within that country. The source of data is European Commission (2001b).
8. Such a pattern cannot but be enhanced by the EU prospective enlargement towards the East. Indeed, the Europe agreements already allow all ten Central European and Baltic countries to define their entire territories as less favoured regions (Objective 1).
9. The model adopted reproduces the basic features of Dixit and Stiglitz (1977) using different functional forms. As discussed in Ottaviano, Tabuchi and Thisse (2002), compared with the standard CES implementation of Dixit and Stiglitz's insights, the present model's comparative advantage lies in neater comparative statics results and more straightfoward welfare analysis with heterogenous agents.
10. Since $r_H(\gamma)$ is decreasing while $r_F(\gamma)$ is increasing in γ, if they cross, they do so only once.
11. The appendix solves the trade costs minimization problem to argue that transport saving is indeed the driving force behind the HME. That is why some degree of HME is always optimal.
12. Given quasi-linear utility and workers' ownership of capital, the exact way income taxes are raised is immaterial in so far as we think in terms of a net investment subsidy.
13. One may wonder, then, why the EU regional budget has been growing through time? The answer is ongoing enlargement. In the present model, the simplest way to capture the joint phenomena of deeper integration between old central members and additional inclusion of new peripheral ones is to have σ rising (the centre grows) and τ rising (the periphery gets more distant) at the same time. On both counts, by equation 8.36, the optimal subsidy rises.
14. Indeed, in the present setting, since marginal costs are zero, trade costs minimization is equivalent to total costs minimization.

REFERENCES

Brander, J.A. (1995) 'Strategic trade policy', in G.M. Grossman and K. Rogoff (eds.), *Handbook of International Economics*, vol. 3, Amsterdam: North Holland.
Brander, J.A. and P.R. Krugman (1983), 'A reciprocal dumping model of international trade', *Journal of International Economics*, **15**, 313–23.
Brander, J.A. and B.J. Spencer (1984), 'Tariff protection and imperfect competition', in H. Kierzkowski (ed.), *Monopolistic Competition and International Trade*, Oxford: Oxford University Press.
Braunerhjelm, P., R. Faini, V. Norman, F. Ruane and P. Seabright (2000), *Integration and Regions in Europe: How the Right Policies Can Prevent Polarization*, Monitoring European Integration 10, London: Centre for Economic Policy Research.
Brülhart, M. and F. Trionfetti (2001), 'Industrial structure and public procurement: theory and empirical evidence', *Journal of Economic Integration*, **16**, 106–27.
Davis D.R. (1998), 'The home market effect, trade, and industrial structure, *American Economic Review*, **88**, 1264–76.
Davis D.R. and D.E. Weinstein (1998), 'Market access, economic geography and comparative advantage: an empirical assessment', NBER Working Paper No. 6787.
Davis D.R. and D.E. Weinstein (1999), 'Economic geography and regional produc-

tion structure: an empirical investigation', *European Economic Review*, **43**, 379–407.
Dixit, A.K. and J.E. Stiglitz (1977), 'Monopolistic competition and optimum product diversity', *American Economic Review*, **67**, 297–308.
European Commission (1995), Free movement of people, *DGX European Dialogue*, 1.
European Commission (2001a), *Regional State Aid Map 1999*, DG Competition, http://europa.eu.int/comm/competition.
European Commision (2001b), *EU Structural Funds 2000–2006*, DG Employment and Social Affairs, http://europa.eu.int/comm/employment social.
Feenstra R.C., J.R. Markusen and A.K. Rose (1998), 'Understanding the home market effect and the gravity equation: the role of differentiated goods', CEPR Discussion Paper No. 2035.
Feenstra R.C., J.R. Markusen and A.K. Rose (2001), 'Using the gravity equation to differentiate between alternative models of trade', *Canadian Journal of Economics*, **34**, 430–47.
Fujita, M., P. Krugman and A.J. Venables (1999). *The Spatial Economy. Cities, Regions and International Trade*, Cambridge, MA: MIT Press.
Head, K. and T. Mayer (2000), 'Non-Europe. The magnitude and causes of market fragmentation in the EU', *Weltwirtschaftliches Archiv*, **136**, 285–314.
Head, K. and J. Ries (forthcoming), 'Increasing returns versus national product differentiation as an explanation for the pattern of US–Canada trade, *American Economic Review*.
Head, K., T. Mayer and J. Ries (2000), 'On the pervasiveness of the home market effect', *Economica*, **69**, 371–90.
Helpman, E. (1990), 'Monopolistic competition in trade theory', *Special Paper in International Economics*, **16**, Princeton University, International Finance Section.
Helpman, E. and P.R. Krugman (1985), *Market Structure and Foreign Trade*, Cambridge, MA: MIT Press.
Helpman, E. and P.R. Krugman (1989), *Trade Policy and Market Structure*, Cambridge, MA: MIT Press.
Krugman, P.R. (1980), 'Scale economies, product differentiation, and the pattern of trade', *American Economic Review*, **70**, 950–59.
Krugman, P.R. (1993) 'The hub effect: or, threeness in international trade', in W.J. Ethier, E. Helpman and J.P. Neary (eds), *Theory, Policy and Dynamics in International Trade*, Cambridge: Cambridge University Press.
McCallum, J. (1995), 'National borders matter: Canada–US regional trade patterns', *American Economic Review*, **85**, 615–23.
Midelfart-Knarvik, K.H., H.G. Overman, S.J. Redding and A.J. Venables (2000), 'The location of European industry', European Commission, DG Economic and Financial Affairs, Economic Paper No. 142.
Ottaviano, G.I.P. and J.-F. Thisse (2002). 'Integration, agglomeration and the political economics of factor mobility', *Journal of Public Economics*, **83**, 429–56.
Ottaviano, G.I.P., T. Tabuchi and J.-F. Thisse (2002), 'Agglomeration and trade revisited', *International Economic Review*, **43**, 409–43.
Trionfetti, F. (1998), 'On the home market effect: theory and empirical evidence', CEP Working Paper No. 987, London School of Economics.
Weder, R. (1997) 'British and American exports: an empirical analysis of comparative home-market advantage', University of British Columbia, mimeo.

9. Empirical evidence on the strategic behaviour of US MNEs within the framework of dynamic differentiated networks

Fragkiskos Filippaios, Constantina Kottaridi, Marina Papanastassiou and Robert Pearce

9.1 INTRODUCTION

One of the seminal contributions towards a realistic understanding of the global economy of the past half-century belongs to Hymer (1960) who challenged the existing theories of foreign direct investment (FDI)[1] with his empirical analysis. The main claim of these theories was that FDI would flow from capital abundant, and hence low rate of return on capital, countries, to capital poor, thus high rate of return countries. According to this argument FDI would be expected to flow mainly from developed to developing countries on the one hand, while on the other hand most countries would be almost exclusively either exporters or recipients of FDI capital. What Hymer demonstrated with his investigation of the immediate post-war period was that FDI was a two-way flow among advanced economies and that most countries (even the USA) were both recipients and providers of FDI capital. An exclusively macro-level theory of FDI as being determined only by relative capital availability seemed inadequate.

Conceptual thinking in explaining this newly observed behaviour added two new elements in the relevant literature. First, that firms carrying out FDI were doing so not just by being motivated by capital considerations, but also as a way of utilizing more effectively other, more firm-specific, sources of competitiveness (technology, marketing and managerial expertise). Secondly, those foreign investors were often making their decisions within a strategic context in response to competitive needs determined by industry structure[2] (that is, by the capabilities and behaviour of other firms). This latter point gave rise to two alternative strands. Hymer himself considered international expansion of national firms as a means of extending the horizons of, competition-suppressing, collusion or cartelization.

Other analysis (Knickerbocker, 1973; Vernon, 1974; Flowers, 1976; Graham, 1978) saw it as a competitive response within industries that were becoming internationalized oligopolies.[3]

One very considerable area of investigation that can be seen to derive from Hymer's critique moved the perspective to the micro-level analysis of the agents that carry out FDI (that is, the multinational enterprise [MNE]). An alternative has sought to retain a predominantly macro-level focus on FDI as reflecting inter-country differences but to broaden the framework in order to encompass a greater range of factors that could determine firm behaviour.[4] The purpose of the present chapter is to formalize important implicit complementarities between these two strands of literature. Thus we retain the view that any meaningful modelling of FDI needs realistically to reflect the decision processes of MNEs. Further we suggest that one enlightening way of categorizing these decision-making processes is by embodying some mix of a set of strategic imperatives. The way in which the mix of strategic motivations varies between individual FDI decisions is likely to reflect the characteristics of attracting potentials in particular host countries, which then leads our approach back to the concerns and variables embodied in much of recent mainstream FDI analysis.

The next section introduces the background in terms of strategic aims of MNEs, while section 9.3 states the hypotheses and the independent variables tested. Section 9.4 describes the datasets and sources along with the statistical methodology adopted. Section 9.5 then presents and interprets the results and, finally, section 9.6 presents the conclusions drawn from the previous analysis.

9.2 CONCEPTUAL FRAMEWORK

This chapter models FDI as indicating patterns in the strategic expansion of MNEs' operations as they approach globalized competition through organizational structures configured as 'dynamic differentiated networks'. Thus at a point in time an MNE's competitive posture is activated through a range of different *types* of subsidiaries addressing different facets of its strategic needs.[5] Across time this network is subject to continual expansion (new operations) and restructuring (changing roles of existing subsidiaries) as competitive needs alter and the potentials of different host countries develop (or are reinterpreted).[6] Here a tripartite typology of strategic imperatives or motivations[7] for FDI is adopted with the hypothesizing in the next section relating these to particular aspects of potential host countries.

Market seeking (MS) refers to production within a country with the objective of supplying the local market or/and a broader region in which this market belongs.[8] Two distinct elements condition the choice of MS operations in a country. The first states that the target market should be a worthwhile (that is, currently or potentially significantly profitable) part of the firm's logical competitive environment, while the second refers to the reasons for which local production rather than trade is a preferable way of servicing the market. The historical prevalence of MS activity (MNEs operating through what Porter [1986] terms a multi-domestic strategy), as many companies made their initial international expansions, was attributed primarily to the existence of high trade protection.[9] A notable residual persistence of an MS motive in MNEs' operations (despite sustained and significant lowering of trade restraints) may be due to a more positive element of this imperative. This takes the form of local responsiveness, reflecting benefits believed to accrue from reacting to (or, indeed, learning from) distinctive elements of local tastes and market conditions (for example, regulations) through product (or process) adaptation.

Although falling barriers to international transactions have weakened the MS motivation in what is regarded as its original emergence, this has often been a co-option within the framework of a second strategic imperative taking the form of efficiency seeking (ES). This involves relocation of production of specific existing goods to a particular country aiming at sharpening the cost-efficiency of their manufacture in order to enhance (or defend) MNEs' competitiveness in those (usually higher-income) markets where they are already well established. Compared to the multi-domestic context of MS subsidiaries, such export-oriented ES activities indicate the emergence of more interdependent global strategies and manifest one aspect of the modern MNE as a differentiated network.

Both MS and ES represent ways in which MNEs seek to enhance the benefits they can secure from their mature competitive technologies as embodied in successful established products. By contrast our third strategic motivation, knowledge seeking (KS), relates to the internationalization of the ways in which these companies pursue the medium- and long-term regeneration of their competitive scope. This reflects a second development (alongside freer trade) that has conditioned the strategic evolution of globally competing enterprises, that is, the greatly increased dispersion of the sources from which they can acquire key inputs into their creative/learning processes (market heterogeneity and technological heterogeneity [Papanastassiou and Pearce, 1999]). Of the variety of ways in which MNEs exercise the KS motivation (in effect involve themselves within the national system of innovation [Lundvall, 1992; Nelson, 1993] of their host countries), localized product development[10] is the one most likely to be reflected in the FDI flows analysed here.

9.3 UNDERLYING HYPOTHESES

The hypotheses relating to MNEs' broad strategic motivations to the location of US FDI involve our seven indicators outlined below.

1. Gross domestic product (*GDP*): the most widely tested hypothesis of MS behaviour in previous studies of FDI determinants has been the direct relationship between the current size (*GDP*) of a country's national market and new investments by MNEs (Culem, 1988; Veugelers, 1991; Wheeler and Mody, 1992; Barrell and Pain, 1996a; Braunerhjelm and Svenson, 1996). This direct relationship between FDI and market size is endorsed within the modelling here. In addition to that, an indirect supplement to the hypothesis argues that larger host markets are more appealing to potential investors as economies of scale are more likely to be captured in local production (Krugman, 1980; Amiti, 1998) so that the option of supply through trade (other constraints on trade assumed constant) is more readily foregone.
2. GDP growth rate (*GDPGR*): alongside the absolute measure of market size, annual growth rates, assumed to represent long-term strategic commitments by MNEs[11] (Culem, 1988; Kobrin, 1979; Veugelers, 1991), complement, in effect, our testing of MS investments. However, *GDPGR* is intended here to reflect a specific aspect of the decision-making process relating to MS, by suggesting that short-term growth rates are read as signals that indicate the strategic potentials of economies and thus determine the location and timing of this element of MNE expansion.
3. Income levels (*GDPPC*): while *GDP* reflects the absolute size of national markets, GDP per capita seeks to test other aspects of MS motivation through a more qualitative characterization of these markets. A traditional mode of hypothesizing here (consonant with trade theories derived from the work of Linder, 1961; McPherson, Redfearn and Tieslau, 2000) perceives products as generated in the home country of the MNE (here the USA) and then marketed successfully in similar economies. This provides the basis for a positive relationship between FDI and *GDPPC* (that is, the richer the host country the more likely it will assimilate US firms' goods). An alternative argument may, however, derive from recent work on the willingness of MNEs to respond competitively to host-country differences. Thus it may be that the more different a country's *GDPPC* from that of the USA (given a sufficiently high GDP or perceived growth potential) the greater the benefits of internal supply (FDI rather than trade) in order to respond to local needs through adapted or newly developed products. With the

US GDPPC near the top of the OECD countries covered, this points to the alternative hypothesis of a negative relationship between this variable and US FDI.

4. Competitiveness (*COMP*): that is, exports divided by exports plus imports. This variable serves as an indicator of a country's current status in terms of international trade competitiveness. Within the context of purely ES behaviour, therefore, we can hypothesize that US firms will respond positively to *COMP* as a measure of a country's revealed capacity to support investments that are aimed at competitiveness in wider markets. However, in contexts where countries have become increasingly part of free-trade situations (Europe in the present analysis, most countries of which form the EU), *COMP* may also come to reflect the more widely conceived dimension of MS. Thus increasingly new US FDI in Europe (also that by Japanese and other Asian MNEs) may be perceived as initially primarily MS-oriented (perhaps reflecting a fear of 'fortress Europe') but with *COMP* then operating within this decision-making process by influencing where in the free-trade area an investment targeting the whole region is most effectively located.
5. Unit labour costs (*ULC*): *ULC* comprise a very precise element of ES behaviour under the hypothesis of a negative relationship with FDI. As many of the industries or stages in production processes that are most strongly associated with the presence of an ES motivation remain relatively labour intensive, the potential savings in this input can represent a strongly important element for undertaking FDI. Besides that, *ULC* may also function as a quantitative measure that is fairly easily compared (across countries and through time) and as such may serve as a broader indicator of labour-market conditions (including regulatory environment) or cost circumstances generally. Labour costs and productivity have a pervasive presence in FDI analyses (Cushman, 1987; Culem, 1988; Veugelers, 1991; Wheeler and Mody, 1992; Barrell and Pain, 1996; 1999a, 1999b).
6. R&D employment (*RDEMPL*): serves as an input measure of a country's ability to support the KS motivation in MNEs' strategic development. Thus the degree of commitment to the education and training of scientific personnel suggests a country's ability to provide sustained support to MNEs' knowledge-creation and product-development aims. *RDEMPL* may also serve as an indicator of the likelihood of a country's science-base producing the types of new technology which MNEs position their KS investments (product mandate subsidiaries and independent R&D laboratories) to monitor and tap into.

7. Patenting (*NPAGDP*): that is, national patent applications normalized by GDP. Related to the knowledge-seeking behaviour of firms, the patents of a country provide an output measure of the current knowledge generation capacity of an economy, as manifest in patentable scientific results. In a manner that can be associated with the forces of agglomeration and science-oriented clustering, it can be suggested that MNEs will seek to position KS FDI within economies, which demonstrates established and ongoing trajectories of scientific creativity and technology generation. Kogut and Chang (1991) and Neven and Siotis (1996) initiated the investigation of R&D intensity as not only a factor underpinning the ability of firms to compete internationally, but as an element in countries' ability to attract MNEs' investments. The analysis of agglomeration factors in attracting FDI (Wheeler and Mody, 1992; Head, Ries and Swenson, 1995; Braunerhjelm and Svensson, 1996; Barrell and Pain, 1999a) often embodies the implications of R&D spillovers and knowledge-related learning processes.

Consequently the model we incorporate takes the following form according to the hypotheses analysed above:

$$FDI_{it} = a_0 + a_1 GDP_{it} + a_2 GDPGR_{it} + a_3 GDPPC_{it} + a_4 COMP_{it} + a_5 ULC_{it} + a_6 RDEMP_{it} + a_7 NPAGDP_{it} + \mu_i + \varepsilon_{it} \quad (9.1)$$

Where $i = 1,\ldots, 28$ represents country i, $t = 1982,\ldots,1997$ represents time, μ_i are the fixed-effects and ε_{it} is the error term.

9.4 DATA AND METHODOLOGY

Our sample of countries hosting US FDI covers the 28 OECD members during the last two decades, that is, from the early 1980s (1982) to the later 1990s (1997). The extended time span and country coverage allowed comparative testing of selected sub-samples. In terms of time periods, we separate the 1980s (1982–89) from the 1990s (1990–97). This permits the detection of strategic development in MNEs as reflected in a changing balance of motivations and therefore in attracting host-country characteristics. Furthermore, in order to better understand differing MNE strategies, as implemented in variegated contexts, we divided the full OECD sample into two sub-groups, that is, a European countries group[12] and a non-European group. Data was compiled from various issues of a number of OECD publications including the *Main Economic Indicators*, *Main Science and Technology Indicators*, *International Direct Investment Statistics*

Yearbook and a database in electronic format, the *OECD Statistical Compendium*. This range of publications and databases facilitated the coverage of the relevant economic variables and the valuably extended time frame (for all OECD countries during their period of membership).

The dependent variable tested in the analysis is annual US direct investment flows to individual OECD countries, from the *International Investment Statistics Yearbook*. The independent variables used and the hypotheses relating to them are introduced in section 9.4.[13]

In order to allow for specific country unobserved characteristics, that is, industrial, cultural and so on, the study used the fixed effects panel estimation technique. The value of the dependent variable (here US FDI flows) for the ith unit at time t, y_{it}, depends on K exogenous variables $(x_{Ait},\ldots,x_{Kit}) = x'_{it}$ that differ among individuals in a cross-section at a given point of time and also exhibit variation through time.

The general form of the model is

$$y_{it} = \alpha_i + \beta' X_{it} + u_{it} \tag{9.2}$$

where $i = 1,\ldots,$ n represents the member countries of the OECD participating in the sample and $t = 1,\ldots,$ t (covering the relevant time period).

β' is a $1 \times k$ vector of coefficients constant over time and α_i is a 1×1 scalar constant representing the effects of those variables peculiar to the ith individual in the same fashion over time.

We formulate the error term u_{it} in a way that represents the effects of the omitted variables that are specific to both the individual units and time. We moreover assume that u_{it} is an independently identically distributed random variable with

$E(u_{it}) = 0$
$E(u_{it}u'_{it}) = \sigma_u^2 I_T$ where I_t is a $T \times T$ identity matrix.
$E(u_i u_j) = 0$ if $i \neq j$

The ordinary least squares (OLS) is the best linear unbiased estimator (BLUE).

Finally, testing for unit roots in panels is relatively recent. We nevertheless applied the Im, Pesaran and Shin (1997) test (IPS). We used this test for two reasons. First, it allows for heterogeneity across the individual i's and secondly overall the IPS t-bar test has the most stable size (Choi and Ahn, 1999). More precisely the test is constructed as follows:

Consider the model:

$$y_{it} = \rho_i y_{it-1} = z'_{it}\gamma + u_{it},\ i = 1,...,N; t = 1,...,T \qquad (9.3)$$

where z_{it} is the fixed effects and

$$u_{it} = \sum_{j=1}^{p_i} \phi_{ij} u_{it-j} + \varepsilon_{it} \qquad (9.4)$$

which means that u_{it} are serially correlated with different serial correlation properties across cross-sectional units. We combine the two equations (9.3) and (9.4) and we get:

$$y_{it} = \rho_i y_{it-1} + \sum_{j=1}^{p_i} \phi_{ij} \Delta y_{it-j} + z'_{it}\gamma + \varepsilon_{it} \qquad (9.5)$$

The null hypothesis is $H_0 : \rho_i = 1$

For all *i* and the alternative is $H_\alpha : \rho_i = <1$ for at least one *i*. The IPS t-bar statistic is defined as the average of the individual Augmented Dickey Fuller (ADF) statistic as:

$$\bar{t} = \frac{1}{N} \sum_{i=1}^{N} t_{\rho_i} \qquad (9.6)$$

where t_{ρ_i} is the individual t-statistic of testing the H_0 in equation 9.5. Using some manipulation[14] we get that:

$$t_{IPS} = \frac{\sqrt{N}(\bar{t} - E[t_{iT} | \rho_i = 1])}{\sqrt{Var[t_{iT} | \rho_i = 1]}} \Rightarrow N(0,1) \qquad (9.7)$$

The values for $E[t_{iT} | \rho_i = 1]$ and $Var[t_{iT} | \rho_i = 1]$ have been computed by IPS using simulations techniques for different values of T and p_is. The results of the IPS test are presented in Table 9.1 and show no evidence of the existence of a unit root.

Finally concerning the validity of breaking up the sample into the selected time and country sub-samples, we carried out Chow tests, the results of which support our distinction (Table 9.2).

Table 9.1 Im, Pesaran, Shin unit root test

Series	Lags	t-bar	Psi (t-bar)	Prob. Value	Obs
FDI	2	−0.982	2.220	0.013	318
GDP	2	−0.552	4.360	0.000	366
GDPGR	1	−2.890	−7.035	0.000	363
GDPPC	2	−0.527	4.486	0.000	366
COMP	2	−1.809	−1.897	0.029	366
ULC	2	5.442	34.188	0.000	356
RDEMP	2	−0.665	3.799	0.000	366
NPAGDP	2	1.774	15.937	0.000	342

Notes:
The lag length was selected in order to eliminate the existence of autocorrelation in the residuals. Prob. Value refers to the probability of accepting the existence of a unit root in the series.

Table 9.2 Chow tests (F-statistic) for structural breaks in the sample

F-test of equality in equations (time dimension)	
	F-statistic
FULL	495.64
EUROPE	330.95
NON-EUROPE	143.88
F-test of equality in equations (regional dimension)	
	F-statistic
EUROPE vs NON-EUROPE	373.70

Note: The null hypothesis is that of no structural break in the sample.

9.5 RESULTS AND INTERPRETATION

OECD Sample[15] and Sub-samples, Full Period 1982–97

All three regressions in Table 9.3 cover the full period 1982–97, first for all OECD countries and then for its European and non-European subsets. Among the three potential driving forces of MS investments, *GDPPC* is the one that emerges as consistently significantly positive in these regressions. By contrast we observe a high positive significance for the absolute measure of the market, *GDP*, in the Europe sample, whilst this turns out to be negative – but not significant – for non-Europe. On the other hand, *GDPGR*

Table 9.3 Econometric results for the full sample, Europe and non-Europe OECD, with US FDI flows as dependent variable

	Full sample	Europe	Non-Europe
GDP	0.490	3.553***	−0.932
	(1.28)	(3.35)	(−1.07)
GDPGR	−0.527	−50.936	110.219
	(−0.01)	(−0.64)	(1.47)
GDPPC	0.103***	0.071***	0.1614957*
	(4.66)	(3.14)	(1.60)
COMP	−3.704	8.609*	−10.406***
	(−1.23)	(1.73)	(−3.40)
ULC	−0.046*	−2.577***	−0.057
	(−1.92)	(−2.55)	(−1.47)
RDEMP	−3.778	−15.153	13.925**
	(−0.69)	(−1.59)	(2.45)
NPAGDP	−0.211	0.399	1.657
	(−1.21)	(1.50)	(0.65)
C	1857.851	−7054.418**	2680.9
	(1.25)	(−2.41)	(1.57)
R-square	0.1069	0.174	0.199
F-statistic	6.34***	8.05***	3.46***
Sigma_u	1717.53	1716.43	1531.165
Sigma_e	2200.82	2337.81	1421.09
Rho	0.378	0.350	0.537
Obs.	405	294	111
N. of groups	27	20	7

Notes:
t-statistics are in parenthesis, with ***, ** and * denoting significance at the 1 per cent, 5 per cent and 10 per cent level.
Fixed-effects estimation with robust standard errors. The fixed effects accompanied with an F-test for their significance can be found in Appendix 9.2.
An unbalanced panel fixed effects estimator was used to correct for the missing observations before 1990, for the three Eastern European countries.

does not appear to comprise an important factor, though the positive sign for non-Europe may mirror its negative one for *GDP* by suggesting that while current absolute GDP does not yet determine MS FDI in these countries (overlapping tastes being more relevant), their growth rates may be emerging as indicators of new mass-market potential and thus betoken more influence for GDP.

Turning to our two measures of the ES imperative we obtain interesting results with the significant negative sign on *COMP* for the non-Europe sample and the positive one for the Europe sample. This would suggest that the factors that determine national trade competitiveness across the former group of countries actually tend to alienate US FDI. By contrast combining the positive sign of *COMP* and the stimulating negative one of *ULC* for Europe indicates a conventional short-term ES behaviour.

Of the KS measures *NPAGDP* does not appear to exert any significant influence in our samples, while it seems that it is the input version *RDEMPL* that impinges more on FDI decisions. Bearing in mind the absence of ES response to current sources of competitiveness for the non-Europe sample, the significant role of *RDEMPL* suggests that US foreign investors are attracted by the creative potential of an economy's commitment to generation of scientific capability. By contrast and very speculatively the negative – though non-significant – sign on *RDEMPL* in the Europe sample may mirror the suggestion of conventional ES motivation there. Thus, it may be that higher levels of *RDEMPL* may be perceived as targeting forward-looking creative aims that offset strident current cost-competitiveness in national strategy and, thereby, alienate US MNEs that are mainly pursuing immediate ES objectives.

OECD Sample and Sub-samples, Sub-periods 1982–89 and 1990–97

The tests reported in Table 9.3 for the full time span of 1982–97 reflect the FDI evolution of US MNEs through a period where most of these firms will already have adopted global strategies based around a mix of competitive aims and behaviour patterns. Nevertheless, rapid developments in the international setting may have induced a change in this mix both due to exogenous factors (the location characteristics of current or potential host countries) or endogenous ones (increased or decreased, willingness or capability to embrace particular types of dispersed strategic behaviour). Thus it is plausible to detect strategic modifications and reorientations in US MNEs' investment decisions during this period, especially in the two decades of 1980s and 1990s. Therefore, dividing our sample into two sub-periods, namely 1982–89 and 1990–97, is an effective way to deepen our understanding of the strategic motivation of US MNEs. Table 9.4 reports regression results for the OECD sample and its Europe and non-Europe subsets. A notable observation here is that for all our samples the regressions are less successful for 1990–97 than for 1982–89.

Under the presence of an ongoing degree of globalization with the accompanying intensification of competition and the dramatic increase of technology and created assets as core competencies, especially in the last decade, this phenomenon comes to confirm our claim of the existence of strategic restructuring (in terms of location influences on FDI). It may be argued, therefore, that US MNEs had not (in the early 1990s) settled into

Table 9.4 Econometric results for time-divided full sample, Europe and non-Europe OECD, with US FDI flows as dependent variable

	Full sample		Europe		Non-Europe	
	1982–89	1990–97	1982–89	1990–97	1982–89	1990–97
GDP	0.733	1.731	3.124*	6.018	−0.833	1.205*
	(1.48)	(1.50)	(1.76)	(1.48)	(−1.29)	(1.77)
GDPGR	30.426	40.944	4.006	−21.287	113.00***	246.847*
	(0.80)	(0.33)	(0.09)	(−0.15)	(2.63)	(1.95)
GDPPC	0.0532*	0.0541	0.074	0.0427	0.194	−0.013
	(1.69)	(0.99)	(1.38)	(0.73)	(1.32)	(−0.26)
COMP	−9.297**	12.786*	−8.331*	18.734*	−7.461***	10.290
	(−2.41)	(1.79)	(−1.60)	(1.68)	(−2.60)	(1.21)
ULC	−0.114	−0.041	−1.303	−2.438**	−0.218	−0.049
	(−0.37)	(−1.41)	(−0.65)	(−2.12)	(−1.21)	(−0.66)
RDEMP	−14.127	13.771	−46.589	10.281	0.996	51.460*
	(−1.43)	(1.26)	(−1.52)	(0.75)	(0.35)	(1.89)
NPAGDP	1.549	−0.180	5.021	0.044	7.251	1.883
	(1.10)	(−0.82)	(1.53)	(0.15)	(0.74)	(0.55)
C	5058.529**	−7015.079*	7782.561	−12720.62	856.989	−8594.298
	(2.35)	(−1.84)	(1.48)	(−1.56)	(0.42)	(−1.60)
R-square	0.127	0.042	0.232	0.067	0.2241	0.1652
F-statistic	3.35***	1.14	4.84***	1.36	1.73	1.16
Sigma_u	988.12	3192.36	1692.84	3473.64	1193.18	4458.18
Sigma_e	844.26	2556.13	829.87	2807.01	756.90	1525.51
rho	0.578	0.609	0.806	0.604	0.713	0.8951
Obs.	192	213	136	158	56	55
N. of groups	24	27	17	20	7	7

Notes: t-statistics are in parenthesis, with ***, ** and * denoting significance at the 1 per cent, 5 per cent and 10 per cent level. Fixed-effects estimation with robust standard errors. The fixed effects accompanied with an F-test for their significance can be found in the Appendix 9.2.

a decisively formulated new configuration of motivations. The tests in Table 9.4 do provide some intriguing indications of the nature of this strategic evolution of US FDI and we now comment on these.

Within the MS variables the most notable result is the loss for both sub-samples of the significant positive sign on *GDPPC* in the second period. In terms of our hypothesis for this variable, this may be interpreted as the USA becoming less motivated to invest in similarly high-income countries in order to benefit from taste overlap and sell their centrally created (that is, US innovated) goods. For non-Europe, *GDPGR* is much more strongly positive than elsewhere in both periods, while *GDP* itself moves from clearly negatively signed to clearly (statistically significant) positively signed. This supports our speculation, in Table 9.1, that in this subset of countries current growth rates are interpreted as reflecting future GDP potential, with GDP itself, in turn, therefore asserting its place in MS motivation (alongside its persistently significant positive result in the Europe sample).

Of the ES variables *ULC* is always correctly (negatively) signed. It becomes significant for Europe in the second period. An interesting result emerges in our second ES variable, *COMP*, for both sub-samples. *COMP* switches from being significantly negative in 1982–89 to clearly significant and positively signed in 1990–97. This provides a clear-cut indication of the presence of a strategic refocusing across time, with US MNEs initially appearing to be alienated by the (non-labour-cost) sources of national competitiveness manifest in sample countries, while beginning to assert importance to them.[16] The output indicator of KS (*NPAGDP*) is positive for Europe for 1982–89 (just misses significance) but though always correctly signed, is never otherwise significant. Evidence for some movement towards KS is more available in the results for *RDEMPL*. For Europe this variable is negatively in 1982–89 but then becomes weakly positive for 1990–97, while it achieves a significant positive result for non-Europe in the second period. Complementing the argument above for *COMP*, this suggests that knowledge-related sources of competitiveness become more attractive to US MNEs (who may previously have felt that the overheads of creative investments compromised short-run cost competitiveness).

9.6 CONCLUDING REMARKS

The chapter has adapted traditional approaches to the analysis of FDI drivers to explore how the ongoing changing features of potential locations within the framework of profound changes in the global economic environment can impact on investment decisions through the range of strategic motivations that define MNEs' global competitive profiles. The dynamic differentiated network through which MNEs operate is perpetually open to reconfiguration as host-countries' needs and potentials themselves evolve.

In this chapter we analyse the determinants of US FDI in the OECD area. Our sample covers the 28 OECD countries hosting US FDI during the last two decades, that is, 1982–97. The results support in particular the hypothesizing of strategic repositioning of US MNEs' activities in Europe, in response to further moves towards an integrated market. Consonant with that, the decline of conventional (national) market-seeking influences suggests a more decisive acknowledgement of an integrated union wide competitive context. Furthermore, there is an evident reorientation in US MNEs' strategic plans evaluating positively the presence of national sources of competitiveness during the latter years, with cost considerations being more relevant for the European countries.

An important overall perspective emerging from this analysis is that MNEs' operations in a particular country can evolve in ways that are supportive of sustained processes of economic development (Pearce, 2001). Thus, as a country's comparative advantage moves away from standardized cost-effective production inputs towards higher levels of skill and the emergence of distinctive local technology competences and R&D capacity, MNEs can co-opt these creative scopes within the development-oriented facets of their own heterogeneous strategic profiles.

APPENDIX 9.1

Table A9.1 Variables description and descriptive statistics

Description of Variables

Variable	Description
FDI	Direct investment position by country (year end), bn US$ (1990)
GDP	GDP (1990), bn US$
GDPGR	GDP (1990), bn US$ growth
GDPPC	GDP per capita (1990), US$
IMP	Imports of goods and services (1990), bn US$
EXP	Exports of goods and services (1990), bn US$
COMP	EXP/(IMP + EXP)
ULC	Unit labour cost (1990)
NPA	National patent applications submitted to all destinations
RDPER	Total R&D personnel, persons
EMP	Employment total, 1000 persons
RDEMP	RDPER/EMP

Descriptive Statistics of Samples for the Full Period (1982–97)

	Full time period								
	FDI	GDP	GDPGR	GDPPC	ULC	COMP	RDEMP	NPA	NPAGDP
FULL									
Mean	1.143	390.621	0.034	14295.770	101.864	0.501	0.009	44367	176.490
St. Dev.	2.783	675.178	0.157	9489.941	55.391	0.044	0.004	66406	253.019
Obs.	407	458	439	458	386	458	458	458	457
EUROPE									
Mean	1.159	313.883	0.038	15539.090	105.386	0.499	0.009	35920	202.287
St. Dev.	3.069	433.511	0.177	9304.964	59.451	0.044	0.004	29485	289.011
Obs.	295	332	315	332	296	332	332	332	332
NON-EUROPE									
Mean	1.101	592.821	0.024	11019.720	90.280	0.505	0.008	66626	107.974
St. Dev.	1.840	1054.584	0.092	9222.878	37.150	0.042	0.005	114591	77.101
Obs.	112	126	124	126	90	126	126	126	125

Sources: OECD *Main Economic Indicators*, OECD *Main Science and Technology Indicators* (various issues).

APPENDIX 9.2

Table A9.2 Fixed effects of the samples

Fixed Effects for Full Sample

Full period		1982–89 period		1990–97 period	
Austria	−1566.804***	Austria	−513.753*	Austria	−2002.301**
	−3.60		−1.67		−2.33
Bel-Lux	−560.5256	Bel-Lux	267.0441	Bel-Lux	−847.6895
	−1.28		0.82		−0.77
Canada	1762.729**	Canada	1336.533*	Canada	2360.532**
	2.17		1.94		1.95
Czech Rep	57.03877	Czech Rep	(dropped)	Czech Rep	−825.1951
	0.12				−0.78
Denmark	−1810.917***	Denmark	−331.816	Denmark	−3229.951***
	−3.91		−1.29		−3.21
Finland	−1376.641***	Finland	13.89032	Finland	−3172.776***
	−3.10		0.04		−3.66
France	−89.35023	France	709.4135	France	−2385.551
	−0.16		1.28		−1.58
Germany	−325.911	Germany	1020.674	Germany	−3503.94*
	−0.49		1.23		−1.70
Greece	−991.0889**	Greece	−1635.952**	Greece	886.1259
	−2.01		−2.15		0.76
Hungary	191.9756	Hungary	(dropped)	Hungary	−130.2279
	0.47				−0.13

Iceland	−1740.05***	Iceland	−372.6501	Iceland	−2235.496***
	−3.98		−1.26		−2.58
Ireland	192.07	Ireland	262.8306	Ireland	−445.661
	0.45		0.99		−0.55
Italy	−707.0889	Italy	−160.3589	Italy	−2169.171
	−1.42		−0.42		−1.61
Japan	−2716.913**	Japan	−103.5345	Japan	−10131.8**
	−2.28		−0.15		−2.15
Korea	99.0672	Korea	1593.707	Korea	−1056.819
	0.20		1.31		−1.27
Mexico	1255.717*	Mexico	397.7986	Mexico	2913.183**
	1.84		0.97		2.23
Netherlands	1719.918	Netherlands	1302.234**	Netherlands	1936.093
	1.48		2.37		0.88
New Zealand	−643.1546	New Zealand	−523.3657*	New Zealand	−729.6189
	−1.56		−1.63		−0.88
Norway	−1789.641***	Norway	−85.39491	Norway	−2909.497**
	−3.64		−0.25		−2.60
Poland	195.7251	Poland	(dropped)	Poland	−415.5365
	0.46				−0.42
Portugal	−776.0058*	Portugal	−1204.306**	Portugal	845.5278
	−1.63		−2.14		0.76
Spain	−589.1471	Spain	−234.572	Spain	−1068.409
	−1.34		−0.77		−1.26
Sweden	−829.912	Sweden	24.48894	Sweden	−1881.136
	−1.23		0.06		−1.44
Switzerland	−1092.617*	Switzerland	481.9861	Switzerland	−1624.419
	−1.84		0.93		−1.07

Table A9.2 (continued)

Fixed Effects for Full Sample

Full period		1982–89 period		1990–97 period	
Turkey	−153.2656	Turkey	−425.8606	Turkey	1035.233
	−0.33		−1.11		0.84
UK	6610.756***	UK	3195.684**	UK	9356.824***
	3.11		2.26		2.65
F(26,371)	8.63***	F(23,161)	4.74***	F(26,179)	7.99***

Fixed Effects for Europe

Full period		1982–89 period		1990–97 period	
Austria	2131.364	Austria	−2724.098	Austria	493.2755
	1.59		−1.16		0.12
Bel-Lux	3343.456**	Bel-Lux	−1082.449	Bel-Lux	1539.86
	2.51		−0.67		0.38
Czech Rep	3967.661***	Czech Rep	(dropped)	Czech Rep	2224.638
	2.89				0.49
Denmark	2053.911	Denmark	−1971.019	Denmark	−636.9987
	1.48		−0.99		−0.15
Finland	2850.75**	Finland	−823.9079	Finland	−349.2286
	2.04		−0.61		−0.08
France	1485.927**	France	−523.3661	France	−4903.295**
	1.97		−0.82		−2.17

Germany	(dropped)	Germany	(dropped)	Germany	−8603.939**
Greece	3703.965**	Greece	−5032.848	Greece	4897.71
	2.34		−1.33		1.08
Hungary	4139.28***	Hungary	(dropped)	Hungary	3089.655
	2.99				0.71
Iceland	2642.806*	Iceland	−1756.818	Iceland	1365.161
	1.76		−0.87		0.29
Ireland	3513.061***	Ireland	−1872.429	Ireland	2225.056
	2.59		−0.84		0.54
Italy	4193.159**	Italy	−1849.782	Italy	(dropped)
	2.33		−0.58		
Netherlands	5145.973***	Netherlands	268.3944	Netherlands	3687.308
	3.33		0.23		0.91
Norway	2135.717	Norway	−1298.937	Norway	−253.2768
	1.49		−0.76		−0.06
Poland	3032.606**	Poland	(dropped)	Poland	2021.525
	2.39				0.52
Portugal	3647.292**	Portugal	−3885.233	Portugal	4341.837
	2.40		−1.24		1.00
Spain	2268.671*	Spain	−3041.997	Spain	231.217
	1.90		−1.17		0.09
Sweden	3183.255**	Sweden	−877.385	Sweden	501.374
	2.09		−0.68		0.12
Switzerland	3270.161**	Switzerland	110.5783	Switzerland	740.9234
	2.35		0.11		0.16
UK	8783.147***	UK	2156.574***	UK	8180.038**
	3.82		3.02		2.24
F(19,267)	7.55***	F(16,112)	5.50***	F(19,131)	6.72***

Table A9.2 (continued)

Fixed Effects for non-Europe Sample

Full period		1982–89 period		1990–97 period	
Canada	2216.617***	Canada	1248.093*	Canada	2972.778**
	2.78		1.81		2.58
Japan	185.8799	Japan	742.4744	Japan	−8344.449***
	0.12		1.23		−2.89
Korea	−13.41141	Korea	892.5763*	Korea	−1254.773
	−0.01		1.64		−1.22
Mexico	3828.321***	Mexico	3099.988	Mexico	5295.523*
	2.62		1.28		1.94
New Zealand	−124.9046	New Zealand	−80.25131	New Zealand	4.948395
	−0.23		−0.37		0.00
Turkey	1875.101	Turkey	2443.968	Turkey	3435.716
	1.49		0.93		1.22
F(6,97)	7.39***	F(6,42)	2.09*	F(6,41)	7.39***

Notes: t-statistics are in parenthesis, with ***, ** and * denoting significance at the 1 per cent, 5 per cent and 10 per cent level.

APPENDIX 9.3

Table A9.3 Correlation matrices for the samples

Full Sample (Obs. 405)

	FDI	GDP	GDPGR	GDPPC	COMP	RDEMP	NPAGDP
FDI	1						
GDP	0.2099	1					
GDPGR	−0.0153	0.0093	1				
GDPPC	0.2117	0.3975	−0.01	1			
COMP	0.0458	0.2427	−0.0648	0.369	1		
RDEMP	0.1902	0.3696	0.0000	0.5927	0.4729	1	
NPAGDP	−0.0777	−0.1608	−0.0604	0.1085	−0.0183	0.1544	1

Europe Sample (Obs. 294)

	FDI	GDP	GDPGR	GDPPC	COMP	RDEMP	NPAGDP
FDI	1						
GDP	0.3949	1					
GDPGR	−0.0201	0.0117	1				
GDPPC	0.2043	0.2503	0.0073	1			
COMP	0.0797	0.1473	−0.0446	0.4579	1		
RDEMP	0.2357	0.3811	−0.0343	0.5844	0.6245	1	
NPAGDP	−0.0785	−0.2397	−0.0807	0.0741	−0.0217	0.103	1

Non-Europe Sample (Obs. 111)

	FDI	GDP	GDPGR	GDPPC	COMP	RDEMP	NPAGDP
FDI	1						
GDP	0.0379	1					
GDPGR	0.0068	0.0053	1				
GDPPC	0.2857	0.7815	−0.052	1			
COMP	−0.0823	0.3569	−0.1224	0.2556	1		
RDEMP	0.0908	0.4896	0.0795	0.572	0.2689	1	
NPAGDP	−0.1471	−0.0013	0.1220	0.1218	0.1681	0.4818	1

NOTES

1. For reviews and critiques of Hymer's work see Yamin (2000), Cantwell (2000, pp. 13–17), Dunning and Rugman (1985) and Horaguchi and Toyne (1990).
2. Part of Hymer's criticism of FDI theory pointed to an industry-specific component. Thus, in a way that could not be explained by economy-wide capital availability, some industries were persistently and substantially involved in FDI and others to only a limited and sporadic degree.
3. A recent strand of literature (for example, Graham, 1998; Veugelers, 1995) has applied game theoretical approaches to aspects of MNEs' competitive behaviour.
4. Recent studies providing wide-ranging surveys of this literature are Chakrabarti (2001) and Scyf (2001).
5. Papanastassiou and Pearce (1999, ch. 2) provides an overview of various categorizations of MNE subsidiaries and presents (ibid., pp. 24–30) a typology that correlates closely to the motivation typology used here.
6. Birkinshaw and Hood (1998) include a collection of papers relating to evolutionary processes in MNE subsidiaries.
7. The typology of motivations used here adapts earlier approaches of Behrman (1984) and Dunning (1993).
8. For example, the specific nature of MS behaviour in Western Europe has evolved as individual countries have entered the EU (Tavares, 2001a; 2000b; Tavares and Pearce, 2001), while MS has proved to be a major reason for MNEs' initial operations in the CEE transition region (Lankes and Venables, 1996; Mutinelli and Piscitello, 1997; Manea and Pearce, 2001).
9. In industrial economies, MS investments by MNEs often emerged within the protectionist response to the 1930s' recession, and were sustained by higher growth and continued trade restraints in the immediate post-war decades. The protectionist import-substitution strategies of the developing economies in the 1950s/1960s also induced MS investment by MNEs. Levels and changes of various protectionist policies and instruments as determinants of FDI have been included in several influential studies (Culem, 1988; Kogut and Chang, 1991; Neven and Siotis, 1996; Barrell and Pain, 1999a; 1999b).
10. This would probably be carried out by product mandate subsidiaries (Bonin and Perron, 1986; Roth and Morrison, 1992; Birkinshaw and Morrison, 1995; Birkinshaw, 1996) which are authorized (by the parent MNE) to take full responsibility for the development of a new product, for its manufacture and sustained competitive evolution. Complementary concepts that embody KS and have received recent analysis include centres of excellence (Forsgren and Pedersen, 1998; Moore, 2001) and dispersed R&D networks in MNEs (Kuemmerle, 1999a; 1999b; Pearce, 1999; Pearce and Papanastassiou, 1999; Håkanson and Noble, 2000).
11. Though not relevant to the empirical context here, Culem (1988) and Kogut and Chang (1991) found growth in the US economy was not significant in attracting inward FDI.
12. US companies' investment in Europe provided the context for a major early wave of studies of determinants of FDI. For summaries and critiques of these see Dunning (1997), Yannopoulos (1990), Clegg (1996) and Tavares (2001a). More recent extensions of analysis of this context include Barrell and Pain (1999a).
13. Tabulations of descriptive statistics for the variables, by subgroup and time period, are available from the authors.
14. Using the properties of the residuals and the Lindeberg-Levy central limit theorem.
15. See Appendix 9.1 for definitions of variables and descriptive statistics of the full-period sample.
16. For an analysis of how KS motivations deploy within Europe, that is, EU core–EU periphery, see Filippaios et al. (2002). For complementary evidence on EU core, see Kottaridi, Filippaios and Papanastassiou (2002).

REFERENCES

Amiti, M. (1998), 'New trade theories and industrial location in the EU: a survey of evidence', *Oxford Review of Economic Policy*, **14**, 45–53.

Barrell, R. and N. Pain (1996), 'An econometric analysis of US foreign direct investment', *Review of Economics and Statistics*, **78**, 200–207.

Barrell, R. and N. Pain (1999a), 'Domestic institutions, agglomerations and foreign direct investment in Europe', *European Economic Review*, **43**, 925–34.

Barrell, R. and N. Pain (1999b), 'Trade restraints and Japanese direct investment flows', *European Economic Review*, **43**, 29–45.

Behrman, J.N. (1984), *Industrial Policies: International Restructuring and Transnationals*, Lexington, MA: Lexington Books.

Birkinshaw, J.M. (1996), 'How multinational subsidiary mandates are gained and lost', *Journal of International Business Studies*, **27**, 467–95.

Birkinshaw, J.M. and N. Hood (1998), 'Multinational subsidiary evolution: capability and charter change in foreign-owned subsidiary companies', *Academy of Management Review*, **23**, 773–93.

Birkinshaw, J.M. and A.J. Morrison (1995), 'Configurations of strategy and structure in subsidiaries of multinational corporations', *Journal of International Business Studies*, **26**, 729–54.

Bonin, B. and B. Perron (1986), 'World product mandates and firms operating in Quebec', in H. Etemad and L. Séguin Dulude (eds), *Managing the Multinational Subsidiary*, London: Croom Helm.

Braunerhjelm, P. and R. Svensson (1996), 'Host country characteristics and agglomeration in foreign direct investment', *Applied Economics*, **28**, 833–40.

Cantwell, J.A. (2000), 'A survey of theories of international production', in C.N. Pitelis and R. Sugden (eds), *The Nature of the Transnational Firm*, London: Routledge.

Chakrabarti, A. (2001), 'The determinants of foreign direct investment: sensitivity analyses of cross-country regressions', *Kyklos*, **54**, 89–114.

Choi, I. and B.C. Ahn (1999), 'Testing the null of stationarity for multiple time-series', *Journal of Econometrics*, **88**, 41–77.

Clegg, J. (1996), 'US foreign direct investment in the EU: the effects of market integration in perspective', in F. Burton, M. Yamin and S. Young (eds), *International Business and Europe in Transition*, Basingstoke, Macmillan.

Culem, C.G. (1988), 'The locational determinants of direct investments among industrialised countries', *European Economic Review*, **32**, 885–904.

Cushman, D.O. (1987), 'The effects of real wages and labour productivity on foreign direct investment', *Southern Economic Journal*, **54**, 174–85.

Dunning, J.H. (1993), *Multinational enterprises and the global economy*, Wokingham: Addison-Wesley.

Dunning, J.H. (1997), 'The European internal market programme and inbound foreign direct investment – parts 1 and 2', *Journal of Common Market Studies*, **35**, 1–30 and 189–223.

Dunning, J.H. and A.H. Rugman (1985), 'The influence of Hymer's dissertation on the theory of foreign direct investment', *American Economic Review: Papers and Proceedings*, **75**, 228–32.

Filippaios, F., C. Kottaridi, M. Papanastassiou and R. Pearce (2002), 'A macro-level analysis of the strategic behavior of US foreign direct investment flows: some

empirical evidence', mimeo, Department of International and European Economic Studies, Athens University of Economics and Business.
Flowers, E.B. (1976), 'Oligopolistic reaction in European and Canadian direct investment in the United States', *Journal of International Business Studies*, **1**, 43–55.
Forsgren, M. and T. Pedersen (1998), 'Centres of excellence in multinational companies: the case of Denmark', in J. Birkinshaw and N. Hood (eds), *Multinational Corporate Evolution and Subsidiary Development*, Basingstoke: Macmillan.
Graham, E.M. (1978), 'Transatlantic investment by multinational firms: a rivalistic phenomenon', *Journal of Post-Keynesian Economics*, **1**, 82–99.
Graham, E.M. (1998), 'Market structure and the multinational enterprise: a game-theoretic approach', *Journal of International Business*, **29**, 67–84.
Håkansson, L. and R. Nobel (2000), 'Technology characteristics and reverse technology transfer', *Management International Review*, **40**, 29–48.
Head, K., J. Ries and D. Swenson (1995), 'Agglomeration benefits and location choice: evidence from Japanese manufacturing investments in the United States', *Journal of International Economics*, **38**, 223–47.
Horaguchi, H. and B. Toyne (1990), 'Setting the record straight: Hymer, internalisation theory and transaction cost economics', *Journal of International Business Studies*, **21**, 487–94.
Hymer, S. (1960), *The International Operations of National Firms: A Study of Foreign Direct Investment*, PhD thesis, Massachusetts Institute of Technology, published (1976), Cambridge, MA: MIT Press.
Im, K.S., M.H. Pesaran and Y. Shin (1997), 'Testing for unit roots in heterogeneous panels', manuscript, Department of Applied Economics, University of Cambridge, UK.
Knickerbocker, F.T. (1973), *Oligopolistic Reaction and the Multinational Enterprise*, Cambridge, MA: Harvard University Press.
Kobrin, S.J. (1979), 'Political risk: a review and reconsideration', *Journal of International Business Studies*, **10**, 67–80.
Kogut, B. and S.J. Chang (1991), 'Technological capabilities and Japanese foreign direct investment in the United States', *Review of Economics and Statistics*, **73**, 401–13.
Kottaridi, C., F. Filippaios and M. Papanastassiou (2002), 'The evolution of FDI determinants among industrialized countries: an empirical assessment', mimeo, Department of International and European Economic Studies, Athens University of Economics and Business.
Krugman, P. (1980), 'Scale economies, product differentiation and the pattern of trade', *American Economic Review*, **73**, 950–59.
Kuemmerle, W. (1999a), 'The drivers of foreign direct investment into research and development: an empirical investigation', *Journal of International Business Studies*, **30**, 1–24.
Kuemmerle, W. (1999b), 'Foreign direct investment in industrial research in the pharmaceutical and electronics industries – results from a survey of multinational firms', *Research Policy*, **28**, 179–93.
Lankes, H.-P. and A.J. Venables (1996), 'Foreign direct investment in economic transition: the changing pattern of investments', *Economics of Transition*, **4**, 331–47.
Linder, S.B. (1961), *An Essay on Trade and Transformation*, New York: Wiley.
Lundvall, B.-Å. (1992), *National Systems of Innovation, Towards a Theory of Innovation and Interactive Learning*, London: Pinter.

Manea, J. and R. Pearce (2001), 'Multinational strategies and sustainable industrial transformation in CEE transition economies: the role of technology', in J.H. Taggart, M. Berry and M. McDermott (eds), *Multinationals in a New Era*, Basingstoke: Palgrave.

McPherson, M.A., M.R. Redfearn and M.A. Tieslau (2000), 'A re-examination of the Linder hypothesis: a random-effects tobit approach', *International Economic Journal*, **14**, 123–36.

Moore, K.J. (2001), 'A strategy for subsidiaries: centres of excellences to build subsidiary specific advantages', *Management International Review*, **41**, 275–90.

Mutinelli, M. and L. Piscitello (1997), 'Differences in the strategic orientation of Italian MNEs in Central and Eastern Europe: the influence of firm-specific factors', *International Business Review*, **6**, 185–205.

Nelson, R.R. (ed.) (1993), *National Systems of Innovation: A Comparative Study*, Oxford: Oxford University Press.

Neven, D. and G. Siotis (1996), 'Technology sourcing and FDI in the EC: an empirical evaluation', *International Journal of Industrial Organisation*, **14**, 543–60.

OECD (Organization for Economic Co-operation and Development) (2000), *International Direct Investment Statistical Yearbook: 1999*, OECD Industry Services and Trade, vol. 2000, no. 6, March, pp. 1–452.

OECD (Organization for Economic Co-operation and Development) (2000), *Main Economic Indicators* (*Principaux indicateurs economiques*), various issues.

OECD (Organization for Economic Co-operation and Development) (2000), *Main Science and Technology Indicators* (*Principaux indicateurs de la science et de la technologia*), vol. 2000, no. 1, July, pp. 1–86.

OECD (Organization for Economic Co-operation and Development) (2000), *OECD Statistical Compendium*, electronic version can be found at http//www.sourceoecd.com/content/html/portal/statistics/statistics.htm?comm=statisti0000%3F.

Papanastassiou, M. and R. Pearce (1999), *Multinationals, Technology and National Competitiveness*, Cheltenham, UK, and Lyme, USA: Edward Elgar.

Pearce, R. (1999), 'Decentralised R&D and strategic competitiveness: globalised approaches to generation and use of technology in multinational enterprises', *Research Policy*, **28**, 157–78.

Pearce, R. (2001), 'Multinationals and industrialisation: the bases of "inward investment" policy', *International Journal of the Economics of Business*, **8**, 51–73.

Pearce, R. and M. Papanastassiou (1999), 'Overseas R&D and the strategic evolution of MNEs: evidence from laboratories in the UK', *Research Policy*, **28**, 23–41.

Porter, M.E. (1986), 'Competition in global industries: a conceptual framework', in M.E. Porter (ed.), *Competition in Global Industries*, Boston, MA: Harvard Business School Press.

Roth, K. and A.J. Morrison (1992), 'Implementing global strategy: characteristics of global subsidiary mandates', *Journal of International Business Studies*, **23**, 715–35.

Seyf, A. (2001), 'Can globalisation and global localisation explain foreign direct investment? Japanese firms in Europe', *International Journal of the Economics of Business*, **8**, 137–53.

Tavares, A.T. (2001a), 'Systems, evolution and integration: modelling the impact of economic integration on multinationals' strategies', PhD thesis, University of Reading.

Tavares, A.T. (2001b), 'Multinational enterprises in Ireland: the dynamics of subsidiary strategy', in J.H. Taggart, M. Berry and M. McDermott (eds), *Multinationals in a New Era*, Basingstoke: Palgrave.
Tavares, A.T. and R. Pearce (2001), 'European integration and structural change in the multinational: evidence from foreign subsidiaries operating in Portugal', in M.D. Hughes and J.H. Taggart (eds), *International Business – European Dimensions*, Basingstoke: Palgrave.
Vernon, R. (1974), 'The location of economic activity', in J.H. Dunning (ed.), *Economic Analysis and the Multinational Enterprise*, London: Allen and Unwin.
Veugelers, R. (1991), 'Locational determinants and ranking of host countries: an empirical assessment', *Kyklos*, **44**, 363–82.
Veugelers, R. (1995), 'Strategic incentives for multinational operations', *Managerial and Decision Economics*, **16**, 47–57.
Wheeler, D. and A. Mody (1992), 'International investment location decisions: the case of US firms', *Journal of International Economics*, **33**, 57–76.
Yamin, M. (2000), 'A critical re-evaluation of Hymer's contribution to the theory of the transnational corporation', in C.N. Pitelis and R. Sugden (eds), *The Nature of the Transnational Firm*, London: Routledge.
Yannopoulos, G.N. (1990), 'Foreign direct investment and European integration: the evidence from the formative years of the European Community', *Journal of Common Market Studies*, **28**, 236–59.

10. Intellectual property rights and international location choices: theoretical modelling and simulations

Etienne Pfister

10.1 INTRODUCTION

Intellectual property rights (IPR) have long been a neglected field in international economics. Yet, their introduction in the World Trade Organization (WTO) agenda, notably through the much discussed TRIPs agreement, has motivated several theoretical and empirical papers in order to appreciate the likely consequences of a strengthening of IPR law in developing countries on the patterns of trade and foreign direct investment (FDI) (Combe and Pfister, 2001). In this context, the current chapter seeks to evaluate the role of IPRs in the location choices of multinationals' subsidiaries.

The extent and direction of the impact of IPRs on cross-border goods and capital flows remains extremely ambiguous. Consider international trade (Smith, 1999). On the one hand, stronger protection in the importing country should increase the market share of foreign IPR owners, thus resulting in higher export flows. On the other hand, however, stronger protection also yields greater market power and higher prices, thus leading to *lower* export flows. Some other contributions cast a look at the mode of foreign entry (Fosfuri, 2000; Markusen, 2001): in this setting, it is often shown that foreign direct investment is appropriate when the level of IPR protection is intermediary, that is, high enough to ensure that the local production process will not be counterfeited, yet too low to risk transfering one's technology to a local competitor. These models thus assume that foreign direct investment and licence contracts result in involuntary technology spillovers from the IPR owner to the local firms, an issue which is debated in the empirical literature (Blomström and Kokko, 1998). Alternatively, Siotis (1999) regards foreign direct investment as a tool to assimilate local technologies. In that case, strong protection will act as a barrier to these technology-sourcing strategies and foreign direct investment will decrease. Finally, empirical studies tend to reflect this ambiguity as a wide array of results have been obtained. Beside, the theoretical uncertainty is compounded by the need to separate the role of IPR from the more general regulatory framework (including corruption levels, political system, education and so on) of the importing/local country (see Pfister, 2001, for a survey of these works).

In this chapter, I consider the role of IPR protection in the location of an innovating subsidiary, an issue which, to our knowledge, has never been considered before. Another distinctive feature stems from the assumption that there are no specific technological spillovers due to foreign direct investment. Therefore, the game equilibrium hinges around a purely strategic consideration (how to deter local competition) rather than on the usual issue of preventing involuntary spillovers to local firms. Finally, I explicitly combine industrial strategy (quantity and location choices) with legal parameters (trial win probability) to explore the complementarity/substituability relations between IPR protection and foreign direct investment.

The rest of the chapter is organized as follows. The first section presents the theoretical framework of the game. Then I solve the game and present the equilibrium. Finally, I use some mathematical simulations to examine some situations that were previously ruled out by assumption.

10.2 THEORETICAL FRAMEWORK

Presentation

Consider a firm M as the exclusive owner of an innovation whose (inverse) demand function writes as $p = a - \beta Q$ and which is produced at a constant unit cost c. M can locate in one of two distinct countries denoted H and L. The location choice is assumed to be unique and irreversible. Host countries are perfectly identical except for the level of protection that is granted to IPR owners. Indeed, when firm M launches a trial against those counterfeiters located in H (resp., L), its trial win probability is α_h (resp., α_l), with $\alpha_h > \alpha_l$. Assuming zero trial costs, M always benefits from litigation.[1]

Thus, the game unfolds as follows:

- First, firm M locates either in H or in L given 1) the extent of protection granted in each country, 2) the possibility to export its product into the other country (at a positive unit cost s).
- Regardless of its location choice, imitating firms enter simultaneously into both countries. F designates a fixed imitation cost which is assumed to be identical for all firms and both countries.
- Then, the imitating firms are litigated by firm M before they even begin to produce. Because intellectual property law is country

specific, two separate trials are orchestrated – one against those firms located in H, another against those located in L – and their outcomes are assumed to be perfectly independent.

- Finally, firm M and its (non-)infringing competitors set their production levels in a simultaneous Cournot fashion. Each one sells on its domestic market and exports to the other country at a unit cost s.

Discussion

The model proceeds to several assumptions and simplifications. First, we may note that the multinational firm is risk-neutral and makes no difference between uncertainty-free competitive strategies and uncertain litigation outcomes. Besides, that trials intervene before production is made is often hypothesized in the IPR literature (Choi, 1998) but this clearly contrasts with the dynamics of real-world litigation processes.

Probably more crucial is the absence of any kind of technological spillovers due to foreign direct investment. Hence, there is no involuntary technology transfer between the subsidiary and its local competitors. First, location does not enable the subsidiary to absorb some foreign technology. Accordingly, foreign direct investment cannot be assimilated to a technology sourcing strategy (Siotis, 1999), and we may conjecture that this analysis is more appropriate for location choices in emerging or developing countries. Second, unlike in Markusen (2001), foreign direct investment (relative to exports) does not facilitate imitation. Quite evidently, if spillovers from the subsidiary to the local firms were to increase, so would the incentive to locate in the stronger protection country. From an empirical standpoint, the extent of spillovers due to foreign direct investment remains debated. In a survey, Blomström and Kokko (1998) note that location in the foreign country may make the subsidiary more competitive (indeed, in our model, there is no longer any export or tariff cost), thus diminishing the extent of local competition. This strategic effect had already been discussed by Smith (1987) and is at the core of the present model.

10.3 A FIVE-FIRM GAME

To make things simpler, we restrict the number of (potential) local imitators to two firms per country. Denote by $\Pi_i(J)$ firm i ($i=h$, l)'s expected profit when M locates in country J ($J=H$, L). It can be decomposed into a domestic component $\pi_i^d(J, n)$ and an export component $\pi_i^e(J, n)$, where n designates the total number of competitors. n is determined by the outcomes of the trials faced by the imitators in each country.

Once the imitation has been made, the imitators' profits thus write as:

$$\Pi_l(L) = (1-\alpha_l)\,[\alpha_h(\pi_l^d(L,3) + \pi_l^e(L,3)) + (1-\alpha_h)\,(\pi_M^d(L,5) + \pi_M^e(L,5))] \tag{10.1}$$

Indeed, with a probability $\alpha_h(1-\alpha_l)$, the imitators in country H are excluded while those located in L can legally imitate the product of firm M; hence $n=3$. Alternatively, with probability $(1-\alpha_l)$ $(1-\alpha_h)$, the imitating firms from both countries are allowed to produce so that $n=5$. Finally, with a probability α_l, the imitating firms located in L are excluded, in which case their profits are zero. In a simultaneous Cournot model, equation 1 turns into:

$$\Pi_l(L) = (1-\alpha_l)\left[\alpha_h \frac{m^2 + (m-s)^2}{16\beta} + (1-\alpha_h)\frac{(m+2s)^2 + (m-3s)^2}{36\beta}\right] \tag{10.2}$$

where $m = a - c$. The other profit functions are similarly deduced:

$$\Pi_h(L) = (1-\alpha_h)\left[\alpha_l \frac{(m+s)^2 + (m-2s)^2}{16\beta} + (1-\alpha_l)\frac{(m+3s)^2 + (m-4s)^2}{36\beta}\right] \tag{10.3}$$

$$\Pi_l(H) = (1-\alpha_l)\left[\alpha_h \frac{(m+s)^2 + (m-2s)^2}{16\beta} + (1-\alpha_h)\frac{(m+3s)^2 + (m-4s)^2}{36\beta}\right] \tag{10.4}$$

$$\Pi_h(H) = (1-\alpha_h)\left[\alpha_l \frac{m^2 + (m-s)^2}{16\beta} + (1-\alpha_l)\frac{(m+2s)^2 + (m-3s)^2}{36\beta}\right] \tag{10.5}$$

At this stage, it is easily shown that in a Cournot setting, the imitators' expected profits are lower when they are located in country H ($\Pi_h(H) < \Pi_l$, (L), $\Pi_h(L) < \Pi_l(H)$) since they are facing a higher risk of being excluded. On the other hand, firm M's location in a country I ($I = H, L$) also diminishes the expected profits of those firms located in I relative to the imitators located in the other country: indeed, the former ones are directly confronting the multinational, which no longer has an exportation cost s to bear. Therefore, the expected profits of a firm l can be lower than those a firm h if M has chosen to locate in L and if $\alpha_h < \alpha_h^*$, with:

$$\alpha_h^* = \frac{6\alpha_l m(m-s) + s^2(16-\alpha_l)}{6m(m-s) + s^2(19-4\alpha_l)} \tag{10.6}$$

Even more importantly, to locate in a country may serve to deter entry by imitators and reduce competition if the imitation costs are sufficiently high.

Consider now the expected profits of the multinational firm. These are made of the revenues earned on the location market – $\pi^d_M(n, u)$ – and of the export revenues $\pi^e_M(n, u)$ – where n continues to designate the total number of firms and u denotes the number of competitors in the market where the revenues are made. In a Cournot setting, it can be shown that:

- the profits in the implantation country exceed those in the export market: $\pi^d_M > \pi^e_M$;
- both profits are inversely related to the extent of competition, so that: $\pi^l_M (I, n', u) > \pi^l_M (I, n'', u)$ $(l = d, e)$ when $n' < n''$ and $\pi^l_M (I, n, u') > \pi^l_M (I, n, u'')$ when $u' < u''$

Depending on the imitation costs, three equilibrium settings are distinguished.

First Setting: $F < \Pi_h(H)$

In that setting, the imitation costs are so low that regardless of firm M's location choice, both imitators from both countries enter the market. Foreign direct investment has no strategic impact and the expected profit of M when it locates in H writes as:

$$\begin{aligned}\Pi_M(H) = {} & \alpha_h\alpha_l[\pi^d_M(1, 0) + \pi^e_M(1, 0)] \\ & + \alpha_h(1 - \alpha_l)[\pi^d_M(3, 0) + \pi^e_M(3, 2)] \\ & + \alpha_l(1 - \alpha_h)[\pi^d_M(3, 2) + \pi^e_M(3, 0)] \\ & + (1 - \alpha_h)(1 - \alpha_l)[\pi^d_M(5, 2) + \pi^e_M(5, 2)]\end{aligned} \tag{10.7}$$

Indeed, with a probability $\alpha_h\alpha_l$, firm M is a monopolist in both markets; with a probability $\alpha_h(1 - \alpha_l)$, both counterfeiters in H are excluded on court decision but those located in L are allowed to produce; the opposite situation holds with a probability $\alpha_l(1 - \alpha_h)$; finally, with a probability $(1 - \alpha_h)(1 - \alpha_l)$, neither attempt to exclude the counterfeiters is successful and the multinational firm is facing four competitors.

Translating equation 10.7 into a Cournot setting we get:

$$\begin{aligned}\Pi_M(H) = {} & \alpha_h\alpha_l\frac{m^2 + (m - s)^2}{4\beta} + \alpha_h(1 - \alpha_l)\frac{(m + 2s)^2 + (m - 3s)^2}{16\beta} \\ & + \alpha_l(1 - \alpha_h)\frac{m^2 + (m - s)^2}{16\beta} + (1 - \alpha_h)(1 - \alpha_l)\frac{(m + 2s)^2 + (m - 3s)^2}{36\beta}\end{aligned} \tag{10.8}$$

with $m = a - c$. Likewise, the expected profit of firm M when it locates in L is:

$$\begin{aligned}\Pi_M(L) = {} & \alpha_h\alpha_l[\pi_M^d(1, 0) + \pi_M^e(1, 0)] \\ & + \alpha_l(1-\alpha_h)[\pi_M^d(3, 0) + \pi_M^e(3, 2)] \\ & + \alpha_h(1-\alpha_l)[\pi_M^d(3, 2) + \pi_M^e(3, 0)] \\ & + (1-\alpha_h)(1-\alpha_l)[\pi_M^d(5, 2) + \pi_M^e(5, 2)]\end{aligned} \tag{10.9}$$

which also writes as:

$$\begin{aligned}\Pi_M(L) = {} & \alpha_h\alpha_l\frac{m^2 + (m-s)^2}{4\beta} + \alpha_l(1-\alpha_h)\frac{(m+2s)^2 + (m-3s)^2}{16\beta} \\ & + \alpha_h(1-\alpha_l)\frac{m^2 + (m-s)^2}{16\beta} + (1-\alpha_h)(1-\alpha_l)\frac{(m+2s)^2 + (m-3s)^2}{36\beta}\end{aligned} \tag{10.10}$$

Comparing these profits, we deduce that the strong protection country is chosen when:

$$(\alpha_h - \alpha_l)\,[(\pi_M^d(3, 0) - \pi_M^d(3, 2)) - (\pi_M^e(3, 0) - \pi_M^e(3, 2))] > 0 \tag{10.11}$$

In a Cournot setting, the expression in brackets is always positive because the profit loss due to competition increases with the initial profits (or market share). Thus, entry by imitators incurs a higher loss on the implantation market (*d*) than on the export market (*e*). Indeed, the condition in equation 10.11 also writes as:

$$\frac{3s^2(\alpha_h - \alpha_l)}{4\beta} > 0 \tag{10.12}$$

Given that $\alpha_h > \alpha_l$, M always locates in H. Foreign direct investment has no strategic implication and the most attractive country is that which ensures the greatest protection, that is, the lowest expected competition.

Second Setting: $\Pi_h(H) < F < \Pi_l(L)$

Locating in H now deters the entry by one or both imitators in country H. On the other hand, locating in L continues to have no strategic effect because IPR protection in that country is too low and the expected profits of the local imitators remain high enough even when the subsidiary is located in L.

Let n_h and n_l respectively denote the number of counterfeiters located in

H and L. $\Pi_i(I, n_h, n_l)$ designates the expected profit of firm i ($i=h, l$) when M locates in I ($I=H, L$). Two cases should be distinguished.

First assume that $\Pi_h(H, 2,2)<F<\Pi_h(H, 1, 2)$: the presence of firm M in country H deters entry by only one local imitator. The expected profit of the multinational thus writes as:[2]

$$\begin{aligned}\Pi_M(H, 1, 2) = {} & \alpha_h\alpha_l[\pi_M^d(1, 0) + \pi_M^e(1, 0)] \\ & + \alpha_h(1-\alpha_l)[\pi_M^d(3, 0) + \pi_M^e(3, 2)] \\ & + \alpha_l(1-\alpha_h)[\pi_M^d(2, 1) + \pi_M^e(2, 0)] \\ & + (1-\alpha_h)(1-\alpha_l)[\pi_M^d(4, 1) + \pi_M^e(4, 2)]\end{aligned} \tag{10.13}$$

which also yields:

$$\Pi_M(H, 1, 2) = \alpha_h\alpha_l\frac{m^2 + (m-s)^2}{4\beta} + \alpha_h(1-\alpha_l)\frac{(m+2s)^2 + (m-3s)^2}{16\beta}$$

$$+\alpha_l(1-\alpha_h)\frac{m^2 + (m-s)^2}{9\beta} + (1-\alpha_h)(1-\alpha_l)\frac{(m+2s)^2 + (m-3s)^2}{25\beta} \tag{10.14}$$

In the second case, $\Pi_h(H, 1, 2)<F$: foreign direct investment in H deters entry by both local imitators. Firm M's expected profits thus write as:

$$\begin{aligned}\Pi_M(H, 0, 2) = {} & \alpha_l[\pi_M^d(1, 0) + \pi_M^e(1, 0)] \\ & + (1-\alpha_l)[\pi_M^d(3, 0) + \pi_M^e(3, 2)]\end{aligned} \tag{10.15}$$

or:

$$\Pi_M(H, 0, 2) = \alpha_l\frac{m^2 + (m-s)^2}{4\beta} + (1-\alpha_l)\frac{(m+2s)^2 + (m-3s)^2}{16\beta} \tag{10.16}$$

The expected profit associated to locating in L remains given by equation (10.9). It is easily shown (and intuitive) that $\Pi_M(H, 0, 2)>\Pi_M(H, 1, 2)>\Pi_M(H)>\Pi_M(L)$. In other words, the incentive to locate in H increases with the exclusion effect of foreign direct investment as long as locating in L does not bring any strategic implication. Let us now consider that setting where the imitation cost is high enough and (some) imitators in L are deterred through foreign direct investment.

Third Setting: $\Pi_L(L)<F<\Pi_l(H)$

The imitation cost F is high enough for foreign direct investment to deter at least one local imitator in country L. Quite evidently, locating in H would also deter entry by local imitators. Again, several cases should be distinguished.

Case 1: $\Pi_l(L, 2, 2) < F < Min\{\Pi_h(H, 1, 2); \Pi_l(L, 2, 1)\}$

Regardless of the location choice, foreign direct investment deters entry by only one local firm. The expected profit associated to a location in country *H* is given by equation 10.13. The expected profit associated to a location in country *L* now writes as:

$$\begin{aligned}\Pi_M(L, 2, 1) = \alpha_h\alpha_l[\pi_M^d(1, 0) + \pi_M^e(1, 0)] \\ + \alpha_l(1-\alpha_h)[\pi_M^d(3, 0) + \pi_M^e(3, 2)] \\ + \alpha_h(1-\alpha_l)[\pi_M^d(2, 1) + \pi_M^e(2, 0)] \\ + (1-\alpha_h)(1-\alpha_l)[\pi_M^d(4, 1) + \pi_M^e(4, 2)]\end{aligned} \qquad (10.17)$$

which translates into:

$$\Pi_M(L, 2, 1) = \alpha_h\alpha_l\frac{m^2 + (m-s)^2}{4\beta} + \alpha_l(1-\alpha_h)\frac{(m+2s)^2 + (m-3s)^2}{16\beta}$$

$$+ \alpha_h(1-\alpha_l)\frac{m^2 + (m-s)^2}{9\beta} + (1-\alpha_h)(1-\alpha_l)\frac{(m+2s)^2 + (m-3s)^2}{25\beta} \qquad (10.18)$$

Comparing equations 10.13 and 10.17 demonstrates that firm *M* prefers to locate in the *low protection* country when:

$$(\alpha_h - \alpha_l)\,[(\pi_M^d(2, 1) - \pi_M^d(3, 0)) + (\pi_M^e(2, 0) - \pi_M^e(3, 2))] > 0 \qquad (10.19)$$

The second term in the bracketed expression reflects the following comparison ('weighted' by trial win probabilities). If it locates in *L*, firm *M* is a duopolist in the host country and exports to a country where competition has been eradicated. If it locates in *H*, firm *M* is a monopolist in the host country but it exports to a country where two competitors have entered. Since this term considers only the exports revenues, it is positive.

The first term reflects the trade-off between a lower but geographically close competition and a higher but geographically remote competition. Intuitively, the larger the market and the lower the exportation costs, the more reduced competition is appreciable while geographical considerations are losing significance. Indeed, if we substitute Cournot profit functions to the reduced forms in equation 10.19, we get:

$$(\alpha_h - \alpha_l)\,[14m(m-s) - 101s^2] > 0 \qquad (10.20)$$

Thus, when the imitation costs are sufficiently high for the foreign direct investment to deter imitation even in the low-protection country, that country may be chosen as a location if markets are sufficiently large and export costs sufficiently low. Indeed, either firm *M* locates in the strong protection country, thus abandoning any substantial hope of eradicating imitation in country *L* (since judicial protection is so low there), or it locates in the low protection country to benefit from the strategic, deterring, effect at the cost of exporting to the strong protection country (knowing that it may well exclude its local imitators through a court process).

Solving this trade-off obeys the following intuitions. First, the larger the markets, the more attractive is deterrence since the residual demand faced by the innovator is increased. In that case, locating in the low-protection country allows him to reduce competition in both markets: the court process is favoured in country *H* (where it is most efficient) and foreign direct investment is used in the country *L*.

But locating in *L* nonetheless presents the drawback of distancing oneself from the country where all imitators could be brushed off through a court process. If the exportation costs are low enough, however, the subsidiary still has the possibility of exporting to country *H* and making a high profit there. Thus, *M* locates in *L* if and only if $s < \frac{\sqrt{1463} - 7}{101} m \simeq 0.31m$

Case 2: $\boldsymbol{Max\{\Pi_h(H, 1, 2); \Pi_l(L, 2, 2)\} < F < \Pi_l(L, 2, 1)}$

Now, locating in *H* deters both imitators while locating in *L* still allows entry by one counterfeiter. The strategic impact of FDI is asymmetric and higher in the strong protection country. Would that still allow a location in *L* and under what conditions?

The expected profit associated to locating in *H* (resp., *L*) corresponds to equation 10.15 (resp., 10.17). Substituting Cournot profit function to the reduced forms and comparing these equations, we get that country *L* is chosen provided that:

$$m(m-s)(512\alpha_h + 838\alpha_h\alpha_l - 1188\alpha_l - 162 \\ + s^2(3078\alpha_l - 1053 - 1472\alpha_h - 533\alpha_h\alpha_l) > 0 \qquad (10.21)$$

The mathematical evaluation of this condition reveals[3] that, except for very high values of α_l and α_h (superior to 0.9458), country *L* will be chosen provided that export costs are sufficiently weak relative to market size and that the protection in country *H* is sufficiently strong. Indeed, firm *M* has a natural tendency to locate in *H* and be a local monopolist. As the IPR protection granted in country *H* increases, however, the marginal function of the strategic impact of FDI decreases: exclusion through a court process is likely to be as effective as exclusion through FDI. Therefore, when α_h *is* sufficiently high, we get back to the trade-offs outlined in Case 1. Conversely, location in H is systematically chosen if the IPR protection there is not high enough (relative to that in country L).

Case 3: $\Pi_l(L, 2, 1) < F < \Pi_h(L, 2, 2)$

Foreign direct investment totally eradicates counterfeiting in the country of location, regardless of its identity. Thus, the strategic effect of FDI is symmetric and stronger than in case 1. The expected profit associated to a location in country H is given by equation 10.15. If M locates in country L, its profit becomes:

$$\Pi_M(L, 2, 0) = \alpha_h[\pi^d_M(1, 0) + \pi^e_M(1, 0)] + (1 - \alpha_h)[\pi^d_M(3, 0) + \pi^e_M(3, 2)] \qquad (10.22)$$

In a simultaneous Cournot setting, this becomes:

$$\Pi_M(L, 2, 0) = \alpha_h \frac{m^2 + (m - s)^2}{4\beta} + (1 - \alpha_h)\frac{(m + 2s)^2 + (m - 3s)^2}{16\beta} \qquad (10.23)$$

Comparing equations 10.15 and 10.22, we deduce that country L *is* chosen if:

$$(\alpha_h - \alpha_l)\ [(\pi^d_M(1, 0) - \pi^d_M(3, 0) + (\pi^e_M(1, 0) - \pi^e_M(3, 2)] > 0 \qquad (10.24)$$

or, equivalently:

$$2m(m - s) - 3s^2 > 0 \qquad (10.25)$$

which is always verified since it amounts to $s < \frac{\sqrt{7} - 1}{3} m \simeq 0.55m$ (by assumption, $s < m/3$; otherwise exporting is not a viable strategy). Indeed, those imitators not located in the country of implantation will be litigated. Since IPR protection is higher in H, profit maximization requires that litigation takes place in that country and that M locates in L.

10.4 MATHEMATICAL SIMULATIONS

The above model proceeded to two important simplifications. First, technological spillovers were deliberately ruled out so that FDI could not facilitate imitation. Second, countries H and L had the same technological capabilities so that the imitation threat posed by each country at the outset (that is, the number of potential imitators) was identical. In this section, these assumptions are relaxed and alternative frameworks are considered through mathematical simulations. I first determine firm *M*'s decision rule and then turn to the simulation results.

Firm *M*'s Decision Rule

Let $n_{ij}(i, j = l, h)$ denote the number of imitators i when M locates in country j.[4] If $n_{ii} < n_{ij}$, FDI has a positive strategic impact for the multinational firm since it reduces the number of local competitors. Conversely, if $n_{ii} > n_{ij}$, FDI increases the number of competitors thanks to high technological spill-overs.

If M locates in L, its profit becomes:

$$\Pi_M(L) = \alpha_h\alpha_l\frac{m^2 + (m-s)^2}{4\beta} + \alpha_h(1-\alpha_l)\frac{m^2 + (m-s)^2}{\beta(2+n_{ll})^2}$$

$$+\alpha_l(1-\alpha_h)\frac{(m + n_{hl}s)^2 + (m - (1 - n_{hl})s)^2}{\beta(2+n_{hl})^2}$$

$$+(1-\alpha_h)(1-\alpha_l)\frac{(m + n_{hl}s)^2 + (m - (1 - n_{hl})s)^2}{\beta(2+n_{ll}+n_{hl})^2} \qquad (10.26)$$

while locating in H brings a profit of:

$$\Pi_M(H) = \alpha_h\alpha_l\frac{m^2 + (m-s)^2}{4\beta} + \alpha_l(1-\alpha_h)\frac{m^2 + (m-s)^2}{\beta(2+n_{hh})^2}$$

$$+\alpha_h(1-\alpha_l)\frac{(m + n_{lh}s)^2 + (m - (1 + n_{lh})s)^2}{\beta(2+n_{lh})^2}$$

$$+(1-\alpha_h)(1-\alpha_l)\frac{(m + n_{lh}s)^2 + (m - (1 + n_{lh})s)^2}{\beta(2+n_{hh}+n_{lh})^2} \qquad (10.27)$$

Rearranging and comparing these profits, we deduce that country L is chosen if:

$$2m(m-s)A + Bs^2 \qquad (10.28)$$

where:

$$A = \frac{\alpha_h(1-\alpha_l)}{\beta}\left(\frac{1}{(2+n_{ll})^2} - \frac{1}{(2+n_{lh})^2}\right)$$

$$+\frac{\alpha_l(1-\alpha_h)}{\beta}\left(\frac{1}{(2+n_{hl})^2} - \frac{1}{(2+n_{hh})^2}\right)$$

$$+\frac{(1-\alpha_h)(1-\alpha_l)}{\beta}\left(\frac{1}{(2+n_{ll}+n_{hl})^2} - \frac{1}{(2+n_{lh}+n_{hh})^2}\right) \quad (10.29)$$

$$B = \frac{\alpha_h(1-\alpha_l)}{\beta}\left(\frac{1}{(2+n_{ll})^2} - \frac{(n_{lh}^2+(n_{lh}+1)^2)}{(2+n_{lh})^2}\right)$$

$$+\frac{\alpha_l(1-\alpha_h)}{\beta}\left(\frac{1}{(2+n_{hh})^2} - \frac{(n_{hl}^2+(n_{hl}+1)^2)}{(2+n_{hl})^2}\right)$$

$$+\frac{(1-\alpha_h)(1-\alpha_l)}{\beta}\left(\frac{n_{hl}^2+(1+n_{hl})^2)}{(2+n_{ll}+n_{hl})^2} - \frac{(n_{lh}^2+(n_{lh})^2)}{(2+n_{lh}+n_{hh})^2}\right) \quad (10.30)$$

Unfortunately, neither A, nor B, is of a constant sign,[5] making the solving of that game highly problematic. In the next section, I present instead some simulation results that somehow illuminate the main patterns of the trade-off between the high- and low-protection countries.

Simulation Results

I assume that the number of local competitors goes from 1 to 3, regardless of the extent of national IPR protection and of firm *M*'s location choice. For each country, two protection regimes are considered: $\alpha_h = \{0.25; 0.75\}$ and $\alpha_l = k\alpha_h$, with $k = \{0.25; 0.75\}$. Depending on how FDI impacts on the market structure in each country, four cases can be distinguished.

FDI has no strategic impact, that is, it does not affect the number of local competitors[6]

This situation broadly corresponds to that described in paragraph 1 and the subsidiary should locate in the country where expected competition is the lowest.[7]

Table 10.1 also considers the case where the number of local imitators is

Table 10.1 No strategic effect

Configuration	Parameters						Results
	k	α_h	n_{hl}	n_{lh}	n_{hh}	n_{ll}	
1	—	—	1	1	1	1	*H*
2	—	—	1	2	1	2	*H*
3	—	—	1	3	1	3	*H*
4	—	—	2	2	2	2	*H*
5	—	—	3	3	3	3	*H*
6	—	—	2	3	2	3	*H*
7	.25	.25	2	1	2	1	*L*
	.75	.25	2	1	2	1	*L*
	.25	.75	2	1	2	1	*H*
	.75	.75	2	1	2	1	*H*
8	.25	.25	3	1	3	1	*L*
	.75	.25	3	1	3	1	*L*
	.25	.75	3	1	3	1	*H*
	.75	.75	3	1	3	1	*L*
9	.25	.25	3	2	3	2	*L*
	.75	.25	3	2	3	2	*L*
	.25	.75	3	2	3	2	*H*
	.75	.75	3	2	3	2	*H*

Notes:
H: country *H* is chosen.
L: country *L* is chosen.

higher in country *H* ($n_h > n_l$, configurations 7, 8 and 9)[8] and reveals that the low-protection country will be chosen when its IPR law is *not too weak* relative to the high-protection country, so that expected competition could be lower in *L*.

FDI has a positive strategic impact in both countries, that is, it diminishes the number of local imitators[9]

Table 10.2 reveals that:

- Other things equal, the incentive to locate in *L* increases with the extent of the deterrence effect (see configurations 1 and 2).
- The firm *M* chooses the country where the deterrence effect is stronger (see configurations 4 to 7) but, as shown in Case 2, above, it can also locate in country *L* when the strategic effect of FDI is lower, provided there is a wide gap between the protection levels (see configurations 8 to 11).

Table 10.2 Positive strategic impact of FDI in both countries

Configuration	Parameters						Results
	k	α_h	n_{hl}	n_{lh}	n_{hh}	n_{ll}	
1	.25	.25	2	2	1	1	.31m
	.75	.25	2	2	1	1	.31m
	.25	.75	2	2	1	1	.31m
	.75	.75	2	2	1	1	.31m
2	.25	.25	3	3	1	1	.33m
	.75	.25	3	3	1	1	.33m
	.25	.75	3	3	1	1	.33m
	.75	.75	3	3	1	1	.33m
3	.25	.25	3	3	2	2	.20m
	.75	.25	3	3	2	2	.20m
	.25	.75	3	3	2	2	.20m
	.75	.75	3	3	2	2	.20m
4	.25	.25	3	3	2	1	.65m
	.75	.25	3	3	2	1	L
	.25	.75	3	3	2	1	.35m
	.75	.75	3	3	2	1	.42m
5	.25	.25	2	2	2	1	.75m
	.75	.25	2	2	2	1	L
	.25	.75	2	2	2	1	.34m
	.75	.75	2	2	2	1	.43m
6	.25	.25	3	3	3	1	L
	.75	.25	3	3	3	1	L
	.25	.75	3	3	3	1	.36m
	.75	.75	3	3	3	1	.46m
7	.25	.25	3	3	3	2	.35m
	.75	.25	3	3	3	2	L
	.25	.75	3	3	3	2	.21m
	.75	.75	3	3	3	2	.27m
8	.25	.25	3	3	1	2	H
	.75	.25	3	3	1	2	H
	.25	.75	3	3	1	2	.16m
	.75	.75	3	3	1	2	H
9	—	—	3	3	1	3	H
10	—	—	3	3	2	3	H
11	—	—	2	2	1	2	H
12	—	—	3	1	1	1	H
13	—	—	2	1	1	1	H
14	—	—	3	2	1	2	H
15	—	—	3	2	2	2	H
16	.25	.25	3	1	2	1	>.23m

Table 10.2 (continued)

Configuration	Parameters						Results
	k	α_h	n_{hl}	n_{lh}	n_{hh}	n_{ll}	
	.75	.25	3	1	2	1	>.22*m*
	.25	.75	3	1	2	1	*H*
	.75	.75	3	1	2	1	>.37*m*
17	.25	.25	3	2	3	1	*L*
	.75	.25	3	2	3	1	*L*
	.25	.75	3	2	3	1	.37*m*
	.75	.75	3	2	3	1	.56*m*
18	.25	.25	3	2	2	1	*L*
	.75	.25	3	2	2	1	*L*
	.25	.75	3	2	2	1	34*m*
	.75	.75	3	2	2	1	47*m*
19	.25	.25	3	2	1	1	*H*
	.75	.25	3	2	1	1	>.34*m*
	.25	.75	3	2	1	1	<.31*m*
	.75	.75	3	2	1	1	<.28*m*
20	.25	.25	1	3	1	1	.34*m*
	.75	.25	1	3	1	1	.36*m*
	.25	.75	1	3	1	1	.33*m*
	.75	.75	1	3	1	1	.36*m*
21	.25	.25	2	3	1	1	.32*m*
	.75	.25	2	3	1	1	.33*m*
	.25	.75	2	3	1	1	.33*m*
	.75	.75	2	3	1	1	.33*m*
22	.25	.25	2	3	2	1	.45*m*
	.75	.25	2	3	2	1	.57*m*
	.25	.75	2	3	2	1	.35*m*
	.75	.75	2	3	2	1	.40*m*
23	.25	.25	1	2	1	1	.35*m*
	.75	.25	1	2	1	1	.38*m*
	.25	.75	1	2	1	1	.33*m*
	.75	.75	1	2	1	1	.35*m*
24	.25	.25	2	3	2	2	.24*m*
	.75	.25	2	3	2	2	.27*m*
	.25	.75	2	3	2	2	.21*m*
	.75	.75	2	3	2	2	.24*m*
25	.25	.25	1	3	1	2	.20*m*
	.75	.25	1	3	1	2	.21*m*
	.25	.75	1	3	1	2	.20*m*
	.75	.75	1	3	1	2	.21*m*
26	.25	.25	2	3	1	2	.11*m*

Table 10.2 (continued)

Configuration	Parameters						Results
	k	α_h	n_{hl}	n_{lh}	n_{hh}	n_{ll}	
	.75	.25	2	3	1	2	H
	.25	.75	2	3	1	2	$.18m$
	.75	.75	2	3	1	2	$.06m$
27	—	—	2	3	1	3	H

Notes:
H: country H is chosen.
L: country L is chosen.
xm: country L is chosen if $s < xm$ (unless indicated).

- The number of local competitors in the absence of firm M also matters. If $n_{hl} > n_{lh}$ (configurations 12 to 19), either FDI has no impact in L, in which case country H is chosen if the strategic impact of FDI is strong enough ($n_{hh} > n_{ll}$) (configurations 12 to 15),[10] or FDI also has a positive effect in country L (configurations 17 to 19), in which case the low protection country is chosen if the deterrence effect is superior or equal to that in country H (configurations 17 and 18).[11] Conversely, if $n_{hl} < n_{lh}$ (configurations 20 to 27), the incentive to locate in country L rather than H is positive if $n_{ll} \leq n_{hh}$ (configurations 20 to 24). If $n_{ll} > n_{hh}$ (configurations 25 to 27), country H is chosen if the exportation costs are sufficiently high relative to market size.
- Finally, we can note that the influence of the strategic effect of FDI not only depends on the number of excluded competitors but also on their identity: going from two to one competitor has more influence on the location choice than going from three to two imitators (configurations 1 and 3, 5 and 7 ...).

FDI has a negative impact in both countries, that is, it increases the number of local competitors[12]

Table 10.3 reveals that:

- The firm M tends to favour the country where the negative strategic effect is weaker.[13]
- On the other hand, if the strategic effect of FDI is stronger in country H (configurations 12 to 22), the multinational also pays some attention to the number of firms in country L. That country will be chosen when the exportation costs are low and the IPR protection in both economies is relatively similar.[14]

Table 10.3 Negative strategic impact of FDI in both countries

Configuration	Parameters						Results
	k	α_h	n_{hl}	n_{lh}	n_{hh}	n_{ll}	
1	—	—	1	1	1	2	*H*
2	—	—	1	1	1	3	*H*
3	—	—	1	1	2	3	*H*
4	—	—	2	2	2	3	*H*
5	—	—	2	1	2	2	*H*
6	—	—	2	1	2	3	*H*
7	—	—	2	1	3	3	*H*
8	—	—	3	1	3	2	*H*
9	—	—	3	1	3	3	*H*
10	—	—	3	2	3	3	*H*
11	—	—	1	2	1	3	*H*
12	.25	.25	1	1	3	1	*L*
	.75	.25	1	1	3	1	*L*
	.25	.75	1	1	3	1	.27*m*
	.75	.75	1	1	3	1	.50*m*
13	.25	.25	1	1	2	1	.95*m*
	.75	.25	1	1	2	1	*L*
	.25	.75	1	1	2	1	.22*m*
	.75	.75	1	1	2	1	.41*m*
14	.25	.25	2	1	3	1	*L*
	.75	.25	2	1	3	1	*L*
	.25	.75	2	1	3	1	.19*m*
	.75	.75	2	1	3	1	*L*
15	.25	.25	2	2	3	2	.34*m*
	.75	.25	2	2	3	2	*L*
	.25	.75	2	2	3	2	.11*m*
	.75	.75	2	2	3	2	.22*m*
16	.25	.25	1	2	3	2	.34*m*
	.75	.25	1	2	3	2	.45*m*
	.25	.75	1	2	3	2	.17*m*
	.75	.75	1	2	3	2	.31*m*
17	.25	.25	1	2	2	2	.25*m*
	.75	.25	1	2	2	2	.33*m*
	.25	.75	1	2	2	2	.13*m*
	.75	.75	1	2	2	2	.25*m*
18	.25	.25	1	3	3	3	.22*m*
	.75	.25	1	3	3	3	.30*m*
	.25	.75	1	3	3	3	.13*m*
	.75	.75	1	3	3	3	.25*m*
19	.25	.25	1	3	2	3	.16*m*
	.75	.25	1	3	2	3	.22*m*
	.25	.75	1	3	2	3	.10*m*

Table 10.3 (continued)

Configuration	Parameters						Results
	k	α_h	n_{hl}	n_{lh}	n_{hh}	n_{ll}	
	.75	.75	1	3	2	3	.21m
20	.25	.25	1	2	3	3	.15m
	.75	.25	1	2	3	3	.29m
	.25	.75	1	2	3	3	.17m
	.75	.75	1	2	3	3	.34m
21	.25	.25	2	3	3	3	.16m
	.75	.25	2	3	3	3	.24m
	.25	.75	2	3	3	3	.08m
	.75	.75	2	3	3	3	.17m
22	.25	.25	1	1	3	2	.13m
	.75	.25	1	1	3	2	L
	.25	.75	1	1	3	2	H
	.75	.75	1	1	3	2	H
23	—	—	1	1	2	2	H
24	—	—	2	2	3	3	H
25	—	—	1	1	3	3	H
26	—	—	2	1	3	2	H
27	.25	.25	1	2	2	3	H
	.75	.25	1	2	2	3	.13m
	.25	.75	1	2	2	3	H
	.75	.75	1	2	2	3	H

Notes:
H: country H is chosen.
L: country L is chosen.
xm: country L is chosen if $s<xm$ (unless indicated).

- Finally, the configurations 23 to 27 simulate an identical strategic impact. The most probable location is country H since IPR protection is higher in that country, Country L is chosen if and only if the identity of entering competitors is more damaging to profits in country H, if IPR protection is relatively similar and if the exportation costs are sufficiently low (configuration 27).

Asymmetric strategic impact

In that case, the multinational firm always locates in country H if the strategic impact is positive there (Table 10.4, configurations 1 to 8). It chooses country L only if the positive strategic impact is strong enough and if exportation costs are relatively low (configurations 9 to 16).

Table 10.4 Asymmetric strategic effect

	Parameters						
Configuration	k	α_h	n_{hl}	n_{lh}	n_{hh}	n_{ll}	Results
1	—	—	2	2	1	3	*H*
2	—	—	2	1	1	2	*H*
3	—	—	2	1	1	3	*H*
4	—	—	3	1	1	2	*H*
5	—	—	3	1	2	2	*H*
6	—	—	3	1	1	3	*H*
7	—	—	3	2	1	3	*H*
8	—	—	3	2	2	3	*H*
9	.25	.25	2	2	3	1	*L*
	.75	.25	2	2	3	1	*L*
	.25	.75	2	2	3	1	.36m
	.75	.75	2	2	3	1	.48m
10	.25	.25	1	2	3	1	.59m
	.75	.25	1	2	3	1	.75m
	.25	.75	1	2	3	1	.37m
	.75	.75	1	2	3	1	.46m
11	.25	.25	1	3	3	1	.48m
	.75	.25	1	3	3	1	.55m
	.25	.75	1	3	3	1	.37m
	.75	.75	1	3	3	1	.44m
12	.25	.25	1	2	2	1	.47m
	.75	.25	1	2	2	1	.56m
	.25	.75	1	2	2	1	.35m
	.75	.75	1	2	2	1	.43m
13	.25	.25	1	3	2	1	.41m
	.75	.25	1	3	2	1	.46m
	.25	.75	1	3	2	1	.35m
	.75	.75	1	3	2	1	.41m
14	.25	.25	2	3	3	2	.32m
	.75	.25	2	3	3	2	.42m
	.25	.75	2	3	3	2	.22m
	.75	.75	2	3	3	2	.29m
15	.25	.25	1	3	3	2	.32m
	.75	.25	1	3	3	2	.39m
	.25	.75	1	3	3	2	.24m
	.75	.75	1	3	3	2	.33m
16	.25	.25	1	3	2	2	.27m
	.75	.25	1	3	2	2	.32m
	.25	.75	1	3	2	2	.22m
	.75	.75	1	3	2	2	.29m

Notes: *H*: country *H* is chosen. *L*: country *L* is chosen. xm: country *L* is chosen if $s < xm$ (unless indicated).

10.5 CONCLUSION

This chapter considered how country differences in IPR legislation may affect multinational subsidiaries' location choices. It has been demonstrated that stronger IPR protection may not necessarily entail greater country attractiveness, provided that market size is important relative to exportation costs and that the imitation costs in the host countries are sufficiently high for FDI to deter imitation by local competitors.

How this unexpected relationship really matters should now be appreciated from an empirical standpoint. At this stage, it should be noted that several studies have shown that the influence of IPR protection on trade flows depends upon the importing country's market size and R&D intensity (Maskus and Penubarti, 1995; Smith, 1999). Results on French subsidiaries' location choices by Pfister (2001, ch. 6) tend to confirm the empirical relevance of the model presented here but more work is probably needed to firmly ground these intuitions. More generally, results on the link between IPR protection and multinational firms' strategy remains very fragile.

Finally, this theoretical model has ambiguous implications for the economic analysis of the TRIPs agreement. On the one hand, countries that have implemented the recommendations of the WTO in their IPR legislation may not register important and positive feedbacks in terms of foreign direct investment. On the other hand, it still remains that if all developing countries strengthen IPR protection, foreign direct investment could increase, especially if technological spillovers are high. Besides, the model can be taken to explain the reluctance of some countries to implement the TRIPs agreement. It thus brings some theoretical support to the intervention of the WTO in this matter.

APPENDIX MATHEMATICAL EXAMINATION OF CONDITION (EQUATION) 10.21

Let Δ define the discriminant of the second-order equation in s (condition 10.21). It is easily shown that:

$$\Delta > 0 \Leftrightarrow \alpha_h > 1350 \frac{10\alpha_l - 3}{6409 + 2970\alpha_l} \qquad (10.31)$$

Since $\alpha_h > \alpha_l$, this condition is systematically verified unless $\alpha_l > 0.9459$. If A designates the first term in parenthesis and B the second one, the solutions to equation 10.21 can thus be written as:

$$s_1 = m\frac{-A + \sqrt{A^2 - 4AB}}{2B} \qquad s_2 = m\frac{-A - \sqrt{A^2 - 4AB}}{2B} \tag{10.32}$$

But *A*'s and *B*'s signs are undetermined. Indeed:

$$B_1 < 0 \Rightarrow \alpha_h > 81\frac{38\alpha_l - 13}{1472 + 533\alpha_l} \tag{10.33}$$

Given that $\alpha_h > \alpha_l$, this condition is systematically verified only if $\alpha_l <$ 0.9642. Similarly:

$$A > 0 \Rightarrow \alpha_h > 54\frac{22\alpha_l + 3}{521 + 838\alpha_l} \tag{10.34}$$

Given that $\alpha_h > \alpha_l$, this is systematically verified only if $\alpha_l > 0.9910$.

Consider first the case where $\Delta > 0$ ($\alpha_l < 0.94$). Then, $B < 0$ but A is indeterminate. If α_h is high enough, then $A > 0$ and it exists a unique solution $s_2 > 0$ under which condition 10.21 is fulfilled. If α_h is too low, $A < 0$, s_1, and s_2 are negative and the equation 10.21 is always negative.

Consider now the case where $B > 0$. $\Delta > 0$ only if $\alpha_l > 0.9835$. Either α_h is high enough ($A > 0$) and both s_1, and s_2 are negative: then, condition 10.21 is always fulfilled. Or α_h is too low ($A < 0$) and s_1 is the unique positive solution: country L is chosen if $s > s_1$.

Finally, let us consider the case where $\Delta < 0$ (implying $\alpha_l > 0.9459$). The sign of equation 10.21 is also that of B. If $0.9459 < \alpha_l < 0.9642$, $B < 0$, H is systematically chosen. If $\alpha_l > 0.9642$, either α_h is weak enough and L is always chosen, or it is high enough and H is chosen.

ACKNOWLEDGEMENTS

This chapter benefited from funding by the Commissariat Général au Plan. I also thank A. Bouët, C. Mathieu, E.M. Mouhoud, J.-L. Mucchielli, and seminar participants at the GRATICE/University of Paris XII and AFSE conference for their comments and suggestions. A shorter version of this chapter has been published in 2003 in the *Revue Economique*.

NOTES

1. If the litigation/trial costs are too high, a settlement agreement might be preferred or the trial threat may not be credible. These costs are likely to be very negligible given the sheer financial strength of the multinational firm.

2. Here, it is assumed that a defeat at trial does not entail the entry of the second imitator: the latecomer continues to face a risk of exclusion despite the fact that a first court decision has ruled that there was no infringement. In other words, a trial defeat does not entail the invalidation of the IPR. This assumption will also hold for country *L*. Relaxing this assumption would diminish the attractiveness of a court-based exclusion strategy for the risk associated to a trial is much greater (Choi, 1998).
3. See the appendix to this chapter.
4. Hence, n_{lh} denotes the number of imitators in country *L* when *M* locates in country *H*.
5. For instance, if FDI has a positive strategic effect (it reduces the number of local competitors), the first term in *A* is positive, the second one is negative while the last one is indeterminate. The same indetermination prevails for *B* and in the case of a negative strategic impact.
6. Concretely, the imitation costs are too low for FDI to deter local competition while technological spillovers are too low to facilite imitation and encourage entry.
7. Thus, it will choose country *H* when the number of local imitators *h* is equal to or lower than the number of local imitators *l*.
8. This could mean, for instance, that country *H* has a higher technological capability.
9. Concretely, technological spillovers are too low to compensate for the greater competitiveness of the multinational's subsidiary.
10. Note that if $n_{ll} < n_{hh}$ (configuration 16), *M* locates in *L* if α_h is *weak* enough and if the exports costs are *high* enough, which seems to contradict our theoretical results. Actually, *M* locates where (expected) competition is the lowest. It only seeks to diminish competition in country *H* if the exports costs are low enough.
11. When the deterrence effect is stronger in country *H* (configuration 19), *M* locates in *H* provided that α_h is weak enough. Indeed, in that case, it is very unlikely that the local competitors in country *H* will be excluded through a court decision.
12. The technological spillovers due to FDI are sufficiently important to facilitate imitation.
13. Hence, when it is stronger in *L* (configurations 1 to 11), country *H* is systematically preferred.
14. Indeed, if protection is much stronger in country *H*, the expected number of competitors is lower in that economy, despite the strategic effect of FDI. High exportation costs also allow firm *M* to benefit fully from its potential monopoly by being isolated from the competition in country *L*.

REFERENCES

Blomström, M. and A. Kokko (1998), 'Multinational corporation and spillovers', *Journal of Economic Surveys*, **12** (3), 247–77.

Choi, J. (1998), 'Patent litigation as an information transfer mechanism', *American Economic Review*, **88** (5), 1249–65.

Combe, E. and E. Pfister (2001), 'Le renforcement international des droits de propriété intellectuelle: quels effets en attendre?', *Economie Internationale-La Revue du CEPII*, **85** (1), 63–81.

Fosfuri, A. (2000), 'Patent protection, imitation and the mode of technology transfer', *International Journal of Industrial Organization*, **18**, 1129–49.

Markusen, J. (2001), 'Contracts, intellectual property rights and multinational investment in developing countries', *Journal of International Economics*, **3**, 481–519.

Maskus, K. and M. Penubarti (1995), 'How trade-related are intellectual property rights', *Journal of International Economics*, **39**, 227–48.

Pfister, E. (2001), Droits de Propriété Industrielle et Stratégies des Firmes: *Eléments Théoriques et Empiriques*, thèse de doctorat, Université de Paris 1.

Siotis, G. (1999), 'Foreign direct investment strategies and firms' capabilities', *Journal of Economics and Management Strategy*, **8** (2), 251–70.
Smith, A. (1987), 'Strategic investment, multinational corporations and trade policy', *European Economic Review*, **31**, 89–96.
Smith, P. (1999), 'Are weak patent rights a barrier to US exports?', *Journal of International Economics*, **48**, 151–77.

Index

Ades, A. 91
advertising, product differentiation by 26, 28
agglomeration effects 44, 46–7, 48, 49
  significance of 50, 51, 52, 55
Ahn, B.C. 184
Alonso-Villar, O. 91
Amemiya, T. 60, 64, 71, 73
Amiti, M. 13, 181
Anderson, J.E. 3–4, 73
Armington, P.S. 140, 141–2, 143, 152, 154
Arromdee, V. 40, 46
Augmented Dickey Fuller (ADF) statistic 185
Austria
  EU regional aid to 159, 160
  geographical concentration of production of leading firms originating from 30
  US FDI in 194, 196
Auto Decrees 78
automobile industry
  determinants of automobile production in Mexico 4, Ch. 4
  geographical concentration of 23, 24
    French-owned firms 44
    Japanese-owned firms 130, 135

Baltagi, B. 62
Banque de France 56
Barrell, R. 77, 181, 182, 183, 200
Bartik, T.J. 42
Behrman, J.N. 200
Belgium
  average regional potential market 53
  average regional wage level 54
  EU regional aid to 159, 160
  French FDI in 36, 37, 44, 45
  Japanese FDI in 123
  see also Belgium/Luxembourg
Belgium/Luxembourg
  leading firms originating from 19, 20
    geographical concentration of production of 29
  share in foreign firm production 22
  share of EU leading firms' production located in 18
  share of production accounted for by foreign-owned firms 21
  US FDI in 194, 196
  see also Belgium; Luxembourg, EU regional aid to
Ben-Akiva, M. 39
Benz 80
Berry, C.H. 33
bifurcation diagram 99–100
bilateral trade flows, border effects and, *see* border effects and trade flows
Birkinshaw, J.M. 200
Blomström, M. 78, 205, 207
Blonigen, B.A. 77
Bonin, B. 200
border effects and trade flows 3–4, Ch. 3
border regions, development of 105–7, 108
Brainard, S.L. 2–3
Brander, J.A. 116, 117, 119, 120, 121, 136, 142, 143, 161, 170
Braunerhjelm, P. 157, 160, 181, 183
Breusch, T. 60, 62, 64, 65, 72, 73
Brülhart, M. 13, 142, 154, 156–7
Brussels 36, 45
business cycles 60

Canada, US FDI in 194, 198
Canon 1
Cantwell, J.A. 200
capital intensity 13, 162
car industry, *see* automobile industry

Cardano's formula 149
Carlton, D. 114
Carrère, C. 74
cartelization 178
Cecchini Report 11
Central and Eastern Europe
  EU accession 1, 91
  French FDI in 45–6
  see also Eastern Europe
centres of excellence 200
CES function 94
Chakrabarti, A. 200
Chang, S.J. 183, 200
Chen, C.-H. 40
Choi, I. 184
Choi, J. 207, 226
Chow tests 185, 186
Chrysler 80, 81
Clegg, J. 200
Cobb-Douglas utility function 93, 114
Combe, E. 205
COMEXT database 61
Common Agricultural Policy (CAP) 159
competitiveness, as motivation for FDI 182, 186–7, 190
concentration index (Ellison-Glaeser) 114, 115
  compared with dartboard production 118–25, 127, 129, 130, 131, 132–5
  significance test for 127, 129
conditional logit models 39, 43, 113, 114, 122, 123
  estimation results of 48–52, 115, 125–6, 127, 129, 131
  IIA property of 39–42
  significance test for 127
congestion cost 13, 101, 102, 113
constant returns to scale 140, 141, 142, 143, 152, 153, 154, 161, 162
consumer surplus 166, 169
corruption 206
cost externalities 97, 100, 102
cost seeking variables 44, 46, 48–52, 54–5, 180, 182, 186–8, 190, 191; *see also* unit labour costs; wages
Coughlin, C.C. 40, 46
Cournot segmented markets (CSM) model 114, 116, 140
cross-elasticity of demand 157
Crozet, M. 4, 40, 47
CSM model, *see* Cournot segmented markets (CSM) model
Culem, C.G. 181, 182, 200
Cushman, D.O. 182
Czech Republic, US FDI in 194, 196

dartboard model 118–19, 123–5
  concentration index compared with 118–25, 127, 129, 130, 131, 132–5
  HME models compared with 119–22, 123, 125, 136–8, 154, 156
  spillover model compared with 122, 123
Davies, S.W. 16, 25, 33
Davis, D.R. 141, 156, 157
De Sousa, J. 4
decreasing returns 13
Delios, A. 30
demand externalities 97, 100, 102
demand function 94, 206
Denmark
  EU regional aid to 159, 160
  leading firms originating from 20
    geographical concentration of production of 29
  share in foreign firm production 22
  share of EU leading firms' production located in 18
  share of production accounted for by foreign-owned firms 21
  US FDI in 194, 196
Devereux, M.P. 40
difference in profits equation 116, 117–18
differentiated products 5, 12–13, 25–6, 28, 83, 92, 100, 114, 116, 140, 141, 142–3, 153, 156, 157, 162–3, 164, 165, 168
discrete choice models 38, 39–42
Disdier, A.-C. 4
diversification strategy 83
Dixit, A. 94, 142, 169, 176
Dornbush, R. 141, 143, 144

dumping 165, 170
Dunning, J.H. 77, 200
dynamic differentiated networks 179, 180, 190

Eastern Europe
free trade area in 76–7
see also Central and Eastern Europe
economic aid, EU expenditure on 159
efficiency seeking variables, *see* cost seeking variables; unit labour costs; wages
Egger, P. 60
Ellison, G. 113, 114, 115, 116, 119–25, 127, 129, 130
Enquête-Filiales DREE 2000 36, 38, 43, 48, 49
Entropy Between index 17, 23, 24, 26, 27, 28
Entropy index 16, 17
Entropy Within index 17, 23
European Commission 13, 160, 176
European Union (EU)
border effects and trade flows within 3–4, Ch. 3
enlargement of 1, 4, 91
EU-12 member states (1987) 16
firm-level location choices determinants within 3, Ch. 2
geographical concentration of manufacturing production in 3, Ch. 1; *see also* Single Market Programme (SMP)
Japanese FDI in, *see* Japanese FDI, explanations for geographical concentration of
location patterns inside countries within 4–5, Ch. 5
regional funding in 4, 91, 158–62, 172–3
Eurostat 48, 49, 61, 131, 156
eviction effect 77
exchange rate evolution 60–61, 65–72 *passim*
export platforms 77, 79, 84
exports
automobiles produced in Mexico 80–82
home market effect and 141, 156
externalities 47, 55, 97, 100, 102
FDI, *see* Foreign Direct Investment (FDI)
Feenstra, R.C. 77, 85, 114, 156, 157
Ferrer, C. 35, 46, 52
Figuirdo, O. 40
Filippaios, F. 6, 200
Finland
EU regional aid to 159, 160
French FDI in 37
geographical concentration of production of leading firms originating from 30
US FDI in 194, 196
Fisher, S. 141, 143, 144
fixed effects estimator, *see* within estimator
Flowers, E.B. 179
Ford, S. 35, 40, 46, 47
Ford Motor Co. 80, 81
Foreign Direct Investment (FDI)
French FDI outflows 35, 36
see also French multinationals' location decisions, determinants of
intellectual property rights and, *see* intellectual property rights, and FDI strategy
Japanese investment in the USA and Europe, *see* Japanese FDI, explanations for geographical concentration of
regional integration agreements (RIAs) and 76–8
see also North American Free Trade Agreement (NAFTA); Single Market Programme (SMP)
strategic motivations for, *see* strategic motivations for location of US MNEs' FDI
Forsgren, M. 200
Forslid, R. 13
Fosfuri, A. 205
France
EU regional aid to 159, 160
FDI outflows from 35, 36
see also French multinationals' location decisions, determinants of
Japanese FDI in 123

leading firms originating from 20
geographical concentration of production of 29, 30
share in foreign firm production 22
share of EU leading firms' production located in 18
share of production accounted for by foreign-owned firms 21
US FDI in 194, 196
French multinationals' location decisions, determinants of 3–4, Ch. 2
Friedman, J. 40, 46, 56
Fujita, M. 2, 13, 47, 95, 175

Gao, T. 15
General Motors 80, 81
Gerlowski, D.A. 40, 46, 56
Germany
average regional potential market 53
average regional wage level 54
EU regional aid to 159, 160
French FDI in 36, 37, 44, 45
Japanese FDI in 123
leading firms originating from 20
geographical concentration of production of 29
share in foreign firm production 22
share of EU leading firms' production located in 18
share of production accounted for by foreign-owned firms 21
US FDI in 194, 197
Gini index 114
Girma, S. 77
Glaeser, E.L. 91, 113, 114, 115, 116, 119–25, 127, 129, 130
Graham, E.M. 179, 200
gravity equation of trade 60–61, 156
Greece
EU regional aid to 159, 160
French FDI in 37
leading firms originating from 20
geographical concentration of production of 29
share in foreign firm production 22
share of EU leading firms' production located in 18
share of production accounted for by foreign-owned firms 21
US FDI in 194, 197
greenfield investment 123
Griffith, R. 40
gross domestic product (GDP), as motivation for FDI 181, 186, 190
gross domestic product (GDP) growth, as motivation for FDI 181, 186, 190
Grosse, R. 85
Guillotin, Y. 65
Guimarães, P. 40, 42

Håkanson, L. 200
Hansen, R.E. 42
Hanson, G. 4, 85, 91, 141
Harris, C. 56
Hausman, J. 60, 63, 64, 65, 70, 73, 74
Hausman test 63, 68–73
Head, K. 3, 5, 40, 41, 42, 47, 56, 59, 61, 65, 74, 114–15, 116, 117, 119, 141–3, 152, 154, 157, 163, 175, 183
Heckman's correction 59
Heckscher-Ohlin model 140, 141, 143, 152
Helliwell, J.F. 59, 60, 74
Helpman, E. 13, 116, 117, 119, 136, 137, 141, 156, 157, 161
Henderson, V. 92, 107
Herfindahl index 33, 121, 122, 124, 125
hierarchical decision structure 39–43
Hirsch, S. 46
HME, *see* home market effect (HME)
home-biased demand 142, 145–7, 150
home market effect (HME)
compared with spillover effect, as source of observed concentration 5, Ch. 6
definition of 140
in a Ricardian model with a continuum of goods 5, Ch. 7
welfare implications of 5–6, Ch. 8
homogenous products 142, 143, 153, 156, 157, 162
Hood, N. 200

Horaguchi, H. 200
hub-city case 105
Hungary, US FDI in 194, 197
Hymer, S. 178

IBM 43
iceberg transport technology 93, 94, 116, 144
Iceland, US FDI in 195, 197
IIA property, *see* Independence of Irrelevant Alternatives (IAA) property
Im, K.S. 184
imitation costs 6, 206, 224
 equilibrium settings for different levels of 209–14
imperfect competition models 13, 94
 and home market effect (HME) 5, 113, 115, 116, 140–43, 153, 157, 158, 161, 162, 173
  compared with dartboard model 119–22, 123, 125, 136–8, 154, 156
implicit function theorem 150
inclusive value 42–3, 52–3
income elasticity 73
income levels, as motivation for FDI 181–2, 185–6, 188–9
income taxes 172
increasing returns to scale 2–3, 13, 25, 26
 and home market effect (HME) 5, 6, 114, 140, 141, 142, 154, 156, 158, 161, 162, 168, 173, 181
Independence of Irrelevant Alternatives (IIA) property 39–42
indirect utility function 162–3
industrial price index 94, 95
instrumental variables estimators 59–60, 63–5
 results of border effects estimations using 68–73
intangible assets 30, 43
intellectual property rights, and FDI strategy 6, Ch. 10
IPS t-bar test 184–5, 186
Ireland
 EU regional aid to 159, 160
 Japanese FDI in 123
 leading firms originating from 20
  geographical concentration of production of 29
 share in foreign firm production 22
 share of EU leading firms' production located in 18
 share of production accounted for by foreign-owned firms 21
 US FDI in 195, 197
Italy
 average regional potential market 53
 average regional wage level 54, 55
 EU regional aid to 159, 160
 French FDI in 36, 37, 44, 45
 Japanese FDI in 123
 leading firms originating from 19, 20
  geographical concentration of production of 29
 share in foreign firm production 22
 share of EU leading firms' production located in 18–19, 21
 share of production accounted for by foreign-owned firms 21
 US FDI in 195, 197

Jacquemin, A. 33
Japan, US FDI in 195, 198
Japan Economic Institute (JEI) 123, 131
Japan External Trade Organization (JETRO) 123, 131
Japanese FDI, explanations for geographical concentration of 5, Ch. 6
JEI, *see* Japan Economic Institute (JEI)
JETRO, *see* Japan External Trade Organization (JETRO)
Jianping, D. 41, 46
Johanson, J. 30, 46

Klayman, L. 85
Knickerbocker, F.T. 179
knowledge-seeking variables 6, 180, 182–3, 187–8, 190, 191; *see also* intellectual property rights, and FDI strategy
Kobrin, S.J. 181
Koenig-Soubeyran, P. 4
Kogut, B. 183, 200

Kokko, A. 78, 205, 207
Korea, US FDI in 195, 198
Kottaridi, C. 6, 200
Krugman, P.R. 2, 4–5, 11, 12, 13, 47, 91, 92, 95, 97, 101–3, 105, 107, 114, 115, 116, 117, 119, 120, 121, 136–8, 141–2, 143, 152, 154, 156, 157, 161, 170, 175, 181
Kuemmerle, W. 200

labour costs, *see* unit labour costs; wages
language, common 60–62, 65–73 *passim*
Lankes, H.-P. 200
leading firms, definition of 15
Lerman, S.R. 39
Li, Q. 62
licence contracts 205
Linder, S.B. 181
Livas, R. 4–5, 91, 101–3, 105
local content requirements 78, 79
localized product development 180
Lombardy region 36, 37, 45
London 36
lumpiness problem 114, 115, 119
Lundvall, B.-Å. 180
Luxembourg, EU regional aid to 159, 160; *see also* Belgium/ Luxembourg

MaCurdy, T. 60, 64, 71, 73
Madrid 36, 45
magnification effect 147–54
Makino, S. 30
Manea, J. 200
manufacturing sector
  determinants of geographic concentration of French firms in, *see* French multinationals' location decisions, determinants of
  geographical concentration of manufacturing production in EU, *see* Single Market Programme (SMP)
marginal cost pricing 169–71, 174
market access advantage 167–9, 171
market crowding 167–8, 171
market integration
  and FDI flows 76–8
    see also North American Free Trade Agreement (NAFTA); Single Market Programme (SMP)
market seeking variables 44–6, 48–51, 53–4, 179–82, 185–6, 188–90, 191
market share matrix (MSM) 15–16
  changes in MSM geographical concentration
    at aggregate level 18–23, 32
    at firm level 27–31, 32
    at industry level 23–7, 32
  measuring geographic concentration using 16–17
market size effect, *see* home market effect (HME)
Markusen, J.R. 114, 142–3, 156, 157, 205, 207
Marshall, A. 46
Martinez-Espineira, R. 74
Maskus, K. 224
Mayer, T. 3, 5, 35, 40, 41, 42, 46, 47, 52, 59, 61, 65, 74, 114–15, 116, 117, 119, 142–3, 157, 163, 175
McCallum, J. 3, 59, 60, 163
McFadden, D. 39, 42, 43
McPherson, M.A. 181
mergers and acquisitions 14, 123
Mexico
  distribution of automobile production between US and 4, Ch. 4
  regional development within 4, 91
  strategic motivation for US FDI in 195, 198
Midelfart-Knarvik, K.H. 14, 21, 156–7
Mizon, G. 60, 64, 72, 73
Mody, A. 181, 182, 183
Monfort, P. 91, 105
Montout, S. 4, 77
Moore, K.J. 200
Morgan, C. 77
Morrison, A.J. 200
motor cycles and cycles industry, *see* automobile industry
Motta, M. 76–7

Mucchielli, J.-L. 3, 35, 40, 41, 42, 43, 46, 47, 52
multi-domestic strategy 180
Mutinelli, M. 200

NACE classification 43, 44, 61
NAF 60 classification 43
NAFTA, *see* North American Free Trade Agreement (NAFTA)
Napa Valley 114
Nash equilibrium 164
national borders, *see* border effects and trade flows
national systems of innovation 180
natural advantages 114
Neary, P. 77
Nelson, R.R. 180
nested logit model 42–3
  empirical results of 51, 52–5
Netherlands
  average regional potential market 53
  average regional wage level 54
  EU regional aid to 159, 160
  French FDI in 36, 37, 44, 45
  Japanese FDI in 123
  leading firms originating from 20
    geographical concentration of production of 29
  share in foreign firm production 22
  share of EU leading firms' production located in 18
  share of production accounted for by foreign-owned firms 21
  US FDI in 195, 197
Neven, D. 183, 200
new economic geography 2, 5, 12–13, 91, 92, 95, 97, 101, 175
New Zealand, US FDI in 195, 198
Nicolini, R. 91, 105
Nissan Motors 80, 81
Nitsch, V. 60
Noble, R. 200
Norman, G. 76–7
North American Free Trade Agreement (NAFTA)
  and regional development in Mexico 91
  and relocation of production from USA to Mexico 1, 4, Ch. 4
  signatories 76
Norway
  geographical concentration of production of leading firms originating from 30
  US FDI in 195, 197

Objective 1 regions 175
Objective 2 regions 175–6
OECD, *see* Organization for Economic Co-operation and Development (OECD)
OLS regressions, *see* ordinary least squares (OLS) regressions
ordinary least squares (OLS) regressions 59, 62, 184
  results of border effects estimations using 65–8, 73
Organization for Economic Co-operation and Development (OECD)
  publications and databases 48, 89, 183–4, 193
  strategic motivations for US MNEs' FDI decisions in OECD countries, *see* strategic motivations for location of US MNEs' FDI
Ottaviano, G.I.P. 5–6, 115, 116, 117, 119, 120, 136, 138, 142, 143, 158, 162

Pagan, A. 62, 65
Pain, N. 77, 181, 182, 183, 200
Paluzie, E. 91, 92, 105
panel data, econometric methods of 61–5
Papanastassiou, M. 6, 180, 200
patenting 183, 187, 190
Pearce, R. 6, 180, 191, 200
Pedersen, T. 200
Penubarti, M. 224
perfect competition 13, 161, 162
  and home market effect (HME) 5, 140, 141, 142, 143, 144, 152, 153, 154, 157
Perot, R. 1
Perron, B. 200
Pesaran, M.H. 184
Pfaffermayr, M. 60
Pfister, E. 6, 205, 206, 224

Philips 1
Piscitello, L. 200
Poland, US FDI in 195, 197
Porter, M.E. 180
Portugal
  average regional potential market 53
  average regional wage level 54
  EU accession 1
  EU regional aid to 159, 160
  French FDI in 36, 37, 44, 45
  Japanese FDI in 123
  leading firms originating from 20
    geographical concentration of production of 29
  share in foreign firm production 22
  share of EU leading firms' production located in 18–19, 21
  share of production accounted for by foreign-owned firms 21
  US FDI in 195, 197
price–cost margins 157, 161, 169, 171
price discrimination 163
price-elasticity of demand 157
product development, localized 180
product differentiation 5, 12–13, 25–6, 28, 83, 92, 100, 114, 116, 140, 141, 142–3, 153, 156, 157, 162–3, 164, 165, 168
product homogeneity 142, 143, 153, 156, 157, 162
productivity 85, 87, 182
profit maximization 39, 42, 94, 116, 164
property rights, intellectual, *see* intellectual property rights, and FDI strategy
protectionism 180
proximity–concentration model 3
Puech, F. 3, 47

R&D, *see* Research and Development (R&D)
random effects estimator 62–3
  results of border effects estimations using 65–8, 73
Raybaudi-Massilia, M. 15
Redfearn, M.R. 181
regional attractiveness measure 37
regional development patterns within countries, effect of trade liberalization on, *see* trade liberalization, and regional development patterns within countries
regional funding, EU 4, 91, 158–62, 172–3
regional integration agreements (RIAs)
  and FDI flows 76–7
    see also North American Free Trade Agreement (NAFTA); Single Market Programme (SMP)
regulatory framework, general 206
Relative Entropy index 16–17, 21, 23–6, 28–9, 31
rent shifting 161
Research and Development (R&D)
  decentralized 200
  employment in, and location choice 6, 182, 187–8, 190, 191
  product differentiation by 26, 28
Ricardian trade model, home market effect (HME) in, *see* home market effect (HME)
Ries, J. 5, 40, 41, 42, 47, 56, 114–15, 116, 117, 119, 141–3, 152, 154, 157, 175, 183
risk-neutrality 207
Rolfe, R.J. 42, 85
Rose, A.K. 114, 156, 157
Roth, K. 200
Roy's identity 163
Rugman, A.H. 200
rules of origin 79

Samuelson, P. 141, 143, 144
scale economies 2–3, 13, 25, 26
  and home market effect (HME) 5, 6, 114, 140, 141, 142, 154, 156, 158, 161, 162, 168, 173, 181
Schmidt, P. 60, 64, 72, 73
Sevestre, P. 65
Seyf, A. 200
share equation 116, 118, 122, 123
  estimates of 126–7, 129, 131
Shin, Y. 184
SIC industry classification 123, 129, 130, 131, 132–5
Silberman, J. 40, 46, 56
Silicon Valley 114

Single Market Programme (SMP), impact on geographical concentration of manufacturing production in EU 3, Ch. 1
Siotis, G. 183, 200, 205, 207
Sleuwaegen, L. 3
Smith, A. 207
Smith, P. 205, 224
SMP, *see* Single Market Programme (SMP)
social aid, EU expenditure on 159
social welfare function 169–70
Spain
average regional potential market 53
average regional wage level 54
EU accession 1
EU regional aid to 159, 160
French FDI in 36, 37, 44, 45
Japanese FDI in 123
leading firms originating from 19, 20
geographical concentration of production of 29
share in foreign firm production 22
share of EU leading firms' production located in 18–19, 21
share of production accounted for by foreign-owned firms 21
US FDI in 195, 197
Spencer, B.J. 161
spillovers 46–7, 55, 183
home market effect versus 5, Ch. 6
intellectual property rights and international location in absence of technology spillovers 206, 207, 214, 226
international property rights and international location with technology spillovers 205, 215–16, 224, 226
staged model of internationalization 30
state aid caps 160
Statistics Canada World Database 156
Stevens, G. 76
Stiglitz, J.E. 94, 142, 169, 176
Strange, R. 35, 40, 46, 47
strategic motivations for location of US MNEs' FDI 6, Ch. 9
strategic seeking variables 44, 46–52, 55
Structural Funds, EU 158–62, 172–3
sunk costs 25–6, 32
sustain point 102–5
Sutton, J. 26
Svensson, R. 181, 183
Sweden
EU regional aid to 159, 160
French FDI in 37
geographical concentration of production of leading firms originating from 30
US FDI in 195, 197
Swenson, D. 40, 41, 42, 47, 56, 183
Switzerland
geographical concentration of production of leading firms originating from 30
US FDI in 195, 197
symmetry conditions 145, 146

Tabuchi, T. 115, 116, 117, 119, 120, 136, 142, 143, 158, 162
Taglioni, D. 74
tariff-jumping motive 77
tariff reductions, NAFTA 78–9
Tavares, A.T. 200
Taylor, W. 60, 63, 64, 65, 70, 73, 74
TEAM 6
technology spillovers, *see* spillovers
Terza, J.V. 40, 46
Thisse, J.-F. 2, 115, 116, 117, 119, 120, 136, 138, 142, 143, 158, 162
Thomas, D.E. 85
Tieslau, M.A. 181
Tobit model 86, 89, 127, 131
Torstensson, J. 13
Toyne, B. 200
trade balance equation 146–7
trade costs
and location choice 2–3, 5, 6, 13, 32, 77, 91, 93, 94, 95, 97–107, 116, 127, 141–2, 144, 151–3, 154, 157, 158, 167, 168, 169, 170, 171, 172–3, 174–5
market size effect in absence of 5, 143, 147–50, 154

trade flows
border effects and, *see* border effects and trade flows
intellectual property rights and 205, 224
trade liberalization, and regional development patterns within countries 4–5, Ch. 5
transaction costs, *see* trade costs
Treaty of Rome 160
tree structure 42–3, 45, 48, 52–3
trial win probability 206, 208, 209, 210, 212, 213, 214, 216, 224–5
Trionfetti, F. 5, 142, 154, 156–7, 175
TRIPs agreement 205, 224
Turkey, US FDI in 196, 198

UNCTAD 35
unemployment rate 46, 48, 49
unit labour costs 182, 187, 190
United Kingdom
average regional potential market 53
average regional wage level 54
EU regional aid to 159, 160
French FDI in 36, 37, 44, 45
Japanese FDI in 123
leading firms originating from 20
geographical concentration of production of 29
share in foreign firm production 22
share of EU leading firms' production located in 18
share of production accounted for by foreign-owned firms 21
US FDI in 196, 197
United States
distribution of automobile production between Mexico and 4, Ch. 4
Japanese FDI in, *see* Japanese FDI, explanations for geographical concentration of
strategic motivations for US MNEs' FDI decisions in OECD countries, *see* strategic motivations for location of US MNEs' FDI
unobservable characteristics 59, 60, 61–2, 65, 73, 184
US Bureau of the Census 131

Vahlne, J.E. 30
value added tax (VAT) 158
van Wincoop, E. 3–4
Vandermerwe, S. 14
Venables, A.J. 2, 11, 12, 13, 47, 95, 142–3, 175, 200
Vernon, R. 179
Veugelers, R. 3, 15, 19, 181, 182, 200
VISA database 61
Volkswagen 80, 81, 84

wage equation 95
wages 3, 4, 14, 46, 48, 49–52, 54–5, 77, 83, 84, 87, 89, 97, 98–9, 102, 113; *see also* unit labour costs
Wakelin, K. 77
Weder, R. 141, 156
Wei, S.-J. 59, 60, 61
Weibull distribution 39
Weinstein, D.E. 141, 156
welfare implications of HME, *see* home market effect (HME)
Wheeler, D. 181, 182, 183
White, H. 65
Wiedersheim-Paul, F. 46
WIFO 13
within estimator 59, 63, 184
results of border effects estimations using 68, 69, 73
Wolf, H.C. 59, 60
Woodward, D.P. 40, 41, 42, 85
Wooton, I. 13
World Trade Organization (WTO) 205, 224

Xiang, C. 141

Yamin, M. 200
Yannopoulos, G.N. 77, 200

Zitouna, H. 4, 77